AF570190

REGIONAL MECHANISMS OF COLLECTIVE SECURITY

THE NEW FACE OF CHAPTER VIII OF THE UN CHARTER?

“Diplomacy and Strategy”
English Series
Directors: Fouad Nohra and Michael J. Strauss

Diplomacy and Strategy is a collection initiated by the academic directorate of the Centre d’Etudes Diplomatiques et Stratégiques to promote the outstanding scientific work presented by Ph.D. graduates, professors and researchers. The scope of subjects covered is as wide as international relations itself, encompassing disciplines such as political science, economic science, international law and sociology.

OTHER TITLES

SOLVIT Samuel, *Dimensions of War. Understanding War as a Complex Adaptive System*, 2012.

DUQUESNE Isabelle, *Nepal, Zone of Peace. A Revised Concept for the Constitution*, 2011.

STRAUSS Michael J., *The Viability of Territorial Leases in Resolving International Sovereignty Disputes,* 2010.

Alena F. Douhan

REGIONAL MECHANISMS OF COLLECTIVE SECURITY

THE NEW FACE OF CHAPTER VIII OF THE UN CHARTER?

Preface by Fouad Nohra

By the Same Author:

Принцип невмешательства во внутренние дела государств: современные тенденции [The Principle of Non-Intervention into the Domestic Affairs of States: Contemporary Challenges] (Economy and Law, Minsk, 2009)*

Co-Authored Works:

Экономический Суд Содружества Независимых Государств: 15 лет [The Economic Court of the Commonwealth of Independent States: 15 Years] (Kovcheg, Minsk, 2008)*

Исследование о соответствии национального законодательства Республики Беларусь нормам международного гуманитарного права по вопросу о защите культурных ценностей в период вооруженных конфликтов [Study on the Implementation in Belarusian Legislation of Norms of International Humanitarian Law concerning the Protection of Cultural Values during Armed Conflicts] (Minsk, 2009)*

Collective Security Treaty Organization (2002-2009) (Procon, Geneva/ Minsk, 2010)

*In Russian

5-7, rue de l'Ecole-Polytechnique, 75005 Paris

http://www.librairieharmattan.com
diffusion.harmattan@wanadoo.fr
harmattan1@wanadoo.fr

ISBN : 978-2-343-00082-4
EAN : 9782343000824

TABLE OF CONTENTS

ACKNOWLEDGMENTS

This book is the result of protracted work on issues of collective security done at the Belarusian State University and the Max Planck Institute for Comparative Public Law and International Law.

I would hereby like to thank all of the people who supported me on my way and believed that the issue under consideration would be interesting for legal scholars and students.

First of all, I would like to thank Professor R. Wolfrum and Professor A. von Bogdandy, directors of the Max Planck Institute for Comparative Public Law and International Law, for the possibility to spend a wonderful year at the Institute, which gave me the chance to work on this book, and also for their priceless support and advice.

I am also grateful to the directors of the Center for Diplomatic and Strategic Studies in Paris for their material support in publishing this book.

My special gratitude is for Professor M. Strauss at the Center for Diplomatic and Strategic Studies, who believed in my ability to accomplish this task and kindly agreed to edit the book.

I would also like to thank my colleagues from the International Law Department of the Belarusian State University and the fellows and guests of the Max Planck Institute for Comparative Public Law and International Law for their valuable comments.

Finally – and most of all – I would like to thank my family for their understanding, tolerance, patience and support.

ABBREVIATIONS

AU – African Union
CFSP – Common Foreign and Security Policy (of the European Union)
CIS – Commonwealth of Independent States
CHS – Council of the Heads of State (of the CIS)
CJEU – Court of Justice of the European Union
CMF – Collective military forces
CRRF – Collective Rapid Reaction Forces (of the CSTO)
CSBM – Confidence- and security-building measures
CSTO – Collective Security Treaty Organization
DARIO – Draft Articles on the Responsibility of International Organizations, 2011
DARS – Draft Articles on Responsibility of States for Internationally Wrongful Acts, 2001
DPRK – Democratic People's Republic of Korea
DRC – Democratic Republic of Congo
ECHR – European Convention on Human Rights (Convention for the Protection of Human Rights and Fundamental Freedoms), 1950
ECOWAS – Economic Community of West African States
ECOMOG – ECOWAS Monitoring Group
EU – European Union
GUAM – Georgia, Ukraine, Azerbaijan and Moldavia (organization)
ICCPR – International Covenant on Civil and Political Rights, 1966
ICJ – International Court of Justice
ILC – International Law Commission
NATO – North Atlantic Treaty Organization
OAS – Organization of American States
OSCE – Organization for Security and Cooperation in Europe
OWT – Organization of Warsaw Treaty (Warsaw Pact)
PDK – Party of Democratic Kampuchea
SCO – Shanghai Cooperation Organization
TCS – Treaty of Collective Security, 1992
TEU – Treaty on European Union (Treaty of Maastricht), 1992
TFEU – Treaty on the Functioning of the European Union, 2007
TNC – Transnational company
UK – United Kingdom
UN HRC – United Nations Human Rights Committee
UN – United Nations

UNASUR – Union of South American Nations (Unión de Naciones Suramericanas)
UNITA – National Union for the Total Independence of Angola
US, USA – United States, United States of America
USSR – Union of Soviet Socialist Republics
WANGO – World Association of Non-Governmental Organizations
WEU – Western European Union

PREFACE

According to the main assumption presented by Thomas Hobbes four centuries ago, and developed by Kenneth Waltz at the end of the last century, security is mainly "individual" and each state is concerned by its own survival as a state within the framework of an anarchic order. Unlike the domestic order that is hierarchic, the international order is submitted to no supranational power and is subject to violent competition between sovereign subjects. Each state is bound by a realistic approach to foreign policy in order to face the threats to its own interests and beyond this to its own existence as a sovereign state. This could be a case against the current implementation of the concept of collective security. The concept would be deemed to be ignored and in the best case to be instrumented by the states themselves in order to legitimate and to dissimulate their own political agendas.

Nevertheless, the anarchic structure of the international order was supposed to be moderated during the bipolar era, when the effects of an unsteady multipolar system were replaced by a new kind of competition that could in no way lead to a total confrontation between the two superpowers, but rather to a mixture of sectoral conflicts balanced by implied compromises.

Did the downfall of the second superpower after 1989 bring us again to a traditional multipolar system almost one decade after the United States failed in establishing itself as the only remaining superpower? The comeback of Russia and the emergence of China as the second economic power in the world do not get us back to the thirties of the twentieth century. Some radical change occurred in the nature of the worldwide system.

It is hardly worth emphasizing the unipolar moment that allowed the United States to transform the Security Council of the United Nations into an efficient body, relieved of the paralysis of the Cold War and of more than three hundred vetoes over four decades. We can easily argue that the many resolutions voted and the multiple international agreements that made UN-based multilateralism work weren't considered by the provisionally sole superpower as a way to foster collective security as such, but rather as a way of removing the threats and challenges that US hegemony could face.

The assumption that security is first of all linked to the states individually could remain credible if state sovereignty were not jeopardized by the hyper-concentration of global capital that resulted in the rapid growth of the economic power of multinational companies, qualified as transnational companies (TNC). This contributed to limiting the actual sovereignty of states, and resulted in a progressive reduction of their ability to issue protective regulations. International institutions supported the trend toward economic reforms inspired by the "Washington consensus" that affected the economic power of states and their economic sovereignty, submitting a wide range of sectors and public services to the rule of the TNCs and the stock markets.

This is to say that the rise of the transnational centers of power has changed the level of concern in the field of international security. As long as certain issues cannot be handled by the states on their own, especially if the states are small or medium-sized in an economic sense, compelled to satisfy the TNCs' quest for optimality, the issues become dealt with globally, along with the rise of the idea of global answers to the hegemony of global capital. Among these answers, the Global Compact appears to be the very basis for transnational regulation limiting the power of transnational capital.

We should have expected research on "collective security" to emphasize war, terrorism and other militarily backed issues. But it seems that many issues that have been in the past considered as "low politics" – issues such as health, the environment, education and social rights, according to the classification by David Fidler – became progressively part of global concerns.

The history of contemporary international politics seems to move from nationally centered concerns to global concerns and from narrow political and military concerns to a wide range of human concerns like those that were part of low politics.

The concept of "security" is also extended: from a concept meaning the security of a state's territory, international politics moved to a definition of security that includes human security, and this extension is subject to a precise and serious statement in Alena Douhan's research. The extension of security to human concerns including human rights, environmental issues and material survival (through, for instance, water supply, etc.) displays an international system politically and legally abandoning the monopoly of states on the definition of security, and moving toward societies and individuals.

Let's now consider the actors that are responsible for such radical changes. The first actors we refer to are international organizations, which are interstate organizations. United Nations bodies contributed to such a doctrinal shift from the principle of non-interference to the duty of humanitarian intervention through a step-by-step process that actually started with the General Assembly's Resolution 43/131 in December 1988, then with Security Council Resolution 688 on Iraqi Kurdistan in 1991. Regional organizations followed the same path; the African Union moved away from its predecessor, the Organization of African Unity, by emphasizing democracy and expecting an appropriate process of reaction against any takeover of political power by the military. Another international organization, the Union of South American Nations (UNASUR – *Unión de Naciones Suramericanas*), emphasized not only human rights issues but above all the principles of social justice at a time when almost all the continent had moved to the left (except for Colombia and a few others) and was trying to break with the very high degree of inequalities left by the former rightist authoritarian, then liberal regimes.

International organizations, whether universal or regional, weren't working alone. The very dense networks of non-governmental organizations (NGO) did a lot to support such a move. They succeeded in facing the most authoritarian regimes, either by getting and providing information or by extending the field of advocacy to almost all social concerns. The World Association of Non-Governmental Organizations (WANGO) estimated in 2010 that there were more than 49,600 NGOs worldwide that had significant influence, with millions of other smaller ones.

This very dense network of international organizations, NGOs and MNCs contributes nowadays to the weakening of the state's monopoly on domestic affairs as it contributes to the extension of the "international community's" concerns to almost all domestic social issues.

But isn't it preferable to remove the confusing ambiguity between collective security and global security? Both seem to be linked and interrelating. While collective security still recognizes the prominent role of the states and emphasizes common issues and threats that can no more be dealt with by national authorities working alone, the concept of global security jumps over the heads of national authorities as it makes of every domestic issue a global concern on which every international/global actor can interfere.

Interrelation is nevertheless obvious between what is collective and what is global; collective action is needed to face an increasing amount of threats, just because the dimension of the threats becomes global. The Shanghai Cooperation Organization's (SCO) main objectives seem to address these issues: because criminality and terrorism become globalized, interstate cooperation is needed. Furthermore, collective initiatives are praised, and despite the overwhelming character of state initiatives, the collective dimension is far from being absent from the scene of SCO actions;

such is the case for most of the regional organizations in which Russia is a pivotal state actor.

But if an increasing number of fields fall into the sphere of collective security – as is the case with state stability, domestic conflicts, terrorism, criminality, the environment and health – the response to collective concerns has to be collective also, involving regional and universal organizations alike. This link seems to be so obvious that it hides the many problems linked to the collective decision-making process. Here lies the dilemma between justice and efficiency. To be the closest possible to justice, the decision is bound not to hurt the individual states' rights and sovereignty and therefore to extend the rule of unanimity inside the executive bodies. But unanimity is often responsible for paralysis, and most international organizations have experienced this moment several times: from the Common Foreign and Security Policy (CFSP) in the European Union to the mechanisms prevailing within the SCO, unanimity leads to a lack of efficiency. On the other side, the concern for efficiency leads to a breach of equality among member states. The Security Council of the UN is an example of this kind of breach.

But efficiency is also a result of the balance of force within an organization. It has been stated that wherever in the composition of the organization a state has a dominant position, thus working as a pivotal state, the efficiency is higher. For instance, the peacekeeping mission by ECOMOG – the Economic Community of West African States (ECOWAS) Monitoring Group – in Liberia and Sierra Leone would have missed its objective without Nigerian leadership and military involvement (we know that Nigeria's population is 16 times the population of Ivory Coast). In the case of the Community of Independent States (CIS), Russian dominance is crucial in measuring the results of peacekeeping in Central Asia.

On the other hand, whenever the dominant position of a state leads to hegemony, it produces negative reactions among the smaller states, in a way that can jeopardize what remains collective in the collective decision. The dominant position of Russia inside the CIS, whose objectives were at the same time economic and linked to political and security issues, led to disruptive behavior among the smaller states: Uzbekistan decided quickly to withdraw from the common currency in 1994, while other peripheral countries decided to create in 1996 a parallel regional organization called the GUAM (Georgia, Ukraine, Azerbaijan and Moldova) with similar aims and prerogatives and expected peacekeeping missions in order to balance Russian power, thus leading Russia to tighten the links between herself and her close allies within the Collective Security Treaty Organization (CSTO) in 2002, with a smaller number of CIS states, but with a more cohesive structure and greater efficiency in military and security initiatives and intervention.

Another obstacle to a common response to collective security issues is the divergence in doctrinal interpretations of international rules and norms. As long as the coupling of collective security issues with collective responses needs a common doctrinal background, the problem of divergence appears, and this was obvious when the new world order shaped by the United States' hegemony after 1990 shifted from the principle of strict respect of states' sovereignty to the principle of interference for humanitarian and collective security reasons. Consensus was not yet reached among the member states of the United Nations system but apparently drafted by the unbalanced relationship within the Security Council. This dissension deepened in the aftermath of 9/11, when the burden of member states became heavier and they were being forced to cooperate within the sense of the binary slogan "if you don't abide fully you are against us." Resolution 1373 (2001) expresses the standpoint detailed above. With the doctrine of preventive war, the dissension reached its peak. So according to which interpretation of the UN Charter will collective security concern be addressed, if we consider that the Bush Administration was in 2002-03 supported by a wide range of no less than 35 member states?

Maybe the answer lies in common procedural principles similar to those imagined by Mohamed Bedjaoui, who, during the seventies, considered that the decisions taken by the General Assembly of the United Nations, as a genuine representative of the international community, could be binding for all its member states. But the effective balance of force and the very nature of the international order that is anarchic, if we refer to the realist doctrine, doesn't make any procedural foundation this obvious. Such is the case of each regional organization. The League of Arab States suffered from this dilemma despite the common civilizational and nationalistic backgrounds among the Arab states. In the situation in which unanimity was unreachable, a decision taken by a majority of the member states was binding for those that approved, and was nevertheless effective, thus avoiding total paralysis.

We can summarize by stressing the paradoxical pairings concerning collective security:

- Collective security arose within the context of a deepening globalization that limited to a great extent the sovereignty of member states that was the main assumption for all the classical theories of international relations. But at the same time, the globalization of security issues represents a level above collective concern. Global security issues may rather marginalize the role of states, especially if they are not the leading states.

- Collective security issues are growing as international and regional organizations are taking an increasing range of prerogatives from their member states, but the paradoxical situation is that the most efficient collective responses are made by those which are framed by at least one hegemonic state (Nigeria in ECOWAS, Russia in the CIS and CSTO, etc.).
- Therefore, collective responses to collective security issues are subject to the old dilemma between justice and efficiency. Very often, collective actions and agreements undermine the principle of equal treatment among states in order to act efficiently: this is, for instance, the case of the Non-Proliferation Treaty based on the unequal status between nuclear and non-nuclear states.
- Last but not least, addressing collective security issues needs common doctrinal frameworks. Are these progressively being set by the United Nations system, through the accumulation of collective resolutions? It is not so obvious, especially since 9/11, when the US administration launched its doctrinal offensive on the traditional principles of international law by introducing new principles that could become effective thanks to their enforcement by military supremacy and would find justification afterward, thus giving credibility to Blaise Pascal's proverb: "If it is impossible for justice to be empowered, let the power become justice."

– Fouad Nohra
Senior Lecturer, Université Paris Descartes
Academic Director, Centre d'Etudes Diplomatiques et Stratégiques
December 2012

INTRODUCTION

In spite of the initial enthusiasm about the role of the UN Security Council, by the early 1990s it appeared unable to settle an enormous number of internal and interstate conflicts arising in all parts of the world or to handle new threats and challenges faced by the international community. As a result, regional and subregional institutions have increasingly assumed responsibility for the maintenance of international peace and security.

These organizations are hardly comparable with the arrangements and entities imagined by the founders of the United Nations. They aspire to be actively involved in the prevention of hypothetical conflicts and the settlement of existing ones, as well as in the struggle against new threats and challenges. Indeed, it is the regional organizations rather than the United Nations that are able to demonstrate and apply real power, including the establishment of permanent military and peacekeeping forces.

Moreover, due to the inability of the Security Council to bear primary responsibility for maintaining international peace and security in the form envisaged in the UN Charter, some publicists argue that the principles of the United Nations[1] and the primary role and responsibility of the Security Council are obsolete in this sphere.[2] Regional organizations are often put forth as a substitute for the "lame" mechanisms of the United Nations setting criteria of international legitimacy and morality.

Apparently, the whole system of international relations, especially with respect to the maintenance of international peace and security, may serve as a good symbol of duality. We oppose universality to regionalization; total formal control by the UN Security Council to *de facto*

---

[1] Damrosch L.F., "Sanctions against the Perpetrators of Terrorism," *Houston Journal of International Law* 22(1) (1999), p. 65; Simon S., Benjamin D., "America and the New Terrorism," *Survival (The IISS Quarterly)* 42(1) (2000), p. 62; Малеев Ю.Н., "Реабилитация адекватного и пропорционального применения силы" [Maleev Y.N., "Rehabilitation of the Adequate and Proportional Use of Force"], *Moscow Journal of International Law*, 3 (2004), p. 31-47; Гольцов С.Д., Малеев Ю.Н., "Применение вооруженной силы государствами как мера превентивной самозащиты ad hoc от внешней угрозы" [Goltsov S.D., Maleev Y.N., "Use of Military Force by States as a Means of *ad hoc* Preventive Self-Help against the External Threat"], *Moscow Journal of International Law*, 4 (2004), p. 45-58.

[2] Byers M., "Terrorism, the Use of Force and International Law after 11 September 2001," *International and Comparative Law Quarterly*, 51 (2002), part 2, p. 402; Müllerson R., Scheffer, D.J., "Legal Regulation of the Use of Force," in *Beyond Confrontation: International Law for the Post-Cold War Era*, ed. L.F. Damrosh, G.M. Danilenko, R. Müllerson (Boulder: Westview Press, 1995), p. 112.

discretion and arbitrariness of states and regional organizations; subsidiarity in UN-regional relations to complementarity of interorganizational tasks; legality to legitimacy; steep demands in particular situations to absolute blindness in some others; "high" principles and ideals to pragmatic aspirations to secure national interests; "old" rules of the UN Charter and contemporary "exceptional" reality.

In international relations and international law we do not deal with "pure" ideal mathematics. We have to deal with reality – but reality existing within the set of well-recognized and established principles and norms. I will therefore not advocate here for the obsolescence of the UN Charter or the need for its comprehensive amendment or even its rejection. I also do not believe that some "higher values" like democracy, security or human rights may be achieved by breaching fundamental rules of the contemporary world order, the denial of the rule of law. That is why I will stand up for the preservation *in interim* of the UN Charter but at the same time for its reinterpretation, especially concerning the maintenance of international peace and security.

The need for reinterpreting the Charter's rules as well as for reestablishing an effective system of collective security is obvious and can easily be illustrated by situations taking place in every region of the world. Sometimes the calls for reinterpretation are rather far-reaching,[3] and it is thus necessary to decide on the rules and framework of the process.

It would be rather ridiculous to claim that the issue of regional cooperation in maintaining international peace and security is not explored in international law. One may cite hundreds of works on the topic that have appeared since the UN Charter was drafted.[4] At the same time, even the

---

[3] *E.g.*, Canadian author W.A. Knight proposes to extend the application of Chapter VIII to non-state arrangements (Knight W.A., "Towards a Subsidiarity Model for Peacemaking and Preventive Diplomacy: Making Chapter VIII of the UN Operational," *Third World Quarterly*, 17(1) (1996), p. 32.

[4] *E.g.*, Abass A., *Regional Organizations and the Development of Collective Security: Beyond Chapter VIII of the UN Charter* (Oxford/Portland: Hart Publishing, 2004); Weiss T.G., ed., *Beyond UN Subcontracting: Task-Sharing with Regional Security Arrangements and Service-Providing NGOs* (New York: St. Martin's Press, Inc., 1998); Borgen C.J., "The Theory and Practice of Regional Organization in Civil Wars," *New York University Journal of International Law and Politics*, 26 (1994), p. 799-835; Heiskanen V., "The Rationality of the Use of Force and the Evolution of International Organizations," in *The Legitimacy of International Organizations*, ed. J.-M. Coicaud and V. Heiskanen (Tokyo/NY/Paris: UN University Press, 2001), p. 155-185; Körbs H., *Die Friedensdicherung duech die Vereinten Nationen und Regionalorganizationen nach Kapitel VIII der Satzung der Vereinten Nationen* (Bochum: UVB – Unversitätsverlag Dr. N. Brockmeyer, 1997); Lind K., *The Revival of Chapter VIII of the UN Charter: Regional Organizations and Collective Security* (Stockholm: PrintCenter, 2004).

newest works follow the traditional pattern of research as well as a traditional approach to the problem. Activities of regional organizations that have occurred outside the auspices of Chapter VIII in light of inaction by the UN Security Council, problems of accountability to (and of) the Security Council, issues of cooperation in the modern interdependent world as well as regional cooperation in specific parts of this world in the face of new threats and challenges – all of these are simply ignored. More and more often we see appeals to accept a situation or behavior just because it takes place[5] or is not condemned.[6] Attention is often paid to the politics of particular organizations, although only a detailed analysis of the whole set of regional organizations involved in the maintenance of peace and security, and of their counteraction and cooperation with the Security Council, may allow us to reach conclusions on the effectiveness of the mechanism.

This book does not pretend to offer a comprehensive study of all of the issues arising from regional mechanisms of collective security. It is rather selective and focuses only on certain elements. At the same time, it seeks to present a new (or at least revised) vision of Chapter VIII of the UN Charter and to discuss the most urgent and important issues in this area.

The first chapter discusses general issues of collective security, including its history, development and current trends. It refers back to the very notion of security and all the changes it has encountered since the end of World War II.

The second chapter describes the current notions and characteristics of regional arrangements and agencies in accordance with Chapter VIII of the UN Charter, outlines their competences, and discusses their traditional and new activities.

The third chapter focuses on contemporary developments in the most dangerous sphere of activity of regional organizations – that which involves immediate or indirect enforcement elements. Special attention is paid to "broadly prized" – but equally condemned – targeted sanctions and the revival of treaty-based interventions.

---

[5] Fourth Report on State Responsibility, by Mr. Gaetano Arangio-Ruiz, Special Rapporteur, Document A/CN.4/444 and Add. 1-3., in *Yearbook of the International Law Commission* (1992-II), Part I (New York/Geneva: United Nations, 1995), p. 30-32; Borelli S., Olleson S., "Obligations Relating to Human Rights and Humanitarian Law," in *The Law of International Responsibility*, ed. J. Crawford, A. Pellet, S. Olleson (Oxford: Oxford University Press, 2010), p. 1180.

[6] Abass A. *Regional Organizations and the Development of Collective Security*, *op. cit.*, p. 53-54, cited by Ress G., Bröhmer J., "Article 53," in *The Charter of the United Nations: A Commentary*, ed. B. Simma, 2nd ed., vol. 1 (Munich: Verlag C.H. Beck, 2002), p. 866.

The fourth chapter considers in-depth issues of mutual relations and cooperation between the United Nations and organizations acting under Chapter VIII, as well as current and possible mechanisms of control from the side of the UN Security Council.

The last chapter seeks to evaluate the status, competences, tasks and activities of regional organizations acting within the territory of the former Soviet Union (the OSCE, CIS, and CSTO) under the existing legal framework, insofar as the mechanisms of collective security that function in this territory are substantially neglected in the European legal doctrine.[7]

---

[7] See, *e.g.*, Бордюжа Н. "Организация Договора о коллективной безопасности" [Bordyuzha N., "The Collective Security Treaty Organization"], *International Life*, 2 (2005), p. 72-82; Bordyuzha N., "The Collective Security Treaty Organization: A Brief Overview," *OSCE Yearbook,* 16 (2010), p. 339-350; Николаенко В., "10 лет Договору о коллективной безопасности" [Nikolaenko V., "10 Years of the Treaty of Collective Security"], *International Life*, 3 (2003), p. 60-66; Рекута А.Л., "Организация Договора о коллективной безопасности: проблемы и пути развития по предотвращению угроз безопасности в Центрально-Азиатском регионе" [Rekuta A.L., "The Collective Security Treaty Organization: Challenges and Perspectives of Development to Prevent the Threats to Security in the Central Asian Region"], *Military Thought* 11, (2006), p. 2-9.

CHAPTER 1

COLLECTIVE SECURITY IN THE MODERN WORLD

1.1 Security in the Modern World

Art.1(1) of the UN Charter declares the maintenance of international peace and security as the key purpose of the United Nations.[8] Security is one of those vague and indeterminate notions that are well known to everyone, but for which no uniform definition has developed.

In the aftermath of World War II, security was approached very narrowly and was seen basically as ensuring the absence of interstate military conflicts.[9] Subsequent developments demonstrated, though, that international peace and security depend on numerous factors and processes. A military conflict could result from a variety of economic, social, ideological or other reasons. Moreover, the international community has come to face a number of new threats and challenges which include, *inter alia*, intrastate and interregional instability; international terrorism; the proliferation of weapons of mass destruction; illicit trafficking of arms, drugs and human beings; illegal migration; cyber-threats; *etc.*[10] These trends

---

[8] On this point, see Hogan W.N., *International Conflict and Collective Security: The Principle of Concern in International Organization* (Lexington: University of Kentucky Press, 1955), p. 179; de Luca S.M., "The Gulf Crisis and Collective Security under the United Nations Charter," *Pace Yearbook of International Law*, 3(1) (1991), p. 268; Neuhold H., "Collective Security after 'Operation Allied Force,'" *Max Planck Yearbook of United Nations Law*, 4 (2000), p. 74; Kelsen H., "Collective Security and Collective Self-Defense under the Charter of the United Nations," *American Journal of International Law*, 42(4) (1948), p. 783.

[9] *Documents of the UN Conference on International Organization*, San Francisco, 1945, vol. III. General (London/New York, United Nations Information Organizations, 1945), p. 434-440. See also Doehring K., "Collective Security," in *United Nations: Law, Politics and Practice*, ed. R. Wolfrum, vol. I (Munich: Verlag C.H. Beck, 1995), p. 110, 112; Evers F., Kahl M., Zellner W., *The Culture of Dialogue: The OSCE Acquis 30 Years after Helsinki* (Hamburg: CORE, 2005), p. 17; *Documents of the UN Conference on International Organization*, San Francisco, 1945, vol. I. General (London/New York, United Nations Information Organizations, 1945), p. 186; Pronk J., "United Nations: Changes, Challenges, Chances," in *The Role of the United Nations in Peace and Security, Global Development and World Governance: An Assessment of the Evidence,* ed. M. Hordijk, M. van Eerd, K. Hofman (Lewinston: The Edwin Mellen Press, 2007), p. 238.

[10] Charter of Paris for a New Europe, 1990; Astana Commemorative Declaration, "Towards a Security Community," 2010, para. 9; Corfu Informal Meeting of OSCE Foreign Ministers on the Future of European Security, Chair's Concluding Statements to the Press, 2009, para. 4; *A*

have found their way into a range of UN Security Council resolutions that have addressed threats to international peace and security; civil conflicts within a country;[11] gross violations of human rights, including genocide;[12] illegitimate anti-democratic governments;[13] destabilization of situations by refugee flows;[14] shipments of weapons in the course of civil conflict;[15] terrorism;[16] drug trafficking; transnational crimes;[17] *etc.*

Some institutions view threats and challenges to international security much more broadly, adding poverty, disease, environmental degradation and other factors to the range mentioned above.[18]

I will join here the position of professor T.M. Franck in advocating that it is not only the list but also the character of the threats that have changed.[19] Indeed, operationally, threats and challenges are still faced and countered by individual states, but they are not national threats any more. We have now come into the era of transboundary or transnational threats, and no state or regional organization, however strong and developed it may be, can handle them all on its own. Moreover, we can hardly expect this situation to change in the foreseeable future.

More Secure World: Our Shared Responsibility. Report of the Secretary-General's High Panel on Threats, Challenges and Change (New York: United Nations, 2004), p. 14-16, paras. 17-23; Strategic Concept for the Defence and Security of the Members of the North Atlantic Treaty Organization, 2010 (hereafter, NATO Strategic Concept), paras. 4, 8-15; see also Возженикoв А.В., Отв. ред., *Региональная безопасность: геополитический и геоэкономический подходы (теория и практика)* [Vozzhenikov A.V., ed., *Regional Security: Geopolitical and Geoeconomic Approaches*] (Moscow: Russian Academy of State Service, 2006), p. 80-81; Graham K., "Regionalism and Responses to Armed Conflict, with Special Focus on Conflict Prevention and Peace-keeping," in *Regionalisation and Global Governance: The Taming of Globalization?*, ed A.F. Cooper, Chr.W. Hughes, Ph. de Lombaerde (London/New York: Routledge Taylor and Francis Group, 2008), p. 164-165.

[11] UN Security Council Resolution 161 (1961), 21 February 1961.

[12] UN Security Council Resolutions 775 (1992), 28 August 1992; 929 (1994), 22 June 1994; 940 (1994), 31 July 1994.

[13] UN Security Council Resolution 221 (1966), 9 April 1966.

[14] UN Security Council Resolution 812 (1993), 12 March 1993.

[15] UN Security Council Resolution 775 (1992), *op. cit.*

[16] UN Security Council Resolutions 1373 (2001), 12 October 2001; 1511 (2003), 16 October 2003.

[17] Statement by the President of the Security Council, S/PRST/2010/4, 24 February 2010.

[18] *A More Secure World*, *op. cit.*, paras. 17-23; Charter of Paris, *op. cit.*; NATO Strategic Concept, *op. cit.*, paras 4, 8-15; Astana Commemorative Declaration, *op. cit.*, para. 9. See also Danchin P.G., Fischer H., "Introduction: The New Collective Security," in *United Nations Reform and the New Collective Security*, ed. P.G. Danchin, H. Fischer (Cambridge: Cambridge University Press, 2010), p. 14-19.

[19] Franck T.M. "Collective Security and UN Reform: Between the Necessary and the Possible," *Chicago Journal of International Law*, 6(2) (2005-2006), p. 601.

It is thus no surprise that security is currently viewed comprehensively and now includes not only politico-military but also economic, environmental and humanitarian aspects.[20] Security is often associated with and conditioned by the process of development,[21] including sustainable development.[22] Indeed, the broadening of the notion of "security" in all dimensions is a natural and well-grounded process. And it is the only thing that can push states all around the globe, regardless of their development levels, their preferences and dislikes, to work together in order to handle situations and factors (also all around the globe) that may undermine international security as well as their own national security. In the contemporary interdependent and ever-smaller world, economic, environmental and humanitarian problems may ultimately turn into political and military conflicts.

However, this is only one side of the coin. A broad approach to security may also result in the escalation of threats in the politico-military sphere. States and regional organizations seek to impose sanctions on behalf of the "common good," and attempt to apply military force to states that have failed (in the opinion of other states or organizations) to fulfill their duty (responsibility) to protect or to guarantee democracy, the rule of law or anything else. All the more, attempts have already been made to include on the agenda of the UN Security Council issues of climate change, to qualify it as a threat to international peace and security and to establish special "peacekeeping climate change forces" (so-called "*green helmets*").[23]

It is not my purpose here to deny the importance of environmental or humanitarian issues or to negate the dangers they may bring to the world community. At the same time, I would insist that mass dilution of the foundations of the United Nations (including attempts to extend mechanisms of politico-military security to other spheres), even when these efforts are aimed at the protection of common values, may hardly bring stability and security to the world order, promote the "common good" or ensure observance of the rule of law.

---

[20] *A More Secure World*, *op. cit.*, paras. 17-23; Charter of Paris, *op. cit.*; Astana Commemorative Declaration, *op. cit.*, para. 6; Hannay D., "Collective Security and the Use of Force," *International Organizations Law Review*, 2(2) (2005), p. 367-368.

[21] In Larger Freedom: Towards Development, Security and Human Rights for All: Report of the Secretary-General (A/59/2005), p. 16-17.

[22] *A More Secure World*, *op. cit.*; Pronk J., "United Nations: Changes, Challenges, Chances," *op. cit.*, p. 242.

[23] See UN Security Council Reports, 5663rd Meeting, 17 April 2007; 6587th Meeting, 20 July 2011.

The problem of climate change, in fact, offers a good illustration of this point, as it is covered by a detailed legal framework. Besides several special documents on issues under consideration (*e.g.*, the UN Framework Convention on Climate Change of 1992, the Kyoto Protocol of 1997), international law provides for extensive regulation of some associated aspects; there are mechanisms that address liability for environmental damage in different situations[24] and the responsibility of states to take all necessary steps to prevent transboundary harm.[25] Existing gaps will logically be filled through cooperation between states and codification in the realm of the environment. Therefore, it is very unlikely that the Security Council, with its exceptional powers for maintaining international peace and security, could be deemed a proper organ for dealing with environmental issues. Moreover, its involvement would not do any good for settling these problems. On the contrary, it would open a wide path for new abuses pursuant to national or regional interests, and for arbitrary unilateral intervention into the domestic affairs of particular states by making reference to the importance of environmental issues to humanity as a whole.

It is not my purpose here to doubt the correctness and importance of the comprehensive approach to security. I will insist, however, that this approach shall not be directly applied to the activities of the Security Council or regional organizations under Chapter VIII of the UN Charter. The provisions of the Charter shall be interpreted in accordance with established and well-known rules set forth by art. 31 of the Vienna Convention on the Law of Treaties,[26] with due account for the object, purpose and other norms of the UN Charter.[27] The extraordinary powers of the Security Council as well as the activities of regional organizations under Chapter VIII of the Charter (as part of the UN mechanism of collective security) are designed to

[24] See, *e.g.*, Convention on Environmental Impact Assessment in a Transboundary Context, 1991; Convention on Long-range Air Pollution, 1979; Convention on Supplementary Compensation for Nuclear Damage, 1997; Convention on the Transboundary Effects of Industrial Accidents, signed 17 March 1992, entered into force 19 April 2000; UN ILC "Draft Articles on Prevention of Transboundary Harm from Hazardous Activities" (2001), GAOR 56th Session Supplement 10, p. 370 *et seq.*; UN ILC "Draft Principles on the Allocation of Loss in the Case of Transboundary Harm Arising out of Hazardous Activities (with Commentaries)" (2006), GAOR 61st Session Supplement 10, p. 106 *et seq.*

[25] Environmental liability conventions; UN ILC "Draft Articles on Prevention of Transboundary Harm from Hazardous Activities," *op. cit.*

[26] Vienna Convention on the Law of Treaties, 23 May 1969, *1155 UNTS*, 331 *et seq.*

[27] Supported by Thakur R., *The United Nations, Peace and Security: From Collective Security to Responsibility to Protect* (Cambridge: Cambridge University Press, 2006), p. 71-221; Ghebali V-Y., Lambert A., *The OSCE Code of Conduct on Politico-Military Aspects of Security: Anatomy and Implementation* (Leiden: Matinus Nijhoff Publishers, 2005), p. 19.

deal with politico-military aspects of security and may deal only with these aspects.

Due to the expansion of threats and challenges in the modern world, however, these aspects are to be viewed rather broadly in their own right. Besides addressing internal and external conflicts, they include the prevention of even the possibility of conflicts (disarmament, control over armaments, confidence- and security-building measures) and the suppression of contemporary menaces (international terrorism, the proliferation of weapons of mass destruction, transboundary crimes).

1.2 History of Collective Security

Collective security has a long history. As noted by H. Kelsen in 1948, "*Collective security is the main purpose of the United Nations, just as it was the main purpose of its predecessor – the League of Nations.*"[28]

The theoretical possibility of collective security had been discussed as far back as the 12th century. For example, P. Dubois, advisor to the French king Philip the Fair, promoted the idea of cooperation among Christian states, including the possibility of collective self-defense as well as collective enforcement against members of the coalition that infringed its rules.[29] The same issues were later developed in the works of W. Penn (Essay Towards the Present and Future Peace in Europe, 1693); Abbé de Saint-Pierre (Projet pour rendre la paix perpetuelle en Europe, 1713) and E. Kant (Essay on Perpetual Peace, 1795).[30]

In practice, the history of collective security can be traced back to various agreements on collective defense[31] and bi- and multilateral non-

---

[28] Kelsen H., "Collective Security and Collective Self-Defense," *op. cit.*, p. 783. See also Neuhold H., "Collective Security after 'Operation Allied Force,'" *op. cit.*, p. 74; de Luca S.M., "The Gulf Crisis and Collective Security," *op. cit.*, p. 268.

[29] Lorenz J.P., *Peace, Power, and the United Nations: A Security System for the Twenty-first Century* (Oxford: Westview Press, 1999), p. 9.

[30] Cited by Danchin P.G., "Things Fall Apart: The Concept of Collective Security in International Law," in *United Nations Reform and the New Collective Security*, ed. P.G. Danchin, H. Fischer (Cambridge: Cambridge University Press, 2010), p. 47-51.

[31] Weiss T.G., Forsythe D.R., Coate R.A., Pease K.-K., *The United Nations and Changing World Politics,* 5th ed. (Boulder: Westview Press, 2007), p. 4; Goodrich L.M., Hambro E., *Charter of the United Nations: Commentary and Documents,* 3rd ed. (Boston: World Peace Foundation, 1946), p. 183; Herndl K. "Reflections on the Role, Functions and Procedures of the Security Council of the United Nations," *Recueil des Cours/Collected Courses of the*

aggression pacts.[32] At the multilateral level, certain provisions can already be found in the Treaty of Westphalia of 1648, under which all parties were obliged to defend provisions of the treaty toward any third states, and were encouraged to settle their disputes by peaceful means (art. CXXIII) and to assist other parties in collective self-defence (art. CXXIV).[33] The Concert of Europe established after the Vienna Congress in 1815 provided for the possibility of collective self-defense as well as collective action by the great powers,[34] which finally developed into the doctrine of "legitimate interventions" and resulted in military interventions to suppress revolutions in Italy (by Austria, 1821) and Spain (by France, 1822).

It is generally recognized that the system of the Concert of Europe cannot be viewed as a system of collective security in the contemporary sense, although some authors view it as the predecessor[35] or the simplest form of it.[36] In legal terms, the Concert of Europe can be called either a system of a balance of power or a system of alliances. It was aimed at the defense of the territory and the rights of its members,[37] often at the expense of any third state or alliance.[38] In short, this type of system did not intend to protect or promote international peace and security in general or to defend a particular state;[39] rather, it sought to secure the balance of power in a specific

---

Hague Academy of International Law, 206 (1987, VI), (Dordrecht: Martinus Nijhoff Publishers, 1991), p. 302.

[32] Doehring K., "Collective Security," *op. cit.*, p. 111.

[33] Treaty of Westphalia, 24 October 1648.

[34] Danchin P.G., "Things Fall Apart," *op. cit.*, p. 48.

[35] de Wet E., Wood M. "Collective Security," *Max Planck Encyclopedia of Public International Law*; Liska G., *Nations in Alliance: the Limits of Interdependence* (Baltimore: The John Hopkins Press, 1962), p. 10-12.

[36] Kelsen H., "Collective Security and Collective Self-Defense," *op. cit.*, p. 783-784; Thompson K.W., "Collective Security Reexamined," in *From Collective Security to Preventive Diplomacy: Readings in International Organization and the Maintenance of Peace*, ed. J. Larus (New York: John Wiley & Sons, Inc., 1965), p. 285.

[37] Johnson C.H., Niemeyer G., "Collective Security: The Validity of an Ideal," *International Organizations*, 1 (1954), p. 22; Nye J.S., *Understanding International Conflicts: An Introduction to Theory and History,* 3rd ed. (New York: Longman, 2000), p. 63; Rothstein R.L., *Alliances and Small Powers* (New York: Columbia University Press, 1968), p. 238.

[38] Liska G., *Nations in Alliance, op. cit.*, p. 3, 12; Nye J.S., *Understanding International Conflicts, op. cit.*, p. 83; Kelsen H., *Collective Security under International Law* (Washington: US Government Printing Office, 1954), p. 39.

[39] Nye J.S., *Understanding International Conflicts, op. cit.*, p. 55.

region[40] or to change the existing balance on behalf of its members[41] – that is, its members cooperated against a particular state or group of states.[42]

The League of Nations the and UN system, as advanced in the legal doctrine, combined both suppressive and preventive mechanisms as a means of maintaining international peace and security,[43] which was a significant development. They were opposed to the balance of power system[44] and were oriented toward the maintenance of universal peace and security (including the security of every individual state), and as such it is claimed that they constituted a perfectly new notion – the system of collective security.[45] In theory, as H. Kelsen has noted, the very fact of the establishment of the universal organization of collective security, which prohibited the use of force between its member states, was to put an end to alliances directed against third states and organizations.[46] This optimistic approach, however, appeared to be remote from reality. Certain elements of the system of the balance of power remained into the second part of the 20th century.[47] In fact,

---

[40] Organski A.F.K., *World Politics* (New York: Alfred A. Knopf, 1958), p. 273.

[41] Nye J.S., *Understanding International Conflicts*, *op. cit.*, p. 55, 81; Rothstein R.L., *Alliances and Small Powers*, *op. cit.*, p. 47.

[42] Nye J.S., *Understanding International Conflicts*, *op. cit.*, p. 59.

[43] See Elaraby N., "Some Reflections on the Role of the Security Council and the Prohibition of the Use of Force in International Relations: Article 2(4) Revisited in Light of Recent Developments," in *Verhandeln für den Frieden,* ed. J.A. Frowein (Berlin: Springer, 2003), p. 42. At the same time, the League of Nations system is also sometimes viewed as a system of the balance of power; see Ball J.H., *Collective Security: The Why and How* (Boston: World Peace Foundation, 1943), p. 33-35. The same approach may be found in the Russian-language doctrine, although the same authors refer to the League of Nations as a system of collective security; see Бровки Ю. П., Лепешкова Ю. А., Павловой Л. В., Отв. ред., *Международное публичное право. Особенная часть* [Brovka Y.P., Lepeshkov Y.A., Pavlova L.V., ed., *International Public Law. Special Part*] (Minsk: Amalfea, 2011), p. 470; Игнатенко Г. В., Тиунов О. И., Отв. ред., *Международное право: учебник для ВУЗов* [Ignatenko G.V., Tiunov O.I., ed., *International Law: Textbook for Universities*] (Moscow: Norma, 2005), p. 464; Додонов В.Н., Панов В.П., Румянцев О.Г.; Трофимова В.Н., Отв. ред., *Международное право. Словарь-справочник* [Dodonov V.N., Panov V.P., Rumjantsev O.G.; Trofimov V.N., ed., *International Law: Dictionary-Handbook*] (Moscow: INFRA-M, 1997), p. 94.

[44] Hogan W.N., *International Conflict and Collective Security*, *op. cit.*, p. 180; Abass A. *Regional Organizations and the Development of Collective Security*, *op. cit.*, p. 33-35; Hummer W., Schweitzer M., "Article 52," in *The Charter of the United Nations: A Commentary*, 2nd ed., vol. 1, ed. B. Sinna (München: Verlag C.H. Beck, 2002), p. 820.

[45] Johnson C.H., Niemeyer G., "Collective Security," *op. cit.*, p. 22; Karns M.P., Mingst K.A., *International Organizations: The Politics and Processes of Global Governance* (Boulder/London: Lynne Rienner Publishers, 2010), p. 295.

[46] Kelsen H., *Collective Security under International Law*, *op. cit.*, p. 41.

[47] See Danchin P.G., "Things Fall Apart," *op. cit.*, p. 49-50. In the doctrine, the problem of the balance of power has moved to the sphere of politics and political sciences. In this area it

when the UN Charter was drafted, Great Britain proposed preserving the whole system of regional alliances. Sir W. Churchill advanced the idea of a peripheral role for the United Nations with the division of the world into spheres of influence.[48] American President F. Roosevelt advocated endowing the great powers with extraordinary authority to pursue the maintenance of international peace and security and to eliminate the armies of other states.[49]

Some remnants of these drastic proposals still found their way into the UN Charter. Articles 23(1) and 27(3) set forth the special role of five permanent members,[50] and Chapter VIII "*does not preclude the existence of regional arrangements and agencies for dealing with such matters relating to the maintenance of international peace and security as are appropriate for regional action.*" The confrontation of the Western and Soviet blocs during the Cold War period was a clear practical demonstration of balance-of-power politics.[51] Similar tendencies may be observed even now, when proposals for reforming the Security Council are sometimes thinly disguised efforts to grab a privileged position as a permanent or semi-permanent member rather than to make the Council strong and effective.[52]

Despite the general agreement on the universal character of the United Nations as well as of the system of collective security established within it,[53] some publicists distinguished – and still distinguish – between the

---

is viewed as a "*base of interstate relations, foundations of the World politics*" (Organski A.F.K., *World Politics*, *op. cit.*, p. 271, 275-277).

[48] Cited by Eide A., "Peace-keeping and Enforcement by Regional Organizations: Its Place in the UN System," *Journal of Peace Research*, 3(2) (1966), p. 133.

[49] Cited by Sakrasena K.P., *The United Nations and Collective Security: A Historical Analysis* (Delhi: D.K. Publishing House, 1977), p. 27-29.

[50] See Neuhold H., "Collective Security after 'Operation Allied Force,'" *op. cit.*, p. 75; Stromberg R.N., "The Idea of Collective Security," in *From Collective Security to Preventive Diplomacy: Readings in International Organization and the Maintenance of Peace*, ed J. Larus (New York: John Wiley & Sons, Inc., 1965), p. 276, 282.

[51] Lorenz J.P., *Peace, Power, and the United Nations*, *op. cit.*, p. 47; Liska G., *Nations in Alliance*, *op. cit.*, p. 3-4, 12-60.

[52] On the issue of UN reform, see *A More Secure World*, *op. cit.*, p. 80.

[53] See *ibid.*, p. 16 (para. 28); *Documents of the UN Conference on International Organization*, vol. I., *op. cit.*, p. 264-271; *Documents of the UN Conference on International Organization*, vol. III., *op. cit.*, p. 80, 257, 274, 288, 353, 397, 434-440; *Documents of the UN Conference on International Organization*, San Francisco, 1945, vol. XII. Commission III. Security Council (London/ New York: United Nations Information Organizations, 1945), p. 765. See also Weiss T.G. *et al.*, *The United Nations and Changing World Politics*, *op. cit.*, p. 18; Nye J.S., *Understanding International Conflicts*, *op. cit.*, p. 83; Beyerlin U., "Regional Arrangements," in *United Nations: Law, Politics and Practice*, ed. R. Wolfrum, vol. I (Munich: Verlag C.H. Beck, 1995), p. 1051.

universal and regional systems of collective security,[54] while others have rejected the very possibility of the existence of either of them.[55]

1.3 Notion of Collective Security

As follows from the previous paragraphs, the notions and functions of collective security have changed over the course of time, depending substantially on evolving visions of security. In the middle of the 20th century, when the United Nations was created, collective security was considered as a possibility for joint protection against an aggressor, and for the prevention and settlement of interstate conflicts.[56] A broad approach could also include any measures taken by a group of states to defend themselves.[57] Later on, the notion of collective security expanded to include collective mechanisms for maintaining and safeguarding peace and security, preventing conflicts,[58] and minimizing and eliminating the very reasons for conflicts.[59]

Yet neither documents nor doctrine provide any agreed definition of collective security. It may be seen as a purpose (to achieve a situation when neither aggression nor breaches of international peace take place), a state (after the achievement of the aforementioned aim), a principle, a mechanism for collective actions, a method (the functioning of the corresponding organizational and procedural means),[60] a mechanism for cooperation[61] or a

---

[54] Abass A. *Regional Organizations and the Development of Collective Security*, *op. cit.*, p. 66-67; Собакин В.К., *Коллективная безопасность – гарантия мирного сосуществования* [Sobakin V.K., *Collective Security – A Guarantee of Peaceful Coexistence*] (Moscow: International Relations, 1962), p. 101, 299-492.

[55] Danchin P.G., "Things Fall Apart," *op. cit.*, p. 63-64; Stromberg R.N., "The Idea of Collective Security," *op. cit.*, p. 273-284; Thompson K.W., "Collective Security Reexamined," *op. cit.*, p. 301; Hoffmann S., "Is There an International Order?" in *Janus and Minerva: Essays in the Theory and Practice of International Politics* (Boulder: Westview Press, 1985), p. 117.

[56] *Documents of the UN Conference on International Organization*, vol. III., *op. cit.*, p. 380-381; Kelsen H., *Collective Security under International Law*, *op. cit.*, p. 53; de Wet E., Wood M. "Collective Security," *op. cit.*; Ignatenko G.V., Tiunov O.I., ed., *International Law*, *op. cit.*, p. 464.

[57] Weiss T.G. *et al.*, *The United Nations and Changing World Politics*, *op. cit.*, p. 225.

[58] Ball J.H., *Collective Security: The Why and How*, *op. cit.*, p. 31.

[59] Hogan W.N., *International Conflict and Collective Security*, *op. cit.*, p. 110-113, 179.

[60] *Ibid.*, p. 180-181; Тахир М., *Правовые проблемы коллективной безопасности* [Tahir M., *Legal Problems of Collective Security*] (St. Petersburg: St. Petersburg University Publishers, 2004), p. 10-11.

collective struggle of states[62]. S.M. de Luca assesses collective security as "*the commitment by nations to resolve their disputes, regardless of national concern.*"[63] J.H. Joensson understands it as "*an ideal or humanity's collective aspiration and moral indignation to peace [...] as a procedural norm for collective wellbeing.*"[64] So collective security is viewed by him "*as both common ideas and understandings, and as a framework for implementation of those,*" and also "*as a practice in terms of allocation of authority and an international legitimization.*"[65] Ch.A. Kupchan and C.A. Kupchan view collective security as an aggregation of military force against threats to peace.[66] K.P. Sakrasena makes an analogy between the mechanism of collective security and police activity.[67] E.B. Haas' attitude to collective security is very narrow – it is limited to "*a technique used by intergovernmental organizations to restrain the use of force among members.*"[68]

None of these definitions reflects the threats and developments that the international community has to face at present. Even today, it is still possible to find works in which the authors limit collective security to the suppression of aggression and settlement of interstate conflicts.[69]

The concept of collective security being aimed at the protection of common interests (the "common good") has usually been opposed to the concepts of self-help,[70] intervention[71] (including humanitarian intervention[72]) and world government.[73] This rule is not, however, an absolute one. The

---

[61] V.G. Shkunaev and S.A. Malinin, cited by Tahir M., *Legal Problems of Collective Security, op. cit.*, p. 12, 14.
[62] N.V. Zakharova, cited by Tahir M., *Legal Problems of Collective Security, op. cit.*, p. 13.
[63] de Luca S.M., "The Gulf Crisis and Collective Security, *op. cit.*, p. 269.
[64] Joensson J.H., *Understanding Collective Security in the 21st Century: A Critical Study of UN Peacekeeping in the Former Yugoslavia*, doctoral thesis in political and social sciences, European University Institute (Florence, 2010), p. 14-15.
[65] *Ibid.*, p. 17.
[66] Kupchan Ch.A., Kupchan C.A., "The Promise of Collective Security," *International Security*, 20(1) (1995), p. 52.
[67] Sakrasena K.P., *The United Nations and Collective Security, op. cit.*, p. 4-5.
[68] Haas E.B., *Collective Security and the Future International System* (Denver: University of Denver, 1967), p. 33.
[69] Tahir M., *Legal Problems of Collective Security, op. cit.*, p. 40.
[70] Kelsen H., "Collective Security and Collective Self-Defense," *op. cit.*, p. 783.
[71] Sobakin V.K., *Collective Security – A Guarantee of Peaceful Coexistence, op. cit.*, p. 500.
[72] Also, G. Andreopoulos inisists that a collective security system must adapt to be able to handle humanitarian problems (Andreopoulos G., "Collective Security and the Responsibility to Protect," in *United Nations Reform and the New Collective Security*, ed. P.G. Danchin, H. Fisher (Cambridge: Cambridge University Press, 2010), p. 157).
[73] Danchin P.G., "Things Fall Apart," *op. cit.*, p. 41-42, 50; Tahir M., *Legal Problems of Collective Security, op. cit.*, p. 13-14. Sometimes, however, it is seen as an interim concept

right to self defense[74] as well as the possibility of taking retaliatory measures and countermeasures are well recognized in international law – and, for self defense, even set forth in the UN Charter.

As noted above, the very notion as well as the characteristics of collective security are extensively discussed in the international legal doctrine. As for the characteristics, they may be viewed as the following:

- The prohibition of the use of force in international relations and the outlawing of aggression;[75]
- Collective enforcement measures in response to the act of aggression from outside or within the system[76] by military forces.[77] As opposed to the system of a balance of power, no enforcement may be taken in response to the capacity of a state to commit an act of aggression.[78] The UN system (as follows from the first point) also provides for the possibility to apply enforcement measures in response to the threat or use of force;
- State orientation of the system.[79] Despite the increasing interest in and attention to the problems and activities of individuals and private companies, collective security is aimed at the protection of states and may only be achieved through the cooperation and efforts of states and derivative subjects of international law (*e.g.*, international organizations);
- Sovereign equality[80] and an orientation toward universal security, including the security of every member state;[81]

---

between anarchy and world government; see Kelsen H., "Collective Security and Collective Self-Defense," *op. cit.*, p. 783-784; Stromberg R.N., "The Idea of Collective Security," *op. cit.*, p. 277.

[74] Kelsen H., "Collective Security and Collective Self-Defense," *op. cit.*, p. 783.

[75] Thompson K.W., "Collective Security Reexamined," *op. cit.*, p. 285; Jessup Ph.C., *International Security: The American Role in Collective Action for Peace* (New York: Council on Foreign Relations Inc., 1935), p. 110.

[76] de Luca S.M., "The Gulf Crisis and Collective Security, *op. cit.*, p. 269; Sakrasena K.P., *The United Nations and Collective Security*, *op. cit.*, p. 4-5.

[77] Nye J.S., *Understanding International Conflicts*, *op. cit.*, p. 82.

[78] Kelsen H., "Collective Security and Collective Self-Defense," *op. cit.*, p. 783; Murdock J.O., "Collective Security Distinguished from Intervention," *American Journal of International Law,* 56(2) (1962), p. 500.

[79] *A More Secure World*, *op. cit.*, p. 9; Cuéllar M.F., "Reflections on Sovereignty and Collective Security," *Stanford Journal of International Law*, 40(1) (2004), p. 213, 215.

[80] Joensson J.H., *Understanding Collective Security in the 21st Century*, *op. cit.*, p. 15.

[81] de Luca S.M., "The Gulf Crisis and Collective Security", *op. cit.*, p. 269; Organski A.F.K., *World Politics*, *op. cit.*, p. 371.

- The neutrality of states in the system.[82] Under specific conditions, every state may become either a victim or an aggressor.
- The *de facto* recognition of peace as a natural universal value. The effective exercise of collective security can only be achieved when this occurs among states, and when they demonstrate sufficient political solidarity (including their readiness to provide military forces and other resources for enforcement measures),[83] especially among the great powers.

I will, however, advocate that the above characteristics are not sufficient. They concern only traditional aspects of collective security (collective defense,[84] prevention of emerging interstate conflicts and settlement of existing ones[85]) and do not take into account the need to suppress contemporary threats and challenges,[86] prevent and settle internal conflicts, and prevent the hypothetical possibility of conflicts. In this connection, some publicists (*e.g.*, D. Hannay) even insist that the prohibition of the use of force and military mechanisms of collective enforcement have lost their constitutive role in the system of collective security.[87]

1.4 System of Collective Security

Active and effective cooperation in the maintenance of international peace and security can hardly be achieved through *ad hoc* interaction. A

[82] Joensson J.H., *Understanding Collective Security in the 21st Century*, *op. cit.*, p. 15; Organski A.F.K., *World Politics*, *op. cit.*, p. 372.

[83] Johnson C.H., Niemeyer G., "Collective Security," *op. cit.*, p. 20-22; Danchin P.G., "Things Fall Apart," *op. cit.*, p. 45; Thompson K.W., "Collective Security Reexamined," *op. cit.*, p. 290-293. Some publicists advocate for the automatic provision of military forces and other resources; see de Wet E., Wood M. "Collective Security," *op. cit.*; Kupchan Ch.A., Kupchan C.A., "The Promise of Collective Security," *op. cit.*, p. 53; Koskenniemi M., "The Place of Law in Collective Security," *Michigan Journal of International Law*, 17(2) (1995-1996), p. 456-457; Lowe V., ed., *The United Nations Security Council and War: The Evolution of Thought and Practice since 1945* (Oxford: Oxford University Press, 2008), p. 13.

[84] Zacher M.W., *International Conflicts and Collective Security, 1946-1977: The United Nations, Organization of American States, Organization of African Unity, and Arab League* (New York: Praeger Publishers, 1979), p. 1.

[85] Thompson K.W., "Collective Security Reexamined," *op. cit.*, p. 287.

[86] Kupchan Ch.A., Kupchan C.A., "The Promise of Collective Security," *op. cit.*, p. 52.

[87] Hannay D., "Collective Security and the Use of Force," *op. cit.*, p. 368.

system of collective security as an institutionalized mechanism of cooperation is universally recognized to be more appropriate and effective.[88]

Moreover, when the collective security system is an institutionalized mechanism of cooperation, it enjoys all of the intrinsic characteristics of the latter and also some specific additional characteristics (recognized in international law): establishment by international treaty;[89] universal membership, which secures the participation of potential adversaries;[90] the existence of a central organ that is able to take decisions (efficiently[91]) concerning conflicts arising within the system[92] and is able to enforce them.[93]

Some other features are also mentioned as being necessary for the effective functioning of the system: permanent military forces that are able to act as needed immediately after the required decision is taken;[94] consensus and political solidarity among states; agreement about the criteria for armed attack, aggression, threat and the use of force;[95] objectivity;[96] legality and legitimacy of the centralized use of military force;[97] and justice, morality and the rule of law.[98]

These characteristics are very important for guaranteeing the active and effective functioning of a system of collective security – that is, the effective maintenance of international peace and security. Although fulfilling all of them is nearly impossible, this should not result in the conclusion reached by some scholars[99] about the impossibility of establishing a system of collective security because the ideal model is unfeasible. In reality, ideal systems cannot be organized and function in everyday life. Nevertheless, this

---

88 Haas E.B., *Collective Security and the Future International System*, *op. cit.*, p. 33.
89 Doehring K., "Collective Security," *op. cit.*, p. 110.
90 Johnson C.H., Niemeyer G., "Collective Security," *op. cit.*, p. 20; Neuhold H., "Collective Security after 'Operation Allied Force,'" *op. cit.*, p. 74-76; Doehring K., "Collective Security," *op. cit.*, p. 110, 112.
91 Stromberg R.N., "The Idea of Collective Security," *op. cit.*, p. 277, 282.
92 Neuhold H., "Collective Security after 'Operation Allied Force,'" *op. cit.*, p. 74-76.
93 Doehring K., "Collective Security," *op. cit.*, p. 110.
94 Organski A.F.K., *World Politics*, *op. cit.*, p. 373.
95 Danchin P.G., "Things Fall Apart," *op. cit.*, p. 45.
96 *A More Secure World*, *op. cit.*, p. 17, para. 71.
97 *Ibid.*, p. 61-62, 66, paras. 183-184, 186, 204.
98 *Documents of the UN Conference on International Organization*, vol. I., *op. cit.*, p. 184, 186; *Documents of the UN Conference on International Organization*, vol. III., *op. cit.*, p. 293, 313, 323, 379, 398.
99 Danchin P.G., "Things Fall Apart," *op. cit.*, p. 63-64; Stromberg R.N., "The Idea of Collective Security," *op. cit.*, p. 273-284; Thompson K.W., "Collective Security Reexamined," *op. cit.*, p. 301; Hoffmann S., "Is There an International Order?" *op. cit.*, p. 117.

does not prevent us from making and securing law, or from establishing governance and civil society.

It is also believed here that a system of collective security is not homogeneous. It consists of several elements that can be characterized as mechanisms for the maintenance of international peace and security within the system. They are:

- The universal recognition of principles of international law as inalienable elements of collective security.[100] Key attention is mostly paid to the prohibition of the use of force (UN Charter, art. 2(4)),[101] the prohibition of intervention in the domestic affairs of states (UN Charter, art. 2(7))[102] and the principle of sovereign equality,[103] but it is maintained here that the whole set of principles is to be applied;

- The system of peaceful settlement of international disputes (UN Charter, Chapter VI);[104]

- The mechanism of collective enforcement in response to the act of aggression or threat to the peace (UN Charter, art. 24-25, Chapter VII);[105]

- Collective self-defense in accordance with art. 51 of the UN Charter. The importance of protection from external threats for the maintenance of peace and security at a regional level was

---

[100] Sobakin V.K., *Collective Security – A Guarantee of Peaceful Coexistence*, *op. cit.*, p. 24-72.

[101] Doehring K., "Collective Security," *op. cit.*, p. 110; Stromberg R.N., "The Idea of Collective Security," *op. cit.*, p. 277, 282; 44.; Koskenniemi M., "The Place of Law in Collective Security," *op. cit.*, p. 456.

[102] *Documents of the UN Conference on International Organization*, vol. III., *op. cit.*, p. 67-69.

[103] Joensson J.H., *Understanding Collective Security in the 21st Century*, *op. cit.*, p. 15.

[104] Hogan W.N., *International Conflict and Collective Security*, *op. cit.*, p. 179-180; *Documents of the UN Conference on International Organization*, vol. III., *op. cit.*, p. 434-440; Stromberg R.N., "The Idea of Collective Security," *op. cit.*, p. 277; Sobakin V.K., *Collective Security – A Guarantee of Peaceful Coexistence*, *op. cit.*, p. 73-98.

[105] Hogan W.N., *International Conflict and Collective Security*, *op. cit.*, p. 179-180; *Documents of the UN Conference on International Organization*, vol. III., *op. cit.*, p. 434-440; Doehring K., "Collective Security," *op. cit.*, p. 110; Stromberg R.N., "The Idea of Collective Security," *op. cit.*, p. 277; Sobakin V.K., *Collective Security – A Guarantee of Peaceful Coexistence*, *op. cit.*, p. 73-98; Ball J.H., *Collective Security: The Why and How*, *op. cit.*, p. 39-48; Koskenniemi M., "The Place of Law in Collective Security," *op. cit.*, p. 456; Tahir M., *Legal Problems of Collective Security*, *op. cit.*, p. 9.

advocated by professor H. Kelsen in 1951.[106] This position seems very logical (as will be considered in detail later, in the discussion about competences of regional arrangements and agencies). As a result, attempts to oppose mechanisms of collective security and self-defense[107] are hardly founded in international law.

- Regional organizations of collective security. These are often qualified in the legal doctrine as independent "regional" systems of collective security.[108] This qualification, however, is believed here to be inaccurate as it comes from equating the notions of the single international "system of collective security" with "regional arrangements and agencies under Chapter VIII of the UN Charter." Despite this, certain organizations (*e.g.*, the CSTO) expressly claim themselves to be regional systems of collective security.[109]

---

[106] Abass A. *Regional Organizations and the Development of Collective Security*, *op. cit.*, p. 39; Kelsen H., "Is the North Atlantic Treaty a Regional Arrangement?" *American Journal of International Law*, 45(1) (1951), p. 163-165.

[107] See, *e.g.*, Haas E.B., *Collective Security and the Future International System*, *op. cit.*, p. 33; Danchin P.G., "Things Fall Apart," *op. cit.*, p. 41.

[108] Johnson C.H., Niemeyer G., "Collective Security," *op. cit.*, p. 19; Abass A. *Regional Organizations and the Development of Collective Security*, *op. cit.*, p. 66-67; Sobakin V.K., *Collective Security – A Guarantee of Peaceful Coexistence*, *op. cit.*, p. 101, 299-492; *Commission to Study the Organization of Peace*: *Regional Arrangements for Security and the United Nations*. Eighth Report and Papers Presented to the Commission (New York, 1953), p. 65-69; Kelsen H., *Collective Security under International Law*, *op. cit.*, p. 197; Ignatenko G.V., Tiunov O.I., ed., *International Law*, *op. cit.*, p. 464-465; Каламкарян Р.А., Мигачев Ю.И., *Международное право: учебное пособие* [Kalamkarjan R.A., Migachev, Y.I., *International Law*] (Moscow: Yurlitinform, 2003), p. 228; Brovka Y.P., Lepeshkov Y.A., Pavlova L.V., ed., *International Public Law*, *op. cit.*, p. 469-503; Ковалева, А.А., Черниченко, С.В., Отв. ред., *Международное право: Учебник для студентов ВУЗов* [Kovalev A.A., Chernichenko S.V., ed., *International Law*] (Moscow: Omega, 2008), p. 761.

[109] As concerns the CSTO, see Соглашение об учреждении системы управления силами и средствами системы коллективной безопасности ОДКБ [Agreement on the Establishment of the System of Management of Forces and Means of the CSTO Collective Security System], 6 October 2007, *National Register of Legal Acts of Belarus* N 53, 3/2212, preamble, art. 3; Соглашение о статусе формирований сил и средств системы коллективной безопасности ОДКБ [Agreement on the Status of the Forces and Facilities of the CSTO System of Collective Security], 10 December 2010, *Electronic Legal Database Konsul'tant Plus. Technologiia* 3000; Соглашение о порядке формирования и функционирования сил и средств системы коллективной безопасности ОДКБ [Agreement on the Order of Formation and Functioning of Forces and Means of the CSTO System of Collective Security], 10 December 2010, *Electronic Legal Database Konsul'tant Plus. Technologiia 3000*, preamble.

Speaking to the incorrectness of viewing these organizations as independent regional systems is the general recognition of the prohibition of the use of force and the centralized character of enforcement measures as an inalienable feature of the system of collective security.[110] In accordance with the UN Charter, the Security Council is the only body entitled to decide on the use of enforcement (including military) measures (art. 41-42). Therefore, the United Nations as a universal organization that is solely entitled to apply enforcement measures is the only institution capable of being qualified as *the* system of collective security.[111] Regional organizations, despite attempts to present them as independent systems of collective security, may only be considered as elements (parts, or subsidiary mechanisms) of the system; this has been repeatedly recognized by states, including at the San Francisco conference in 1945 that drafted the UN Charter as well as after the Charter's adoption.[112]

The origin of this confusion may be found in the willingness of states and particular organizations to underline and maintain their independence from the United Nations, combined with a formal view that every item consisting of elements may be characterized as a system.[113] (The scope of the notion of regional arrangements and agencies is discussed in the next chapter.)

Disarmament is set forth in the UN Charter (art. 11, 26, 47) and agreed in the legal doctrine[114] as a key mechanism for the maintenance of

---

[110] Johnson C.H., Niemeyer G., "Collective Security," *op. cit.*, p. 20; Neuhold H., "Collective Security after 'Operation Allied Force,'" *op. cit.*, p. 74-76; Doehring K., "Collective Security," *op. cit.*, p. 110, 112.

[111] It should be noted, however, that the vision of a single system of collective security is not that popular in the contemporary legal doctrine; see, *e.g.*, Tahir M., *Legal Problems of Collective Security*, *op. cit.*, p. 138.

[112] *A More Secure World*, *op. cit.*, p. 85-86, para. 272; *Documents of the UN Conference on International Organization*, vol. III., *op. cit.*, p. 434-440; Cuéllar M.F., "Reflections on Sovereignty and Collective Security," *op. cit.*, p. 215; Luck E.C., "Regional Arrangements, the United Nations and the Japanese-American Security Treaty," *Asia Survey*, 35(3) (1995), p. 237-238; Колосов Ю.М., Кривчикова Э.С., Отв. ред., *Международное право: Учебник* [Kolosov Y.M., Krivchikova, E.S., ed., *International Law*] (Moscow: International Relations, 2003), p. 373; Pernice R., *Die Sicherung des Weltfriedens durch Regionale Organisationen und die Vereinten Nationen (eine Untersuchung zur Kompetenzverteilung nach Kapitel VIII der UN-Charta)* (Hamburg: Hansischer Gildenverlag, Joachim Heitmann & Co., 1972), p. 39, 60; Kovalev A.A., Chernichenko S.V., ed., *International Law*, *op. cit.*, p. 688.

[113] A.I. Zybaylo, *e.g.*, insists on the existence of regional systems of collective security but at the same time qualifies them as subjects of the universal system (Brovka Y.P., Lepeshkov Y.A., Pavlova L.V., ed., *International Public Law*, *op. cit.*, p. 493).

[114] Ignatenko G.V., Tiunov O.I., ed., *International Law*, *op. cit.*, p. 439-440, 451; Kelsen H., *Collective Security under International Law*, *op. cit.*, p. 197; Brovka Y.P., Lepeshkov Y.A., Pavlova L.V., ed., *International Public Law*, *op. cit.*, p. 474.

international peace and security. Its importance cannot be disputed. At the same time, due to the increasing number of new threats and challenges as well as the broader cooperation of states in the struggle against these evils, disarmament shall be viewed here as being among measures aimed at preventing the hypothetical possibility of conflict, together with arms control and confidence- and security-building measures.

Some other mechanisms, *e.g.*, the promotion and protection of human rights[115] and provisional measures in accordance with art. 40 of the UN Charter,[116] although having some impact on the maintenance of peace and security, cannot be viewed as elements of the system. The former cannot be derived from the UN Charter as far as it represents an extensively broad approach to security that goes far beyond the politico-military notion. The latter is rather a phase of enforcement measures under chapter VII of the Charter. International conventions, peace-building and humanitarian intervention, cited by some other authors (M.P. Karns, K.A. Mingst),[117] have no origin in the UN Charter. Some of them (*e.g.*, peace-building) may constitute parts of separate mechanisms. Others are altogether disputable from the standpoint of international law (*e.g.*, humanitarian intervention).

Due to the changing nature of threats and challenges as well as an urgent need to counter them as they arise, often with the use of new mechanisms, it seems appropriate to include among the elements of collective security *peacekeeping* and *measures aimed at the struggle against new threats and challenges*.

Conclusions

Visions of security and collective security have come a long way – including since the UN Charter was adopted. They have developed from the absence of international conflicts to the prevention and settlement of internal conflicts, the prevention of the hypothetical possibility of any conflict, and the fight against contemporary threats and challenges.

At the same time, a comprehensive vision of security as including economic, environmental, social and other components can be applied to the

[115] See, *e.g.* ; B.M. Klimenko (Клименко Б.М., Отв. ред., *Всеобъемлющая международная безопасность... Международно-правовые принципы и нормы: справочник*. [Klimenko B.M., ed., *Comprehensive International Security... International Legal Principles and Norms: Handbook*] (Moscow: International Relations, 1990), p. 5).
[116] Ignatenko G.V., Tiunov O.I., ed., *International Law*, *op. cit.*, p. 439-440.
[117] Karns M.P., Mingst K.A., *International Organizations*, *op. cit.*, p. 294.

activities of the UN Security Council and regional organizations of collective security. Such an approach, arguably too expansive, can have the opposite effect; it is likely to be used as a new excuse for the advancement of national interests rather than as an active mechanism for the maintenance of international peace. Nevertheless, the competences, functions and tasks of the Security Council and regional organizations under Chapter VIII of the UN Charter are much broader today that those envisaged when the Charter was drafted.

As a result, definitions of collective security and of the system of collective security, as put forth by numerous publicists,[118] are much outdated today. Currently, the *system of collective security* is based on the prohibition of the use of force and other principles of international law, and is the universal state-oriented institutionalized mechanism for the maintenance of international peace and security. In this context, the latter provide the possibility of centralized collective enforcement in response to the use or threat of force or an act of aggression, and they provide for the application of multilevel measures aimed at eliminating or minimizing potential reasons for conflicts and the suppression of threats to international peace and security in accordance with the purposes and principles of the UN Charter as well as obligations under the Charter.

The system includes the following elements: principles of international law; mechanisms for the peaceful settlement of international disputes; centralized mechanisms of enforcement, self defense, regional arrangements and agencies; peacekeeping, disarmament and control over armaments; confidence- and security-building measures; and mechanisms for cooperation in the struggle against contemporary threats and challenges.

---

[118] Thompson K.W., "Collective Security Reexamined," *op. cit.*, p. 285; Jessup Ph.C., *International Security*, *op. cit.*, p. 110; Sakrasena K.P., *The United Nations and Collective Security*, *op. cit.*, p. 4-5; Kelsen H., "Collective Security and Collective Self-Defense," *op. cit.*, p. 783; *etc.*

CHAPTER 2
REGIONAL ARRANGEMENTS AND AGENCIES

The possibility that regional organizations could exist as useful means of maintaining international peace and security had been recognized in the Covenant of the League of Nations (art. 21).[119] Despite the initial orientation of the United Nations toward the universality of cooperation, the idea of regionalism as well as the remains of the balance of power concept found their way into Chapter VIII of the UN Charter, which sets forth the general framework for the activity of regional arrangements and agencies.[120] Yet neither document defines regional groupings or describes their characteristics.

2.1 Scope and Terminology

The qualification and status of regional arrangements and agencies came to be a matter of intense debate amid tensions during the Cold War (*e.g.*, Cuba, 1960; Haiti, 1963; Panama, 1964). Some of these arrangements (*e.g.*, NATO, OWT, WEU) qualified themselves as organizations of collective defense,[121] allowing them to "cheat" the UN Charter by bypassing both the obligation to get the Security Council's authorization to apply any enforcement measures under art. 53(1)[122] as well as the obligation to inform

---

[119] The Covenant of the League of Nations, 28 June 1919.

[120] Weiss T.G. *et al.*, *The United Nations and Changing World Politics*, *op. cit.*, p. 18; *Documents of the UN Conference on International Organization*, vol. III., *op. cit.*, p. 80, 257, 274, 288, 353, 397, 434-440; *Documents of the UN Conference on International Organization*, vol. I., *op. cit.*, p. 364-371; *Documents of the UN Conference on International Organization*, vol. XII., *op. cit.*, p. 765.

[121] Bentwich N., Martin A., *A Commentary on the Charter of the United Nations* (London: Routledge & Kegan Paul Ltd., 1950), p. 110; Beyerlin U., "Regional Arrangements," *op. cit.*, p. 1050; Wilson G., "Regional Arrangements as Agents of the UN Security Council: Some African and European Organizations Contrasted," *Liverpool Law Review,* 29(2) (2008), p. 186; Doehring K., "Collective Security," *op. cit.*, p. 114; Abass A. *Regional Organizations and the Development of Collective Security*, *op. cit.*, p. 38.

[122] Sarooshi D., *The United Nations and the Development of Collective Security (The Delegation by the UN Security Council of its Chapter VII Powers)* (Oxford: Clarendon Press, 1999), p. 251; C. Walter underlines that control of the UN Security Council under art. 52 and 53 is stronger than under art. 51 (Walter C., *Vereinte Nationen und Regional Organisationen:*

the Security Council of activities undertaken and planned with the aim of maintaining international peace and security (art. 54).[123]

Chapter VIII of the Charter sets forth a general framework for the functioning of regional organizations as elements of the collective security system. In accordance with art. 52, "*Nothing in the present Charter precludes the existence of regional arrangements or agencies for dealing with such matters relating to the maintenance of international peace and security as are appropriate for regional action provided that such arrangements or agencies and their activities are consistent with the Purposes and Principles of the United Nations.*" Regional organizations enjoy priority in the peaceful settlement of local disputes (art. 52(2)). The Security Council may utilize these arrangements and agencies for enforcement action under its authority (art. 53(1)). "*No enforcement action shall be taken under regional arrangements or by regional agencies without the authorization of the Security Council*" (art. 53(1)). "*The Security Council shall at all times be kept fully informed of activities undertaken or in contemplation under regional arrangements or by regional agencies for the maintenance of international peace and security*" (art. 54).

Despite their laconism and apparent clarity, the provisions of Chapter VIII of the UN Charter have caused numerous disputes both in the international legal doctrine and in practice, including the subject of legal regulation. In particular, the Charter contains neither a definition nor clear characteristics of regional arrangements and entities. The terminology used by states at the San Francisco conference varied greatly: "*regional arrangements and groups*" (Egypt);[124] "*regional organizations*" (Uruguay, Columbia, Guatemala);[125] "*regional arrangements*" (Turkey,[126] Venezuela,[127] Costa Rica,[128] France);[129] "*regional agreements*" (Norway);[130] "*agencies of special and limited scope*" (Mexico);[131] "*regional groups, systems and units*" (Venezuela,[132] Chile,[133] Bolivia[134]); "*systems of regional*

Eine Untersuchung zu Kapitel VIII der Satzung der Vereinten Nationen (Berlin: Springer Verlag, 1995), p. 347.

[123] Walter C., *Vereinte Nationen und Regional Organisationen*, *op. cit.*, p. 346.

[124] *Documents of the UN Conference on International Organization*, vol. III., *op. cit.*, p. 460.

[125] *Ibid.*, p. 256; *Documents of the UN Conference on International Organization*, vol. I., *op. cit.*, p. 305, 356.

[126] *Ibid.*, p. 453.

[127] *Ibid.*, p. 517-518.

[128] *Documents of the UN Conference on International Organization*, vol. III., *op. cit.*, p. 277.

[129] *Ibid.*, p. 387.

[130] *Ibid.*, p. 363.

[131] *Ibid.*, p. 82.

[132] *Ibid.*, p. 215.

[133] *Ibid.*, p. 290.

nature" (joint proposal of Chile, Colombia, Costa Rica, Peru, Ecuador);[135] "*regional arrangements, conventions, agencies*" (Czechoslovakia).[136]

A narrow definition proposed by Egypt limited regional arrangements to "*organizations of permanent nature, grouping in a given geographical area several countries which, by reason of their proximity, community of interests or cultural, linguistic, historical or spiritual affinities, make themselves jointly responsible for [...],*"[137] but this was not accepted. No definition was introduced into the Charter (as demonstrated by the variety of terms used) in order to extend the rules of Chapter VIII over all possible structures of cooperation,[138] including treaties of mutual assistance and unions of non-neighboring countries,[139] regardless of whether their character was *ad hoc* or more permanent.[140]

The legal regime of Chapter VIII extends over all these forms. In theory, publicists have distinguished between arrangements and agencies on the basis of institutional structure, defining the former as international treaties or informal understandings[141] aimed at the maintenance of international peace and security and the latter as institutions with some internal structure.[142] The classification by Swedish professor K. Lind is more detailed and rests on two criteria: legal grounds and institutionalization. He

---

[134] *Ibid.*, p. 585.

[135] *Documents of the UN Conference on International Organization*, vol. XII., *op. cit.*, p. 771.

[136] *Ibid.*, p. 773.

[137] *Documents of the UN Conference on International Organization*, vol. III., *op. cit.*, p. 460-461.

[138] *Documents of the UN Conference on International Organization*, vol. XII., *op. cit.*, p. 701; see also Goodrich L.M., Hambro E., *Charter of the United Nations*, *op. cit.*, p. 184; Hummer W., Schweitzer M., "Article 52," *op. cit.*, p. 817; Walter C., "Security Council Control over Regional Action," *Max Planck Yearbook of United Nations Law,* 1 (1997), p. 131-132. As rightly noted by R. Pernice, unions of states under Chapter VIII may or may not have international legal personality; see Pernice R., *Die Sicherung des Weltfriedens*, *op. cit.*, p. 76.

[139] Goodrich L.M., Hambro E., *Charter of the United Nations*, *op. cit.*, p. 184; *Commission to Study the Organization of Peace*, *op. cit.*, p. 19-22.

[140] Weiss T.G. *et al.*, *The United Nations and Changing World Politics*, *op. cit.*, p. 19; Beyerlin U., "Regional Arrangements," *op. cit.*, p. 1040, 1047-1050; Hummer W., Schweitzer M., "Article 52," *op. cit.*, p. 817, 822-823; Wilson G., "Regional Arrangements as Agents of the UN Security Council," *op. cit.,* p. 186.

[141] Goodrich L.M., Hambro E., *Charter of the United Nations*, *op. cit.*, p. 312.

[142] See Akehurst M., "Enforcement Action of Regional Organizations with Special Reference to the Organization of American States," *British Yearbook of International Law,* 42 (1967), p. 178; Alagappa M., "Regional Arrangements, the UN and International Security: A Framework for Analysis," in *Beyond Subcontracting: Task Sharing with Regional Security Arrangements and Service-Providing NGOs,* ed. Th. Weiss (Basingstoke: MacMillan, 1998), p. 6; Pernice R., *Die Sicherung des Weltfriedens*, *op. cit.*, p. 20-21, 76.

distinguishes between interstate cooperation not based on a legal treaty and that based on a legal treaty with or without legal personality.[143]

These differences, however, have no impact on the legal status, regulation or activity of any of these types.[144] Currently, activities pertaining to the maintenance of international peace and security are mostly exercised by international organizations, so the term "regional organizations" has become used in conjunction with Chapter VIII functions.[145] It will also be used in this work as such.

The tendency toward institutionalization and the broad use of the term "regional organizations," however, shall not be meant as eliminating any other forms of regional arrangements or agencies acting in the sphere of international peace and security. Regional arrangements and agencies falling beyond the criteria of international organizations still play an important role in this sphere. The last decade has also been characterized by the establishment and increasing activity of vaguely institutionalized mechanisms of cooperation (*e.g.*, the NATO-Russia Council, the Group of 8 (G8), ASEAN+3),[146] as well as *ad hoc* entities established for particular operations or activities (KFOR, EUFOR ALTHEA). These institutions have non-universal membership and their activities are aimed at the maintenance of international peace and security. The question consequently arises about whether such entities can be, or should be, considered regional arrangements and agencies in accordance with Chapter VIII of the UN Charter, subjecting them to the Chapter's rules.

An entity's permanent character is often cited in the legal doctrine as a decisive criterion for its qualification as a regional organization under Chapter VIII.[147] However, the San Francisco documents and the UN Charter

---

[143] Lind K., *The Revival of Chapter VIII of the UN Charter*, *op. cit.*, p. 71.

[144] On this point, see also Abass A. *Regional Organizations and the Development of Collective Security*, *op. cit.*, p. 37; Legault A., "Euro-Atlantic Multilateral Regimes," in *Multilateralism and Regional Security,* ed. M. Fortmann, S.N. MacFarlane, S. Roussel (Toronto: The Canadian Peacekeeping Press, 1997), p. 152.

[145] Supplement to an Agenda For Peace. A/50/60-S/1995/1, 3 March 1995; Security Council Update Report, "The United Nations and Regional Organizations," No. 3, 23 March 2007; Security Council Update Report, "The United Nations and Regional Organizations," 18 September 2006, No. 3; 2005 World Summit Outcome, A/RES/60/1, 24 October 2005, para. 170.

[146] Annex B. International Security Cooperation Bodies, in *SIPRI Yearbook 2010: Armaments, Disarmament and International Security* (Oxford: Oxford University Press, 2010), p. 509-525.

[147] Körbs H., *Die Friedensdicherung duech die Vereinten Nationen und Regionalorganizationen*, *op. cit.*, p. 173; Lind K., *The Revival of Chapter VIII of the UN Charter*, *op. cit.*, p. 72-75.

as well as later UN materials provide no support for this position.[148] For example, the UN Secretary-General expressly qualified *ad hoc* arrangements under Chapter VIII in para. 61 of the UN Agenda for Peace.[149] State practice after the end of the Cold War also provides a good illustration of this, one recognized even by those publicists who object to the possibility of qualifying *ad hoc* arrangements under Chapter VIII. The recent emphasis on cooperation with and between traditional regional organizations, sometimes cited as an argument against qualifying those that are *ad hoc*,[150] demonstrates a willingness for order and institutionalization in the sphere of maintenance of peace and security rather than for any sort of disqualification of *ad hoc* entities.

It is also notable that many international organizations actively involved in maintaining international peace and security (EU, CIS, ECOWAS) are not focused exclusively on such work; nevertheless (as will be demonstrated later), this does not prevent them from being qualified under Chapter VIII of the UN Charter as concerns the exercise of their functions toward this end.

Before I make any conclusions on the nature and scope of regional organizations under Chapter VIII, I will pay some attention to the Chapter's purpose. The majority of attempts to limit the scope of regional organizations arise from the perception that the UN Charter is intended (as noted by W. Hummer and M. Schweitzer) "*to grant certain international organizations [...] powers to resolve local disputes within their own jurisdiction and on a local basis, and to serve thereby the purposes of the maintenance of international peace and security.*"[151]

The view expressed here is the opposite one – that Chapter VIII was introduced into the UN Charter to impose restrictions. The following arguments may be cited in support of this: regional organizations are generally viewed as elements (subsidiary mechanisms) of the universal system of collective security.[152] The right of United Nations members to

---

[148] See, *e.g.*, Lind K., *The Revival of Chapter VIII of the UN Charter*, *op. cit.*, p. 73.

[149] An Agenda for Peace, "Preventive Diplomacy, Peacemaking and Peace-keeping," A/47/277- S/24111. Report of the UN Secretary-General, 17 June 1992.

[150] See Lind K., *The Revival of Chapter VIII of the UN Charter*, *op. cit.*, p. 75.

[151] Hummer W., Schweitzer M., "Article 52," *op. cit.*, p. 822. See also Pernice R., *Die Sicherung des Weltfriedens*, *op. cit.*, p. 32-33; Geyrhalter B., *Friedenssicherung durch Regionalorganizationen ohne Beschluß des Sicherheitsrates* (Cologne: LIT, 2001), p. 30; Lind K., *The Revival of Chapter VIII of the UN Charter*, *op. cit.*, p. 76, *etc.*

[152] Belgium, Bolivia – *Documents of the UN Conference on International Organization*, vol. I., *op. cit.*, p. 184, 186; Chile, Netherlands, France, Ecuador – *Documents of the UN Conference on International Organization*, vol. III., *op. cit.*, p. 293, 313, 323, 379, 398. The same approach has been developed in the consequent UN documents and international legal

settle their disputes by peaceful means of their choice without any additional authorization from UN bodies is clearly stated in art. 2(3) of the UN Charter. The wording of Chapter VIII as well as the absence of any definition of regional arrangements and agencies demonstate a distinct aspiration of the Charter's drafters to bring any existing or future entity, regardless of its form, grounds for establishment, personality or character (*ad hoc* or permanent), under the limitations of Chapter VIII and the control of the UN Security Council.

Therefore, the approach to the qualification of organizations in this book is a functional one – it is based on what an organization *does*, rather than what it *is*.[153] Without denying the importance of analyzing the structure, functions and activities of well-known arrangements, I would join here H. Körbs, who believed that the key question in the matter is not whether any interstate entity may be qualified as a regional arrangement under Chapter VIII in general but rather whether the activity of a group of states in a particular situation may be characterized as falling under Chapter VIII.[154]

This approach is the only one that provides us with the possibility of subordinating collective activity in the sphere of maintenance of international peace and security to the limitations of Chapter VIII.

2.2 Regionalism, Membership and Territorial Constraints

The wording of art. 52-53 of the UN Charter can be literally interpreted as restricting the types and activities of regional organizations on geographical or territorial grounds. In particular, art. 52(1) recognizes the existence of <u>*regional*</u> arrangements and agencies for dealing with matters that are appropriate for <u>*regional action*</u>. The pacific settlement of <u>*local*</u> disputes (art. 52(2)) is viewed as their primary concern.

---

doctrine (see *A More Secure World*, *op. cit.*, p. 62, 66, paras. 186, 204; Beyerlin U., "Regional Arrangements," *op. cit.*, p. 1040-1051; Schreuer C., "Regionalization," in *United Nations: Law, Politics and Practice,* ed. R. Wolfrum, vol. I (Munich: Verlag C.H. Beck, 1995), p. 1059).

[153] Lind K., *The Revival of Chapter VIII of the UN Charter*, *op. cit.*, p. 32.

[154] Körbs H., *Die Friedensdicherung duech die Vereinten Nationen und Regionalorganizationen*, *op. cit.*, p. 88.

In view of the "regional" orientation of Chapter VIII,[155] it is important to decide what the term "region" means. It is sometimes asserted that the 21st century is a period of the birth[156] or renewal of regionalism.[157]

Regional Organizations

Although both the San Francisco documents and legal doctrine mention geographical proximity as a usual characteristic of regional organizations, neither considers it to be ultimate.[158] The distinction between regional, subregional, interstate or quasi-regional organizations repeatedly cited in the doctrine[159] and UN documents[160] does not affect the exercise of

---

[155] References to regional activity, especially as regards the maintenance of international peace and security, occur often in the UN Charter. This issue has been considered in depth by H. Körbs (see *ibid.*, p. 79-81).

[156] *Ibid.*, p. 4; see Thakur R., van Langenhove L., "Enhancing Global Governance through Regional Integration," in *Regionalisation and Global Governance: The Taming of Globalization?*, ed. A.F. Cooper, C. W. Hughes, Ph. de Lombaerde (London/New York: Routledge Taylor and Francis Group, 2008), p. 23, 25.

[157] Karns M.P., Mingst K.A., *International Organizations*, *op. cit.*, p. 145-153; Forteau M., "Regional Co-operation," in *Max Planck Encyclopedia of Public International Law*, paras. 3, 10.

[158] Weiss T.G. *et al.*, *The United Nations and Changing World Politics*, *op. cit.*, p. 18-19; Schreuer C., "Regionalization," *op. cit.*, p. 1059; Beyerlin U., "Regional Arrangements," *op. cit.*, p. 1040; Kelsen H., "Is the North Atlantic Treaty a Regional Arrangement?" *op. cit.*, p. 162; Hummer W., Schweitzer M., "Article 52," *op. cit.*, p. 820-821; Abass A. *Regional Organizations and the Development of Collective Security*, *op. cit.*, p. 10-11, 13; *Documents of the UN Conference on International Organization*, vol. III., *op. cit.*, p. 82, 214, 256; *Documents of the UN Conference on International Organization*, vol. I., *op. cit.*, p. 371; *Commission to Study the Organization of Peace*, *op. cit.*, p. 20. Geographical proximity as an ultimate criterion had been promoted at the San Francisco conference by delegates of Egypt; see *Documents of the UN Conference on International Organization*, vol. III., *op. cit.*, p. 451.

[159] Körbs H., *Die Friedensdicherung duech die Vereinten Nationen und Regionalorganizationen*, *op. cit.*, p. 95, 167-168; Pernice R., *Die Sicherung des Weltfriedens*, *op. cit.*, p. 24, 33; Walter C., *Vereinte Nationen und Regional Organisationen*, *op. cit.*, p. 32, 124; Sobakin V.K., *Collective Security – A Guarantee of Peaceful Coexistence*, *op. cit.*, p. 334-337; Kolosov Y.M., Krivchikova, E.S., ed., *International Law*, *op. cit.*, p. 267; Ignatenko G.V., Tiunov O.I., ed., *International Law*, *op. cit.*, p. 354; Brovka Y.P., Lepeshkov Y.A., Pavlova L.V., ed., *International Public Law*, *op. cit.*, p. 494; Geyrhalter B., *Friedenssicherung durch Regionalorganizationen*, *op. cit.*, p. 28; Weiss T.G. *et al.*, *The United Nations and Changing World Politics*, *op. cit.*, p. 19; Fawcett L., "The Evolving Architecture of Regionalization," in *The United Nations and Regional Security: Europe and Beyond,* ed. M. Pugh and W.P. Singh Sidhu (Boulder/London: Lynne Rienner Publishers, 2003), p. 15.

[160] 2005 World Summit Outcome, *op. cit.*, para. 170; UN Security Council Resolution 1631 (2005), 17 October 2005; Statement by the President of the Security Council, S/PRST/2010/1, 13 January 2010; Security Council Meeting 6257 (S/PV.6257) – Cooperation between the United Nations and regional and sub-regional organizations in maintaining international peace

their powers under Chapter VIII. The "regional" nature of organizations referred to in Chapter VIII is currently not conditioned by any geographical boundaries. These organizations are viewed as distinct from universal ones, that is, as organizations with limited membership.[161]

Membership

The status of regional organizations summons two more issues that are actively debated in the international legal doctrine. The first concerns the possibility to qualify as regional organizations under Chapter VIII groups which include states (or are established by states) that are *non-members of the United Nations*[162] and, as follows, the applicability of Chapter VIII to their activities. Presently, due to the all-embracing nature of the United Nations, this question has lost most of its actuality and practical impact, but situations do arise from time to time (*e.g.*, Kosovo) to make it relevant.

The second issue is a logical outgrowth of the first. It concerns the *subjects able to establish regional organizations under Chapter VIII*. This question is rather new in the international legal doctrine. The traditional vision limits regional organizations under Chapter VIII exclusively to interstate entities.[163] An innovative approach extends this to include other subjects, including international organizations, parts of federal states and even non-state actors.[164]

Apparently, even in the middle of the 20th century, the UN's founders were able to imagine that non-state actors might become important enough to claim an independent constructive role in the security area. As a result, the UN Charter appears to be a rather flexible mechanism; as correctly noted by C. Walters, it does not limit subjects of art. 52-54

---

and security, 13 January 2010; Security Council Update Report, 18 September 2006, No. 3, *op. cit.*

161 See Pernice R., *Die Sicherung des Weltfriedens*, *op. cit.*, p. 41; Geyrhalter B., *Friedenssicherung durch Regionalorganizationen*, *op. cit.*, p. 28-29; Fawcett L., "The Evolving Architecture of Regionalization," *op. cit.*, p. 11; Eide A., "Peace-keeping and Enforcement by Regional Organizations," *op. cit.*, p. 125.

162 See *e.g.* Pernice R., *Die Sicherung des Weltfriedens*, *op. cit.*, p. 40-41; Körbs H., *Die Friedensdicherung duech die Vereinten Nationen und Regionalorganizationen*, *op. cit.*, p. 165-166.

163 Pernice R., *Die Sicherung des Weltfriedens*, *op. cit.*, p. 41; Körbs H., *Die Friedensdicherung duech die Vereinten Nationen und Regionalorganizationen*, *op. cit.*, p. 88-89, 162; Geyrhalter B., *Friedenssicherung durch Regionalorganizationen*, *op. cit.*, p. 31; Lind K., *The Revival of Chapter VIII of the UN Charter*, *op. cit.*, p. 71.

164 For details on this point, see Walter C., *Vereinte Nationen und Regional Organisationen*, *op. cit.*, p. 116-119, 125.

exclusively to sovereign states.[165] Therefore, international organizations may participate in the establishment of regional organizations under Chapter VIII.

As concerns non-state actors, no-one can deny today that some of them (*e.g.*, transnational corporations or private military companies) may possess resources comparable to those of individual states. Nevertheless, the contemporary system of collective security is still state-oriented. Moreover, the maintenance of international peace and security is an extremely sensitive matter for every state and, indirectly, for every individual. As a result, entities that cannot be qualified as subjects of international law may hardly be endowed with active competences in this area. They do not possess any international personality, and are therefore not bound by provisions of the UN Charter and cannot be held responsible if any breaches of international law take place. Non-state entities may thus only play a subsidiary role in the maintenance of international peace and security when their involvement occurs through recognized subjects of international law, with the latter assuming the risks for their actions.

Another important issue warranting consideration is the *minimal number of members* necessary for an entity to be recognized as a regional organization under Chapter VIII. Theorists usually indicate a minimal number – two,[166] three[167] or five[168] states. The first of these (two members) seems to be the correct one, as the ordinary meaning of collective as opposed to individual does not provide for a minimal threshold. Indeed, due to the broad approach of the UN's founders to the very notion of regional organizations under Chapter VIII, as well as the primary purpose of the Chapter (that is, to subject all local arrangements acting in the peace and security area to its basic restrictions), every collective establishment, or every relevant activity of every collective establishment (including those with only two members) should already be qualified under Chapter VIII.

This minimal number, however, is not applicable when a regional organization under Chapter VIII is established by another international organization, as might occur on an *ad hoc* basis (although the opposite opinion is also cited in the legal doctrine),[169] because the establishing international organization is already a derivative collective entity and it falls

---

[165] *Ibid.*, p. 117-118.

[166] *Ibid.*, p. 120, 125.

[167] Pernice R., *Die Sicherung des Weltfriedens*, *op. cit.*, p. 35; Körbs H., *Die Friedensdicherung duech die Vereinten Nationen und Regionalorganizationen*, *op. cit.*, p. 164; Alagappa M., "Regional Arrangements, the UN and International Security," *op. cit.*, p. 6.

[168] B. Boutros-Ghali, cited by Walter C., *Vereinte Nationen und Regional Organisationen*, *op. cit.*, p. 119.

[169] Walter C., *Vereinte Nationen und Regional Organisationen*, *op. cit.*, p. 126.

under Chapter VIII with regard to its own actions. The last point, however, does not preclude the possibility that organizations may participate in regional organizations under Chapter VIII and take part in regional actions together with states and other organizations; this often happens in practice.

Territorial Constraints

Two other characteristics mentioned in art. 52 – "appropriate for regional action" and "local disputes" – mostly concern the competences of regional organizations with respect to the territorial sphere. In particular, can an organization be entitled to act beyond its territory? Are there any specifics in the peaceful settlement of local disputes or involvement in local matters that are appropriate for regional action? Can a regional organization be utilized by the UN Security Council for enforcement action under its authority beyond the territory of the organization?

As opposed to "local disputes," which are clearly viewed in art. 52(2) as disputes between member states of regional organizations,[170] neither the UN Charter nor the San Francisco documents specify which matters are to be considered as *appropriate* for regional action. Some states[171] and legal publicists[172] have intended to limit such matters to those which require actions only within the territory of the member states of an organization. I would like, however, to join those who support the opposite view,[173] since peace and security in a region can be endangered by events or activity both within and beyond its borders. It is illustrative that this approach has been implemented in recent documents of regional organizations.[174] In the absence of applicable rules, regional organizations can independently decide which matters beyond their territories may be appropriate for regional action.

[170] Goodrich L.M., Hambro E., *Charter of the United Nations*, *op. cit.*, p. 185; Abass A. *Regional Organizations and the Development of Collective Security*, *op. cit.*, p. 31.

[171] *Documents of the UN Conference on International Organization*, vol. III., *op. cit.*, p. 284.

[172] Beyerlin U., "Regional Arrangements," *op. cit.*, p. 1043; Doehring K., "Collective Security," *op. cit.*, p. 110; Hummer W., Schweitzer M., "Article 52," *op. cit.*, p. 821; Walter C., "Security Council Control over Regional Action," *op. cit.*, p. 176.

[173] Kelsen H., "Is the North Atlantic Treaty a Regional Arrangement?" *op. cit.*, p. 163; Bentwich N., Martin A., *A Commentary on the Charter of the United Nations*, *op. cit.*, p. 109.

[174] See, *e.g.*, Strategic Concept for the Defence and Security of the Members of the North Atlantic Treaty Organization, *op. cit.*, paras. 11, 20; Consolidated version of the Treaty on European Union (with Lisbon treaty), *Official Journal of the European Union*, 51 (2008), art. 42(1); Договор о коллективной безопасности [Treaty of Collective Security (TCS)] of 15 May 1992 (with Protocol of 20 December 2010), *Electronic Legal Database Konsul'tant Plus: Technologiia 3000.*

The qualification of disputes as "local" and matters as "appropriate for regional action" has practical, not only theoretical, impact.

It is generally agreed that regional organizations enjoy priority in the peaceful settlement of local disputes.[175] It is believed here, however, that art. 52(1) of the UN Charter ("*Nothing in the present Charter precludes the existence of regional arrangements or agencies for dealing with such matters [...]*") is to be interpreted analogously with the rules of art. 30(2) of the Vienna Convention on the Law of Treaties. It follows, then, that regional organizations shall enjoy priority as concerns any activity on "*matters relating to the maintenance of international peace and security as are appropriate for regional action*" subject to the limitations of the UN's purposes and principles (art. 52(1)), the requirement for them to get authorization from the Security Council for any enforcement action (art. 53(1)) and the obligations arising from the UN Charter (art. 103),[176] including (for the peaceful settlement of international disputes) art. 34 and 35 of the Charter.[177]

It is also advocated here that limiting the dispute settlement competence of regional organizations to the disputes exclusively between member states of organizations[178] is not sufficiently grounded. Due to the right of states to freely select the means of peaceful settlement of international disputes, third states or a member state and a third state may decide to use one or another means of peaceful settlement of international disputes within an organization and within its competence. This is why I would join those who believe that the limitation of art. 52(2) concerns exclusively the application of the subsidiarity rules[179] – that is, priorities in the peaceful settlement of disputes. Art. 52 cannot be interpreted as obliging member states to settle their disputes by local means or obliging a regional

---

[175] *Documents of the UN Conference on International Organization*, vol. III., *op. cit.*, p. 215, 234, 241, 525; Abass A. *Regional Organizations and the Development of Collective Security*, *op. cit.*, p. 32-33; Schreuer C., "Regionalization," *op. cit.*, p. 1063.

[176] See Bernhardt G., "Article 103," in *The Charter of the United Nations: A Commentary,* 2nd ed., vol. 1, ed. B. Simma (Munich: Verlag C.H. Beck, 2002), p. 1295-1296, 1298; UN Security Council Resolutions 660 (1990), 25 September 1990; 713 (1991), 25 September 1991; 724 (1991), 15 December 1991; 787 (1992), 16 November 1992; 1127 (1997), 28 August 1997; 1298 (2000), 17 May 2000, *etc.*; Military and Paramilitary Activities in and against Nicaragua (Nicaragua *v.* United States of America), Jurisdiction and Admissibility, Judgment, *I.C.J. Reports 1984*, p. 440.

[177] Beyerlin U., "Regional Arrangements," *op. cit.*, p. 1041; Bentwich N., Martin A., *A Commentary on the Charter of the United Nations*, *op. cit.*, p. 112; Hummer W., Schweitzer M., "Article 52," *op. cit.*, p. 842; Military and Paramilitary Activities in and against Nicaragua, 1984, *op. cit.*, p. 440, para. 108.

[178] Tahir M., *Legal Problems of Collective Security*, *op. cit.*, p. 135.

[179] Lind K., *The Revival of Chapter VIII of the UN Charter*, *op. cit.*, p. 25.

collective security organization to develop a set of dispute settlement mechanisms, *e.g.*, as with H. Kelsen's assertion that states may be obliged to settle their disputes through means of a regional organization only if it is set forth in its constituent documents.[180]

In a formal legal sense, states are free to choose the means of peaceful settlement of international disputes. At the same time, the constituent documents of most institutionalized agencies set forth one or several means of peaceful settlement. In accordance with art. 52 of the UN Charter, regional organizations enjoy priority over universal mechanisms of peaceful settlement, even if states have recognized the jurisdiction of both regional and universal mechanisms. Formally, this priority is not absolute. As concerns local disputes, it is limited by articles 52(4), 34 and 35 of the UN Charter as concerns disputes and situations that may potentially threaten international peace and security.[181] It is generally agreed that states may formally submit their dispute to the Security Council.[182] In practice, however, the Security Council has sent situations back to regional mechanisms (Haiti/Dominican Republic, 1963; Panama/USA, 1964).[183]

The right of the Security Council to utilize regional organizations under its authority is not limited on territorial grounds;[184] this will be considered in detail in Chapter 3.

2.3 Competence

Purpose

Before we start to examine issues pertaining to the competence of regional organizations, it is necessary to look at the purpose of these entities. Art. 52(1) clearly states that regional security organizations are supposed to deal "*with such matters relating to the maintenance of international peace and security as are appropriate for regional action.*" As a result, the

---

[180] Kelsen H., *Collective Security under International Law*, *op. cit.*, p. 182.
[181] Beyerlin U., "Regional Arrangements," *op. cit.*, p. 1041.
[182] Bentwich N., Martin A., *A Commentary on the Charter of the United Nations*, *op. cit.*, p. 112; Hummer W., Schweitzer M., "Article 52," *op. cit.*, p. 839.
[183] Cited by Abass A. *Regional Organizations and the Development of Collective Security*, *op. cit.*, p. 32-33; Hummer W., Schweitzer M., "Article 52," *op. cit.*, p. 842.
[184] See also Bentwich N., Martin A., *A Commentary on the Charter of the United Nations*, *op. cit.*, p. 113; Abass A. *Regional Organizations and the Development of Collective Security*, *op. cit.*, p. 62. The opposite opinion was expressed by Chile at the San Francisco conference; see *Documents of the UN Conference on International Organization*, vol. III., *op. cit.*, p. 284.

orientation of regional organizations toward the maintenance of regional peace and security is commonly recognized as their defining feature.[185]

Although the early years of the United Nations were characterized by the narrow doctrinal approach to the notion of regional organizations, so that only those substantially aimed at maintaining international peace and security could be characterized as falling under Chapter VIII,[186] practice has shown that international organizations can evolve to include security in addition to their other spheres of activity (*e.g.*, EU, ECOWAS and CIS, which are primarily involved in economic and other sorts of cooperation). It is generally agreed (and it may serve as a good illustration on behalf of the functional approach to qualification) that due to the expanding tasks of international organizations, exclusive or predominant involvement in the maintenance of peace and security is currently not to be assessed as a restrictive criterion.[187]

Some organizations do not possess sufficient competences or facilities for dispute settlement or enforcement action (*e.g.*, the OSCE, the Council of Europe and the EU have no military personnel to accomplish enforcement activity). The question thus arises whether regional organizations can act beyond the methods expressly prescribed by Chapter VIII, and whether they fall under Chapter VIII when they do not possess competences and/or facilities to fulfill all of the tasks set forth by the UN Charter.

"Obligatory" Competences

As noted above, the UN Charter provides a general framework for regional activity in the security area. Chapter VIII refers to the peaceful settlement of international disputes and endows regional organizations with the right, or sets forth their duty, to take enforcement action under the authority of the Security Council.[188] These mechanisms are the only way the Charter

---

[185] Brovka Y.P., Lepeshkov Y.A., Pavlova L.V., ed., *International Public Law*, *op. cit.*, p. 493; Tahir M., *Legal Problems of Collective Security*, *op. cit.*, p. 141; Pernice R., *Die Sicherung des Weltfriedens*, *op. cit.*, p. 41.

[186] See Pernice R., *Die Sicherung des Weltfriedens*, *op. cit.*, p. 41; Körbs H., *Die Friedensdicherung duech die Vereinten Nationen und Regionalorganizationen*, *op. cit.*, p. 171.

[187] See also Walter C., *Vereinte Nationen und Regional Organisationen*, *op. cit.*, p. 91, 125; Geyrhalter B., *Friedenssicherung durch Regionalorganizationen*, *op. cit.*, p. 37; Fawcett L., "The Evolving Architecture of Regionalization," *op. cit.*, p. 19.

[188] C. Walter views art. 52, paras. 2-4 of the UN Charter as a threshold for the distribution of competence between the UN Security Council and regional organizations; see Walter C., *Vereinte Nationen und Regional Organisationen*, *op. cit.*, p. 99.

provides for the activity of regional organizations. It is sometimes disputed whether regional organizations may only be qualified under Chapter VIII if they possess effective mechanisms of peaceful settlement of international disputes[189] as well as mechanisms to undertake enforcement actions.[190]

A single particular form of dispute settlement is usually not sufficient to be qualified under Chapter VIII, as has been noted by the ICJ in the Decision on Military and Paramilitary Activity in and against Nicaragua (Preliminary Objections) concerning the Contadora process (para. 107).[191] At the other extreme, a regional organization cannot be required to have a "*complete system of dispute settlement*"[192] or a developed mechanism of peace enforcement[193] to be qualified under Chapter VIII.[194] No requirement of this type can be found in either the UN Charter or the San Francisco documents.

Expansion of Competences

It is believed here that the list of activities of regional organizations engaged in the peaceful settlement of local disputes and enforcement action

---

[189] Körbs H., *Die Friedensdicherung duech die Vereinten Nationen und Regionalorganizationen, op. cit.*, p. 197-200; Faust D.A., *Effektive Sicherheit. Analyse des Systems kollektiver Sicherheit der Vereinten Nationen und Entwurf eines alternativen Sicherheitssystems* (Wiesbaden: Westdeutscher Verlag, 2002), p. 204; Pernice R., *Die Sicherung des Weltfriedens, op. cit.*, p. 38, 41; Hummer W., Schweitzer M., "Article 52," *op. cit.*, p. 828; Lind K., *The Revival of Chapter VIII of the UN Charter, op. cit.*, p. 89-90.

[190] It is often disputed whether regional organizations may be used by the UN Security Council for enforcement action under its control if their constituent documents do not provide for enforcement mechanisms, but the possibility that organizations under Chapter VIII exist without enforcement mechanisms is not denied; see, *e.g.*, Pernice R., *Die Sicherung des Weltfriedens, op. cit.*, p. 40.

[191] Military and Paramilitary Activities in and against Nicaragua, 1984, *op. cit.*, Preliminary Objections, p. 440.

[192] See Colombia's proposal at the San Francisco conference (*Documents of the UN Conference on International Organization*, vol. XII., *op. cit.*, p. 687); Körbs H., *Die Friedensdicherung duech die Vereinten Nationen und Regionalorganizationen, op. cit.*, p. 200; Faust D.A., *Effektive Sicherheit, op. cit.*, p. 204; Kourula E., "Peace-keeping and Regional Arrangements," in *United Nations Peace-keeping: Legal Essays,* ed. A. Cassese (Alphen aan den Rijn: Stijthoff & Noordhoff International Publishers, 1978), p. 102; Geyrhalter B., *Friedenssicherung durch Regionalorganizationen, op. cit.*, p. 45-46.

[193] Kourula E., "Peace-keeping and Regional Arrangements," *op. cit.*, p. 102. It is correctly noted that most regional organizations traditionally lack freely available military resources (Wilson G., "Regional Arrangements as Agents of the UN Security Council," *op. cit.,* p. 187).

[194] C. Walter even maintains that the existence of regional organizations as a forum for cooperation between states is already a sufficient means of peaceful settlement of disputes (Walter C., *Vereinte Nationen und Regional Organisationen, op. cit.*, p. 100-101).

under the UN Security Council's control is not exhaustive[195]. As for the general scope of competences of regional organizations, the only explicit limitation of Chapter VIII concerns the alignment of their activities with the UN's purposes and principles. Art. 52(1) expressly recognizes the right of regional organizations to deal "*with such matters relating to the maintenance of international peace and security [...] which are appropriate for regional action*" and thus contains no restrictions on the list of activities or competences. The UN Charter had been drafted as a flexible document that could adapt to new circumstances and still provide a sufficient framework for the activities of regional organizations, even in the face of an expansion of new threats and challenges.[196]

In reality, regional organizations are currently adapting their activities to reach all aspects of maintenance of international peace and security. Corresponding UN documents recognize their role in preventive diplomacy; peace-making; early warning; peacekeeping; post-conflict peace-building (including election monitoring and assistance); disarmament;[197] peaceful settlement of international disputes (including facilitation and mediation);[198] fighting international terrorism, genocide, ethnic cleansing, war crimes, crimes against humanity,[199] illegal arms trafficking and the proliferation of weapons of mass destruction; crisis management; implementation of UN Security Council sanctions; establishment of quick-

---

[195] In support of this view, see also Lind K., *The Revival of Chapter VIII of the UN Charter*, *op. cit.*, p. 25. In the early period of existence of regional organizations, only two forms of activity (dispute settlement and enforcement) or three (dispute settlement, enforcement and collective self-defense) in the sphere of maintenance of international peace and security have been recognized (Eide A., "Peace-keeping and Enforcement by Regional Organizations," *op. cit.*, p. 125).

[196] Para. 79 of 2005 World Summit Outcome (*op. cit.*) expressly says that "*the relevant provisions of the Charter are sufficient to address the full range of threats to international peace and security.*"

[197] Supplement to an Agenda for Peace, *op. cit.*, para. 23.

[198] Declaration on the Enhancement of Cooperation between the UN and Regional Arrangements or Agencies (A/RES/49/57), 17 February 1995, para. 2; Perspectives of the UN and Regional Organizations on Preventive and Quiet Diplomacy, Dialogue, Facilitation and Mediation: Common Challenges and Good Practices, February 2011.

[199] 2005 World Summit Outcome, *op. cit.*, paras. 87-88, 93, 100, 139.

reaction forces to support UN peace-keeping operations;[200] and promotion and protection of human rights.[201]

It is thus obvious that the expansion of activities of regional organizations reflects and conforms to an expansion of the notion and vision of security.[202] In addition to measures aimed at the prevention or settlement of a particular conflict (existing or imminent), which besides dispute settlement and enforcement action include peacekeeping measures,[203] there are measures aimed at the prevention of the very possibility of a conflict – so-called "confidence- and security-building measures" (hereafter, CSBMs): disarmament, control over armaments, exchanges of information, mutual inspections, *etc.*; and measures aimed at struggles against particular threats and challenges. The implementation of resolutions of the Security Council, depending on their content, could concern any of these areas. Attention is also paid to the promotion and protection of human rights.

The activity of regional organizations, regardless of its nature, is to be exercised within the framework of the UN's purposes and principles and thus requires the explicit, prior, clear and freely expressed consent of a target/host state[204] for non-forcible measures or the Security Council's authorization of enforcement actions.

---

[200] UN Security Council Resolutions 1631 (2005), *op. cit.*, paras. 2-5; 1809 (2008), *op. cit.*, para. 8; Statement by the President of the Security Council, S/PRST/2010/1, *op. cit.*, paras. 3, 5-7; Security Council Meeting 6257, *op. cit.*, p. 25-28 (speeches of the US and Austrian representatives).

[201] Relationship between the United Nations and Regional Organizations, in Particular the African Union, in the Maintenance of International Peace and Security. Report of the UN Secretary-General, 7 April 2008 (S/2008/18), parts IV-IX.

[202] As concerns the scope of areas recognized by UN bodies, see also UN Security Council Resolution 2033 (2012), 12 January 2012, preamble, paras. 2, 4 (active involvement at all stages of the conflict); UN General Assembly Resolution 66/36, Regional disarmament, 12 January 2012; UN General Assembly Resolution 66/37, Conventional arms control at the regional and subregional levels, 12 January 2012; UN General Assembly Resolution 66/38, Confidence building measures in the regional and sub-regional context, 12 January 2012; Statement by the President of the Security Council, S/PRST/2007/42, 6 November 2007; 2005 World Summit Outcome, *op. cit.*, paras. 87-88, 93, 100, 139.

[203] On the types and forms of peacekeeping operations, see *United Nations Peacekeeping Operations*: *Principles and Guidelines* (New York: UN Department of Peacekeeping Operations, 2010), p. 17-18.

[204] See Certain Expenses of the United Nations (Article 17, Paragraph 2, of the Charter), Advisory Opinion, *I.C.J. Reports 1962* (The Hague: I.C.J, 1962), p. 162; Henkin L., "The Invasion in Panama Under International Law: A Gross Violation," *Columbia Journal of Transnational Law*, 29(2) (1991), p. 299; Draft Articles on Responsibility of States for Internationally Wrongful Acts, with commentaries, 2001, *Yearbook of the International Law Commission*, 2001, vol. II (New York/Geneva: United Nations, 2006), Part Two, p. 73; Bother N., "Peace-keeping," in *The Charter of the United Nations: A Commentary*, ed. B.

Military (Self-Defense) Alliances Within the UN Rules

The qualification of military alliances in relation to the rules of Chapter VIII has been actively debated in international law. A number of authors differentiate between regional organizations and military alliances,[205] referring to different purposes (security in the region for the former, and security against external threats for the latter), legal foundations (Chapter VII for treaties of self-defense and Chapter VIII for regional organizations),[206] permanence (regional organizations as permanent and self-defense as an *ad hoc* mechanism)[207] and legal nature (regional organizations as part of the UN system and self-defense as an exceptional emergency means outside the system),[208] and do not recognize NATO, OSCE, WEU, EU or others as regional organizations under Chapter VIII. Other publicists (H. Kelsen, C. Walters) stand up for the possibility of qualifying self-defense alliances as regional security organizations, insofar as defense against external threats can have an important impact on the maintenance of peace and security in the region, and aggression may be directed not only from the outside but also from inside the organization.[209] A third group insists that collective self-defense is a necessary form of activity within the sphere of maintenance of international peace and security.[210]

At the same time, as C. Walters reasonably asserts,[211] the question of whether an organization is a self-defense alliance or a security organization under Chapter VIII is a misleading one. This is illustrated all the more by the fact that most publicists (even those who distinguish between these groups of

---

Simma, vol. 1 (Munich: Verlag C.H. Beck, 2002), p. 681-682; Helsinki Summit Declaration 1992, paras. 23-24; Siekmann R., "Commentary: OSCE versus UN Peacekeeping," *Helsinki Monitor,* 3(4) (1992), p. 19.

205 The latter are viewed as being much closer to traditional alliances under the balance of power system, when cooperation was oriented against external threats (Pernice R., *Die Sicherung des Weltfriedens*, *op. cit.*, p. 54). For a detailed analysis, see Walter C., *Vereinte Nationen und Regional Organisationen*, *op. cit.*, p. 48-90; Kourula E., "Peace-keeping and Regional Arrangements," *op. cit.*, p. 102.

206 See Doehring K., "Collective Security," *op. cit.*, p. 114; Abass A. *Regional Organizations and the Development of Collective Security*, *op. cit.*, p. 14; Hummer W., Schweitzer M., "Article 52," *op. cit.*, p. 823; Walter C., *Vereinte Nationen und Regional Organisationen*, *op. cit.*, p. 49; Pernice R., *Die Sicherung des Weltfriedens*, *op. cit.*, p. 52-53.

207 Körbs H., *Die Friedensdicherung duech die Vereinten Nationen und Regionalorganizationen*, *op. cit.*, p. 173.

208 *Ibid.*, p. 177-178.

209 See also Kelsen H., "Is the North Atlantic Treaty a Regional Arrangement?" *op. cit.*, p. 163-165; Abass A. *Regional Organizations and the Development of Collective Security*, *op. cit.*, p. 39; Kelsen H., "Collective Security and Collective Self-Defense," *op. cit.*, p. 795; Walter C., *Vereinte Nationen und Regional Organisationen*, *op. cit.*, p. 93-94, 124-125

210 Eide A., "Peace-keeping and Enforcement by Regional Organizations," *op. cit.*, p. 125.

211 Walter C., *Vereinte Nationen und Regional Organisationen*, *op. cit.*, p. 77.

interstate establishments) do not object to the existence of mixed systems and qualify NATO and OSCE as regional organizations due to the proliferation of their competences.[212] Many existing regional organizations are designed, among other things, to repulse armed attacks if they happen.[213]

Moreover, it is maintained here that the distinction between regional organizations under Chapter VIII and collective-defense alliances has nothing to do with the UN Charter. As noted above, the notion of regional arrangements and agencies was initially very broad and included military alliances as well,[214] something that has been asserted, *inter alia*, by the same authors who distinguish between regional organizations and military alliances.[215]

It may thus be concluded that the problem of a distinction between regional security organizations and defense alliances has an artificial origin. During the period of the Cold War, both NATO and OWT intended to exempt their activity from the operation of articles 53 and 54 of the UN Charter to be able to apply some enforcement measures without the sanction of the Security Council and to not be obliged to report to the Council on activity "in contemplation" as required (differently from art. 51) by art. 54 of the UN Charter.

Collective self-defence has an important impact on the maintenance of international peace and security in a region that obviously corresponds to the purpose of regional organizations (to deal "*with such matters relating to the maintenance of international peace and security as are appropriate for regional action*") set forth in art. 52(1). As a result, this activity is also subject to the operation and (no less important) restrictions of Chapter VIII from the moment self-defense has started and regardless of its legal grounds (permanent collective-defense alliances or *ad hoc* groups of states).

---

[212] Doehring K., "Collective Security," *op. cit.*, p. 110; Abass A. *Regional Organizations and the Development of Collective Security*, *op. cit.*, p. 14, 23-24; Beyerlin U., "Regional Arrangements," *op. cit.*, p. 1041, 1050; Wilson G., "Regional Arrangements as Agents of the UN Security Council," *op. cit.,* p. 124.

[213] TCS, *op. cit.*, art. 4; North Atlantic Treaty, 4 April 1949, art. 5; Charter of the Organization of American States, 1948, art. 3(g), 28; Устав Организации Договора о коллективной безопасности [CSTO Charter], 17 October 2002, *Bulletin of International Treaties*, 3 (2004), art. 3, 7(1).

[214] *Documents of the UN Conference on International Organization*, vol. III., *op. cit.*, p. 128.

[215] Weiss T.G. *et al.*, *The United Nations and Changing World Politics*, *op. cit.*, p. 19; Beyerlin U., "Regional Arrangements," *op. cit.*, p. 1040; Hummer W., Schweitzer M., "Article 52," *op. cit.*, p. 817; Akehurst M., "Enforcement Action of Regional Organizations," *op. cit.*, p. 178; Alagappa M., "Regional Arrangements, the UN and International Security," *op. cit.*, p. 6.

In theory, this statement may seem ridiculous insofar as the right of individual and/or collective self-defense is positioned as an independent mechanism and even placed into another chapter (Chapter VII) of the UN Charter. In reality, however, art. 51 also seeks to ensure some minimal restrictions (narrower than those of Chapter VIII) to be implemented when organizations or groups of states claim not to fall under the regime of Chapter VIII. Due to the nature and character of self-defense activity, art. 51 should therefore be viewed as *lex specialis* to the rules of regional security (no obligation to obtain Security Council authorization to start self-defense activity; an obligation to inform the Council concerning only actions already taken but not future actions).

2.4 Limitations

Although the UN Charter does not strictly frame the activity of regional organizations, some limitations do exist nevertheless. In accordance with art. 52(1), regional "*arrangements or agencies and their activities* [shall be] *consistent with the Purposes and Principles of the United Nations*." Art. 103 resolves any conflict between states' obligations under the UN Charter and obligations under any other agreement in favor of the former.[216]

Adherence to the Purposes and Principles of the UN

It follows from the wording of art. 52(2) that both the constituent and other documents of regional organizations as well as their activity shall be consistent with the UN's purposes and principles. In view of the initial aspiration of the drafters of the UN Charter to establish a single universal system of collective security and to subordinate the activity of regional organizations to that of the United Nations,[217] this basically means that no military alliances (balance of power systems) may be established. Regional organizations may exist and function only under the control of the United

[216] See Bernhardt G., "Article 103," *op. cit.*, p. 1295-1296, 1298; UN Security Council Resolutions 660 (1990), *op. cit.*; 713 (1991), *op. cit.*; 724 (1991), *op. cit.*; 787 (1992), *op. cit.*; 1127 (1997), *op. cit.*; 1298 (2000), *op. cit.*, *etc.*; Military and Paramilitary Activities in and against Nicaragua, 1984, *op. cit.*, Preliminary Objections, p. 440.

[217] This was an entirely new approach in the practice of international organizations; *e.g.*, art. 21 of the Covenant of the League of Nations had allowed for the priority of regional action ("*regional arrangements were not considered incompatible with any provisions of the Charter*"). See also Venezuela's position, *Documents of the UN Conference on International Organization*, vol. III., *op. cit.*, p. 214.

Nations and in accordance with its principles. These principles include prohibitions on the use of force in international relations and on intervening in the domestic affairs of states,[218] in addition to other recognized principles of international law.

Because of the priority of obligations under the UN Charter in accordance with art. 103, art. 52(1) establishes a strict and sufficient obligation for regional arrangements and agencies. A reaffirmation of their adherence to the UN's purposes and principles in the constituent documents of an organization (if there are any) therefore has no legal meaning, although it is sometimes cited as necessary.[219] In reality, permanent institutionalized regional organizations usually refer to the UN Charter's purposes and principles in their establishing documents, although with a declaratory (rather then constituent) character, and this may only be useful for the official qualification of a permanent regional entity under Chapter VIII. The UN's purposes and principles may be qualified as "high standards" that are obligatory for all actors in the international arena, including the Security Council itself.[220]

Much more important than a regional organization's "pure" declaration of adherence to the UN's purposes and principles is whether its constituent and other documents are consistent with them. Attempts by particular organizations (*e.g.*, ECOWAS, AU) to advocate for the possibility of applying military force to member states, even through the conclusion of specific treaties (*e.g.*, Protocol Relating to the Mechanism of Conflict Prevention, Management, Resolution, Peacekeeping and Security of 10 December 1999, art. 25;[221] Protocol Relating to the Establishment of the

---

[218] This obligation was fiercely maintained during the San Francisco conference: see the position of Colombia – *Documents of the UN Conference on International Organization*, vol. I., *op. cit.*, p. 364; also see those of Mexico, Venezuela, Guatemala – *Documents of the UN Conference on International Organization*, vol. III., *op. cit.*, p. 82, 214, 215, 256.

[219] Körbs H., *Die Friedensdicherung duech die Vereinten Nationen und Regionalorganizationen*, *op. cit.*, p. 192-193.

[220] Frowein J.A., Krisch N., "Article 41," in *The Charter of the United Nations: A Commentary*, 2nd ed., vol. 1, ed. B. Simma (Munich: Verlag C.H. Beck, 2002), p. 745; Doehring K., "Unlawful Resolutions of the Security Council and Their Legal Consequences," *Max Planck Yearbook of United Nations Law*, 1 (1997), p. 92-93; Orakhelashvili A., *Peremptory Norms in International Law* (New York: Oxford University Press, 2008), p. 425; Orakhelashvili A., "The Impact of Peremptory Norms on the Interpretation and Application of United Nations Security Council Resolutions," *European Journal of International Law*, 16(1) (2005), p. 60-62; Farral J.M., *United Nations Sanctions and the Rule of Law* (Cambridge: Cambridge University Press, 2009), p. 21.

[221] Protocol Relating to the Mechanism of Conflict Prevention, Management, Resolution, Peacekeeping and Security, 10 December 1999.

Peace and Security Council of the African Union of 9 July 2002, art. 4(j)),[222] most probably contradict peremptory norms of international law[223] (this is analyzed in detail in the next chapter) and as a result go counter to the limitations of art. 52(1).

Subordination to the Norms of the UN Charter (art. 103)

Art. 103 was not designed to directly regulate the activity of regional organizations in the sphere of maintenance of international peace and security, but rather to establish a general rule for all members of the United Nations: "*In the event of a conflict between the obligations of the Members of the United Nations under the present Charter and their obligations under any other international agreement, their obligations under the present Charter shall prevail.*"

This obligation, formally relevant only for states that are members of the United Nations, is immediately applicable to any regional organization established by them,[224] including but not limited to those involved in the maintenance of peace and security. It generally means that regardless of an organization's qualification under Chapter VIII, any activity of any regional organization shall always be subject to the provisions of article 103 of the UN Charter.[225] They all are obliged to act in comformity with provisions of the Charter and obligations arising from resolutions of the Security Council.[226]

---

[222] Protocol Relating to the Establishment of the Peace and Security Council of the African Union, 9 July 2002.

[223] See Walter C., "Security Council Control over Regional Action," *op. cit.*, p. 141 Reisman M.W., "Termination of the USSR's Treaty Right of Intervention in Iran," *American Journal of International Law*, 74(1) (1980), p. 150-153; Henkin L., "The Invasion in Panama," *op. cit.*, p. 309.

[224] K. Lind clearly states that "Although regional organizations are not, as such, members of the UN, they are legally bound by the UN Charter" (Lind K., *The Revival of Chapter VIII of the UN Charter*, *op. cit.*, p. 19).

[225] On this point, see Military and Paramilitary Activities in and against Nicaragua, 1984, *op. cit.*, Preliminary Objections, p. 440, para. 107; Walter C., *Vereinte Nationen und Regional Organisationen*, *op. cit.*, p. 91; Abass A. *Regional Organizations and the Development of Collective Security*, *op. cit.*, p. 62; Wippman D., "Treaty-Based Intervention: Who Can Say No?" *The University of Chicago Law Review*, 62(4) (1995), p. 619-620; Henkin L., "The Invasion in Panama," *op. cit.*, p. 309; Bernhardt G., "Article 103," *op. cit.*, p. 1295-1296, 1298; UN Security Council Resolutions 660 (1990), *op. cit.*; 713 (1991), *op. cit.*; 724 (1991), *op. cit.*; 787 (1992), *op. cit.*; 1127 (1997), *op. cit.*; 1298 (2000), *op. cit.*, *etc.*

[226] In the International legal doctrine, obligations arising from the UN Charter are understood rather broadly and include "*all obligations which arise immediately and directly from the Charter*" (Bernhardt G., "Article 103," *op. cit.*, p. 1295, 1300).

Art. 103 may thus be seen as imposing broader limitations than the obligation in art. 52(1) to act in conformity with the UN's purposes and principles.[227] It is believed here that through adopting art. 52(1), the UN's founders sought to reaffirm the general obligations in art. 103 and impose stronger (although narrower) obligations on any regional organization acting in the sphere of maintenance of international peace and security. Initially, this duplication was probably aimed at situations when regional organizations could also be established by non-UN members, which as such did not fall under the effect of art. 103.[228]

2.5 Criteria and Qualification

Because the characteristics of regional arrangements and entities are left very uncertain in the UN Charter and it provides no mechanism of assessment, the qualification of a particular organization as falling within the Chapter VIII requirements often entails debates. Until recently, some academics insisted that only the OAS, LAS and OAU could be qualified as regional organizations.[229] Others argued that NATO and the OWT should be excluded from the operation of Chapter VIII as military alliances.[230] Currently, this approach is not widely supported. After the end of the Cold War, regional organizations drastically changed their approach to the very idea of security, and the shift in their qualifications or characteristics relative to Chapter VIII has been remarkable. All or most regional organizations involved in the maintenance of peace and security are now apprised as falling under Chapter VIII,[231] although, as noted above, the scope of activity of relevant entities can be much broader.

[227] Walter C., *Vereinte Nationen und Regional Organisationen*, *op. cit.*, p. 108-109; Pernice R., *Die Sicherung des Weltfriedens*, *op. cit.*, p. 36-37.

[228] See Lind K., *The Revival of Chapter VIII of the UN Charter*, *op. cit.*, p. 22.

[229] Doehring K., "Collective Security," *op. cit.*, p. 114; Kourula E., "Peace-keeping and Regional Arrangements," *op. cit.*, p. 102-103. In fact, the length of the list of regional organizations depended on their activity in the international arena; *e.g.*, in 1966 most authors recognized the OAS, LAS and OAU as such. (Eide A., "Peace-keeping and Enforcement by Regional Organizations," *op. cit.*, p. 136).

[230] Gelber L., "The Commonwealth and the United Nations," in *Commission to Study the Organization of Peace*, *op. cit.*, p. 49; Eagleton C., "The North Atlantic Treaty Organization," in *Commission to Study the Organization of Peace: Regional Arrangements for Security and the United Nations*. Eighth Report and Papers Presented to the Commission (New York, 1953), p. 92-93, 96.

[231] Ress G., Bröhmer J., "Article 53," *op. cit.*, p. 862; Abass A. *Regional Organizations and the Development of Collective Security*, *op. cit.*, p. 23-24; Beyerlin U., "Regional Arrangements," *op. cit.*, p. 1043-1045, 1047.

Some publicists still insist that an organization, in order to be qualified under Chapter VIII, must correspond to some rather strict criteria, including geographical, institutional and structural tests; provisions for peacekeeping and enforcement mechanisms;[232] being established on the basis of international treaty;[233] having a permanent character;[234] having constituent documents with minimal specific content;[235] being recognized by the UN or by member states of regional organizations;[236] *etc*. This basically corresponds to a narrow traditionalist approach toward the notion of regional organizations.[237]

None of these criteria, as demonstrated above, follows immediately from the provisions of the UN Charter, its purposes and principles, or the San Francisco or any other UN documents. Artificially limiting the scope of regional organizations under Chapter VIII may only serve the purpose of cheating the rule of the Charter and escaping the control of the Security Council.

Some other issues, for example a discussion of competences of regional organizations toward enemy states[238] as well as the qualification of organizations under Chapter VIII based on their competence against enemy states,[239] were common in the 1950s but became irrelevant after the UN expanded to include the overwhelming number of states in the world.

---

[232] Kourula E., "Peace-keeping and Regional Arrangements," *op. cit.*, p. 102.

[233] Pernice R., *Die Sicherung des Weltfriedens*, *op. cit.*, p. 34-35; Hummer W., Schweitzer M., "Article 52," *op. cit.*, p. 822. As rightly noted by B. Geyrhalter, the UN Charter says nothing about the need for any formal agreement to qualify an entity as a regional arrangement under Chapter VIII. With a formal agreement, they could be qualified as treaties rather than arrangements (Geyrhalter B., *Friedenssicherung durch Regionalorganizationen*, *op. cit.*, p. 32); see also Walter C., *Vereinte Nationen und Regional Organisationen*, *op. cit.*, p. 109, 125; Alagappa M., "Regional Arrangements, the UN and International Security," *op. cit.*, p. 6. The restrictive character of a formal treaty as a ground for qualifying an establishment as a regional arrangement had already been recognized by L.M. Goodrich and E. Hambro in 1946; they viewed arrangements as those "*embodied in unwritten understandings*" (Goodrich L.M., Hambro E., *Charter of the United Nations*, *op. cit.*, p. 312).

[234] Körbs H., *Die Friedensdicherung duech die Vereinten Nationen und Regionalorganizationen*, *op. cit.*, p. 173; Lind K., *The Revival of Chapter VIII of the UN Charter*, *op. cit.*, p. 72-75.

[235] Pernice R., *Die Sicherung des Weltfriedens*, *op. cit.*, p. 35; Körbs H., *Die Friedensdicherung duech die Vereinten Nationen und Regionalorganizationen*, *op. cit.*, p. 171-199.

[236] Lind K., *The Revival of Chapter VIII of the UN Charter*, *op. cit.*, p. 35-36.

[237] *Ibid.*, p. 33.

[238] Körbs H., *Die Friedensdicherung duech die Vereinten Nationen und Regionalorganizationen*, *op. cit.*, p. 100-142.

[239] *Commission to Study the Organization of Peace*, *op. cit.*, p. 19-22.

The constituent documents of international organizations usually do not qualify them under Chapter VIII (the only exemption is the OAS Charter, art. 1). Many of these organizations, however, have been viewed as regional security organizations by their drafters (*e.g.*, the African Union)[240] or developed this vision in their everyday activity.[241] Nevertheless, no uniform approach has been established to date.[242]

The UN has protractedly avoided any explicit qualification of this sort. For example, references to Chapter VIII can be found only in three resolutions of the Security Council as regards European and Central Asian conflicts.[243] The General Assembly, although referring to Chapter VIII in resolutions on cooperation with particular regional organizations[244] or in general,[245] does not qualify the organizations as regional. The General Assembly usually relies on autonomous qualification by an organization and expresses its readiness to cooperate with it under Chapter VIII.

Despite the existence of the opposite view in the legal doctrine,[246] it is believed here that the expressed qualification of a regional organization under Chapter VIII by either the organization itself or the UN is not a prerequisite for its activity under Chapter VIII. The UN Charter, although recognizing some rights of regional organizations, primarily imposes constraints on their activities. It is advanced here that for the purpose of safeguarding the rule of law and world order, regional organizations, arrangements or agencies are bound by the framework of Chapter VIII whenever they are involved in the maintenance of peace and security.[247] This

---

[240] See Abass A. *Regional Organizations and the Development of Collective Security*, *op. cit.*, p. 35.

[241] Protocol Relating to the Establishment of the Peace and Security Council of the African Union, 9 July 2002, *op. cit.*, preamble; Helsinki Summit Declaration 1992, *op. cit.*, para. 25; Charter for European Security 1999, para. 7.

[242] Security Council Update Report, 18 September 2006, No. 3, *op. cit.*

[243] UN Security Council Resolutions 757 (1992), 30 May 1992, preamble; 787 (1992), *op. cit.*, para.12; 816 (1993), 31 March 1993, preamble.

[244] On cooperation with the OSCE: UN General Assembly Resolutions 47/10, 28 October 1992; 50/87, 18 December 1995; 55/179, 19 December 2000; 58/55, 8 December 2003. On cooperation with the CSTO: UN General Assembly Resolutions 64/256, 2 March 2010; 65/122, 13 December 2010.

[245] Declaration on the Enhancement of Cooperation (A/RES/49/57), *op. cit.*; Cooperation between the United Nations and Regional and Other Organizations, Report of the UN Secretary-General, A/65/382-S/2010/490, 20 September 2010.

[246] *E.g.* A. Abass asserts that in the absence of expressed qualification, the UN does not consider an international organization as falling under Chapter VIII (Abass A. *Regional Organizations and the Development of Collective Security*, *op. cit.*, p. 20).

[247] This statement can be illustrated by, *inter alia*, the right of the UN Security Council "*to utilize regional arrangements and agencies for enforcement action under its authority*," which basically endows it with the competence to decide which arrangement or agency falls

rule is not conditioned by the recognition of the status of the organization under Chapter VIII.

2.6 Definition

In the course of drafting the UN Charter, the formal definition of regional organizations under Chapter VIII was deemed to be excessive. In 1953, the Commission to Study the Organization of Peace reaffirmed that "*No general characterization of regional arrangements as desirable or as undesirable is possible.*"[248]

That is why only isolated attempts have ever been made to develop any definition as such. For example, R. Pernice defines a regional organization as "*a union of states with limited geographically-based membership, established on the basis of international treaty in conformity with the UN purposes and principles, aimed at the maintenance of international peace and security under the control and within the United Nations, including the effective settlement of regional disputes.*"[249]

In the opinion of C. Walters, a regional organization under Chapter VIII of the UN Charter is "*a conjunction of two or more states (not necessarily UN members), international organizations or other actors with certain international personality under international law (subjects of a federal state) based on the agreement between them (not necessarily in the form of a binding document) established for some period with the purpose of maintenance of international peace and security (also any de facto activity taken with this purpose).*"[250]

W. Hummer and M. Schweitzer assess it as a "*union of states or international organizations based upon a collective treaty or a constitution and consistent with the Purposes and Principles of the UN, whose primary task is the maintenance of peace and security under the control and within the framework of the UN. Its members, whose number must be smaller than that of the UN, must be so closely linked in territorial terms that effective*

under Chapter VIII in a particular case, regardless of its competence, structure or stability. On this issue see Wilson G., "Regional Arrangements as Agents of the UN Security Council," *op. cit.*, p. 186.

[248] *Commission to Study the Organization of Peace*, *op. cit.*, p. 32.

[249] Pernice R., *Die Sicherung des Weltfriedens*, *op. cit.*, p. 41.

[250] Walter C., *Vereinte Nationen und Regional Organisationen*, *op. cit.*, p. 126-127.

local dispute settlement by means of a specially provided procedure is possible."[251]

Each of these definitions presents a personal approach by its author to the problem of regional organizations. The more recent ones demonstrate the expanding vision of this notion. It is believed here, however, that the development of a detailed definition is not only excessive but may also be harmful. In view of current developments and challenges, it is much more important to determine that activity may be characterized and therefore subordinated to the operation of Chapter VIII of the UN Charter.

Conclusions

The spectrum of entities falling under Chapter VIII of the UN Charter is rather broad. The qualification of an arrangement or an entity as regional in the meaning of Chapter VIII is not conditioned by its permanent or temporary nature, the existence or absence of formal constituent documents, its institutional structure or its effective means and facilities for dispute settlement or enforcement.

The list of qualifying criteria is restricted to the following: limited (as opposed to universal) membership that may also include an entity established by two subjects of international law or by one international organization, an orientation (primarily or *inter alia*) toward the maintenance of international peace and security, and adherence to the purposes and principles of the UN as well as obligations arising from the UN Charter itself.

As a result of the primary purpose of Chapter VIII being to subordinate the activity of regional organizations to UN control, its rules extend over any collective action in the sphere of maintenance of international peace and security conducted by subjects of international law, independently from the existence of any formal agreement between or among them. The expressed qualification of a regional organization under Chapter VIII by the organization itself or the UN is not obligatory. Thus, the term "regional organization" has a descriptive meaning rather than one that is contextual or restrictive.

The UN Charter sets no limitations on the scope of competences of regional organizations under Chapter VIII. The expansion of their range of

[251] Hummer W., Schweitzer M., "Article 52," *op. cit.*, p. 828.

recognized activities corresponds to the general expansion of the vision of security. As follows, regional organizations are currently active in the prevention and settlement of international and internal disputes, the prevention of the hypothetical possibility of disputes and the struggle against contemporary threats and challenges.

The only limitations on the functions and activities of regional organizations concern their obligation to be and to act in conformity with the UN's purposes and principles (art. 52(1)) as well as obligations arising from the UN Charter (art. 103). Art. 53, introduced in order to reaffirm the general prohibition on using force in international relations, brings regional organizations under the control of the Security Council with respect to any enforcement action. Meanwhile, regional organizations enjoy priority as concerns any activity aimed at the maintenance of peace and security that does not require the application of enforcement means.

CHAPTER 3

ENFORCEMENT ACTIVITY OF REGIONAL ORGANIZATIONS

This chapter is devoted to the enforcement activity of regional organizations. As noted above, art. 53 of the UN Charter does not grant regional organizations any additional powers (in comparison with art. 52) but primarily introduces mechanisms of control from the side of the United Nations and establishes the role of regional organizations as a subsidiary one in the sphere of enforcement action.

Our focus is only on the first part of art. 53(1); the latter part as well as art. 53(2) have become obsolete, as they concern the specific treatment of the initial Charter signatories' former "enemy states," all of which are currently members of the United Nations, as well as various established regional organizations.

Art. 53(1) of the UN Charter reads: "*The Security Council shall, where appropriate, utilize such regional arrangements or agencies for enforcement action under its authority. But no enforcement action shall be taken under regional arrangements or by regional agencies without the authorization of the Security Council.*"

At first glance, this passage may only be read as imposing clear and rather serious restrictions on the enforcement actions of regional organizations. A closer look shows that it provides, *inter alia*, two different options for the application of enforcement measures, ensuring both passive and active roles for regional organizations. Apparently the wording of art. 53(1) states that regional organizations *may be utilized* by the UN Security Council under its authority; this means that the Security Council will bear all the responsibility for a corresponding operation. The second sentence, however, leaves some autonomy to regional organizations and sets forth their right to initiate the question about application of enforcement measures before the UN Security Council and to apply these measures autonomously after getting *authorization from the Council*. Either way, however, regional organizations are entitled only to a subordinate role[252] under Security Council control.

[252] Villani U., "The Security Council's Authorization of Enforcement Action by Regional Organizations," *Max Planck Yearbook of United Nations Law*, 6 (2002), p. 537; Frowein J.A., "Zwangsmaßnahmen von Regionalorganizationen," in *Recht zwischen Umbruch und*

The history of putting the provisions of art. 53(1) into practice as well as early attempts to contest its validity date back to 1960, when selected economic measures (a partial economic boycott) and a suspension of diplomatic relations were applied to the Dominican Republic by the OAS.[253] During discussion in the UN Security Council, the USSR stresssed the need for prior authorization from the Council in this case, while the US and Great Britain insisted that authorization is necessary only for the application of military measures.[254] No decision was finally taken on this regard, mainly because of the possibility of a veto[255].

Two other situations took place shortly afterward. In 1962, the Conference of the OAS suspended Cuba's membership in the organization and recommended that its member states impose a trade embargo and a sea blockade against it, as well as to break diplomatic relations.[256] And in 1965, the US took military action against the Dominican Republic, referring to the need "*to protect US and other citizens.*"[257]

As occurred in 1960, the Security Council discussion of the situation concerning Cuba had been initiated by the USSR, which insisted that the application of enforcement measures outside the control of the Security Council undermines its authority, but again no decision was taken.[258] Most members of the Security Council concurred that its authorization was not necessary because no decision obliging OAS member states to impose an embargo had been taken[259] – and a recommendation, in accordance with the opinion of the ICJ in the Certain Expenses case, creates no international obligations.[260]

Bewahrung, ed. U. Beyerlin, M. Bothe, R. Hofmann, E.-U. Petersman (Berlin: Springer Verlag, 1995), p. 64.

[253] Some authors refer back to 1948, when LAS took military action in Palestine (see Pernice R., *Die Sicherung des Weltfriedens*, *op. cit.*, p. 94; Körbs H., *Die Friedensdicherung duech die Vereinten Nationen und Regionalorganizationen*, *op. cit.*, p. 475-480, 502-531), or to the operation in Hungary taken by OWT in 1956 (Eide A., "Peace-keeping and Enforcement by Regional Organizations," *op. cit.*, p. 127).

[254] On the histories, see Abass A. *Regional Organizations and the Development of Collective Security*, *op. cit.*, p. 43, 49; Pernice R., *Die Sicherung des Weltfriedens*, *op. cit.*, p. 94-99; Eide A., "Peace-keeping and Enforcement by Regional Organizations," *op. cit.*, p. 127-130; Akehurst M., "Enforcement Action of Regional Organizations," *op. cit.*, p. 188-213.

[255] Pernice R., *Die Sicherung des Weltfriedens*, *op. cit.*, p. 95.

[256] See also Geyrhalter B., *Friedenssicherung durch Regionalorganizationen*, *op. cit.*, p. 62.

[257] Cited by Pernice R., *Die Sicherung des Weltfriedens*, *op. cit.*, p. 97.

[258] Article 53. Supplement 1959-1966.

[259] On the history, see Hummer W., Schweitzer M., "Article 52," *op. cit.*, p. 844-845; Walter C., "Security Council Control over Regional Action," *op. cit.*, p. 135; Geyrhalter B., *Friedenssicherung durch Regionalorganizationen*, *op. cit.*, p. 62-63.

[260] Certain Expenses of the United Nations, *op. cit.*, p. 162-163.

As concerns the invasion of the Dominican Republic in 1965, the US asserted in the Security Council that no enforcement action under art. 53 took place, but rather "*action for restoration of peace.*" Once again, there was no resolution that defined whether these measures could be qualified as enforcement measures under Chapter VIII that required authorization.[261]

These early cases demonstrate three principal justifications that were invoked by states attempting to bypass the requirements of art. 53 – the limitation of enforcement measures only to military measures; the recommendation rather than requirement that member states undertake certain action; and the undertaking of military action with a purpose different from enforcement, in particular action aimed at the restoration of peace. Whether these justifications were reasonable will be considered later in this chapter.

3.1 "Enforcement" under Chapter VIII of the UN Charter

The Notion of "Enforcement"

Art. 53 of the UN Charter regulates the regime of application of "*enforcement action*" by regional organizations. At the same time, neither this nor any other article provides a definition or characteristics of this term. As M. Shaw correctly notes, it could be viewed narrowly or broadly, and therefore the question about the need for UN Security Council authorization may be answered in different ways.[262]

The matter turns even more ambiguous insofar as the term "enforcement action" is not used elsewhere in the UN Charter. Chapter VII of the Charter talks about "*measures not involving the use of armed force*" (art. 41) and "*action by air, sea, or land forces*" (art. 42). It is believed here, however, that these provisions may hardly be interpreted as limiting "enforcement action" under art. 53 to a particular sort of action. The drafters of the UN Charter viewed enforcement action as any sort of enforcement[263] – an opinion that still prevails[264] in the international legal doctrine.[265] Leaning

---

[261] Cited by Pernice R., *Die Sicherung des Weltfriedens*, *op. cit.*, p. 97-98.
[262] See Shaw M.N., *International Law*, 6th ed. (Cambridge: Cambridge University Press, 2008), p. 1275.
[263] Cited by Ress G., Bröhmer J., "Article 53," *op. cit.*, p. 860. See also Geyrhalter B., *Friedenssicherung durch Regionalorganizationen*, *op. cit.*, p. 61; Akehurst M., "Enforcement Action of Regional Organizations," *op. cit.*, p. 186.
[264] Körbs H., *Die Friedensdicherung duech die Vereinten Nationen und Regionalorganizationen*, *op. cit.*, p. 481.

toward the general approach to enforcement, F. Morrison defines enforcement action as "*any action which would itself be a violation of international law, if taken without either some special 'justification' or without the contemporaneous consent or acquiescence of the targeted state.*"[266]

Repeated attempts, however, have been made to confine "enforcement action" under art. 53 to exclusively military action on grounds of its form and intensity,[267] so that non-military action would need no authorization.[268] The same approach is usually taken by those regional organizations that seek to broaden the sphere of their independent action.[269]

---

[265] Akehurst M., "Enforcement Action of Regional Organizations," *op. cit.*, p. 186; Kelsen H., *The Law of the United Nations* (London: Stevens and Sons, 1964), p. 724; Abass A. *Regional Organizations and the Development of Collective Security*, *op. cit.*, p. 47-48; Beyerlin U., "Regional Arrangements," *op. cit.*, p. 1042; Pernice R., *Die Sicherung des Weltfriedens*, *op. cit.*, p. 114-115; Körbs H., *Die Friedensdicherung duech die Vereinten Nationen und Regionalorganizationen*, *op. cit.*, p. 482, 532; Walter C., *Vereinte Nationen und Regional Organisationen*, *op. cit.*, p. 177, 201.

[266] Morrison F.L., "The Role of Regional Organizations in the Enforcement of International Law," in *Allocation of Law Enforcement Authority in the International System* (Proceedings of an International Symposium of the Kiel Institute of International Law, 23-25 March 1994), ed. J. Delbrück (Berlin: Dunker and Humblot, 1994), p. 43.

[267] Körbs H., *Die Friedensdicherung duech die Vereinten Nationen und Regionalorganizationen*, *op. cit.*, p. 485.

[268] See, *e.g.*, Abass A. *Regional Organizations and the Development of Collective Security*, *op. cit.*, p. 43, 45, 46, 49, 53-54; Walter C., "Security Council Control over Regional Action," *op. cit.*, p. 142; Farer T., "Political and Economic Coercion in Contemporary International Law," *American Journal of International Law*, 75 (1985), p. 407; Frowein J.A., "Legal Consequences for International Law Enforcement in Case of Security Council Inaction," in *The Future of International Law Enforcement. New Scenarios – New Law?*, ed. J. Delbrück (Berlin: Duncker & Humblot, 1993), p. 121; Frowein J.A., Krisch N., "Article 42," in *The Charter of the United Nations: A Commentary*, 2nd ed., vol. 1, ed. B. Sinna (Munich: Verlag C.H. Beck, 2002), p. 754; L. Miker, Z. Wolter, cited by Ress G., Bröhmer J., "Article 53," *op. cit.*, p. 864. The starting point for this approach dates back to 1960, when the majority of states did not support a complaint by Cuba against the OAS concerning the application of non-military measures without authorization of the UN Security Council (Ress G., Bröhmer J., "Article 53," *op. cit.*, p. 860; Geyrhalter B., *Friedenssicherung durch Regionalorganizationen*, *op. cit.*, p. 64-65, 72 ; Villani U., "The Security Council's Authorization of Enforcement Action by Regional Organizations," *op. cit.*, p. 539).

[269] Beyerlin U., "Regional Arrangements," *op. cit.*, p. 1042. In 1962, during consideration of Cuba's complaint, states supported the idea of limiting enforcement measures to military action; see Ress G., Bröhmer J., "Article 53," *op. cit.*, p. 860; Abass A. *Regional Organizations and the Development of Collective Security*, *op. cit.*, p. 44; Hummer W., Schweitzer M., "Article 52," *op. cit.*, p. 844-845; see also Walter C., "Security Council Control over Regional Action," *op. cit.*, p. 135; Farer T., "Political and Economic Coercion in Contemporary International Law," *op. cit.*, p. 407; Frowein J.A., "Legal Consequences for International Law Enforcement in Case of Security Council Inaction," *op. cit.*, p. 121; Frowein J.A., "Reactions by Not Directly Affected States to Breaches of Public International Law," in *Recueil des Cours/Collected Courses of the Hague Academy of International Law*,

The absence of condemnation by the UN Security Council of activity taken against Cuba and the Dominican Republic in the 1960s, as well as subsequent state practice, are often cited in support of this.[270]

Moreover, the Security Council's positive responses to requests by regional organizations for help in implementing non-military sanctions already imposed by these organizations have often been qualified as *post facto* authorization[271] (*e.g.*, in Resolution 788 (1992) of 19 November 1992 it commended ECOWAS' efforts in Liberia in 1990-1992 (para. 1)[272] and imposed the UN arms embargo that strengthened the embargo imposed by ECOWAS (para. 8); during the Haiti crisis, it affirmed that resolving the situation should take into account OAS resolutions imposing an embargo against Haiti (Resolution 841 (1993) of 16 June 1993 (para. 1), and imposed a comprehensive UN embargo in support of the OAS measures (paras. 5-6); a similar situation took place regarding ECOWAS sanctions against Liberia in 1997).[273]

Additional confusion in the sphere was caused by the report of the UN Secretary-General "Agenda for Peace" 1995. In the Supplement to the report, B. Boutros-Ghali asserted that sanctions as well as enforcement measures may be independently taken not only by the Security Council but also by regional organizations (para. 24). He also distinguished between enforcement measures, as military measures under art. 42 and 53 and as sanctions ("*measures not involving the use of armed force in order to maintain or restore international peace and security*") in art. 41 (para.66).

"Force" and "Intervention" in International Law

The equally ambiguous nature of the notion of "force" in international law also contributes to the complexity of the matter. Doctrinal

---

248 (1994, IV) (Dordrecht: Martinus Nijhoff Publishers, 1995), p. 388. The same approach is reflected in Supplement to an Agenda for Peace, *op. cit.*, para. 66.

270 See Pernice R., *Die Sicherung des Weltfriedens*, *op. cit.*, p. 111.

271 Walter C., "Security Council Control over Regional Action," *op. cit.*, p. 142.

272 See Doc. S/24811 of 18 November 1992, Annex 1. See also *The Repertoire of Practice of the Security Council (Supplement 1989-1992)* (United Nations: Department of Political Affairs, 1993), p. 270.

273 At the 3822nd meeting of the UN Security Council on 8 October 1997, the representative of Nigeria, acting on behalf of ECOWAS, stated: "ECOWAS was left with no option but to adopt a set of measures in the form of sanctions and embargo as a means of pressuring the regime in Freetown to appreciate the futility of its situation and agree to re-engage ECOWAS in a constructive dialogue which would ensure the early reinstatement of the legitimate Government of President Kabbah" UN Security Council Report, 3822nd Meeting, 8 October 1997, S/PV.3822; see also UN Security Council Resolution 1132 (1997), 8 October 1997.

approaches vary from equating it to an armed attack[274] via exclusively military force,[275] to military and non-military physical force[276] and to any form of pressure including military, economic and diplomatic (this was typical in the the Soviet and Russian doctrine of international law).[277] However, irrespective of the scope of force accepted by particular publicists, it is generally agreed that regional organizations are bound not only by the principle of the non-use of force (art. 2(4) of the UN Charter) but also by the prohibition of intervention (art. 2(7) of the UN Charter).[278] As a result, regardless of whether the vision of intervention includes[279] or excludes[280] the use of military force, its coercive (forcible) nature is universally accepted.[281]

---

[274] Röling B.V.A., "Definition of Aggression," in *The Current Legal Regulation of the Use of Force*, ed. A. Cassese (Dordrecht: Martinus Nijhoff Publishers, 1986), p. 416; Alexandrov S.A., *Self-defense Against the Use of Force in International Law* (The Hague: Kluwer Law International, 1996), p. 109; Farer T., "Political and Economic Coercion in Contemporary International Law," *op. cit.*, p. 124.

[275] Randelzhofer A., "Use of Force," in *Encyclopedia of Public International Law,* vol. 4, ed. R. Bernhard (Amsterdam: North-Holland Publishing Co., 1982), p. 268; Belatchew A., *Prohibition of Force under the UN Charter: A Study of Art. 2(4)* (Uppsala: Iustus Förlag, 1991), p. 64.

[276] Cited by Jackamo T.J., "From the Cold War to the New Multilateral World Order: The Evolution of Covert Operations and the Customary International Law of Non-intervention. Note," *Virginia Journal of International Law*, 32(4) (1992), p. 959; Simma B., ed., *The Charter of the United Nations: A Commentary* (New York: Oxford University Press Inc., 1995), p. 113.

[277] Тункин Т.И., *Право и сила в международной системе* [Tunkin T.I., *Law and Force in International Relations*] (Moscow: International Relations, 1983), p. 23; Лазарев М.И., "Международные правоотношения и международные силоотношения в конце XX – в канун XXI века" [Lazarev M.I., "International Relations in Law and Force at the End of the XXth – Eve of XXIst Centuries], *Russian Yearbook of International Law*, 1998-1999 (Saint Petersburg: Russia-Neva, 1999), p. 251.

[278] Körbs H., *Die Friedensdicherung duech die Vereinten Nationen und Regionalorganizationen, op. cit.*, p. 483; Villani U., "The Security Council's Authorization of Enforcement Action by Regional Organizations," *op. cit.*, p. 538.

[279] Аречага Э.Х. де, *Современное международное право* [Arechaga H. de, *Modern International Law*] (Moscow: Progress, 1983), p. 138-139.

[280] Черниченко С.В., *Теория международного права* [Chernichenko S.V., *Theory of International Law*], vol. 1 (Moscow: NIMP, 1999), p. 232; Arechaga H. de, *Modern International Law, op. cit.*, p. 174.

[280] Ушаков Н.А., *Невмешательство во внутренние дела государств* [Ushakov N.A., *Non-Intervention into Domestic Affairs*] (Moscow: International Relations, 1971), p. 51.

[281] Verzijl J.H.W., *International Law in Historical Perspective* (Leiden: A.W. Sijhoff, 1968), vol. 1, p. 308; Rajan M.S., *United Nations and Domestic Jurisdiction*, 2nd ed. (London: Asia Publishing House, 1961), p. 9; Скакунов Э.И., *Самооборона в международном праве* [Skakunov E.I., *Self-Defense in International Law*] (Moscow: International Relations, 1973), p. 15; Waldock C.H.M., "The Regulation of the Use of Force by Individual States in International Law," *Recueil des cours/Collected Courses of the Hague Academy of International Law*, 1952 (II), p. 461; Simma B., ed., *The Charter of the United Nations: A Commentary, op. cit.*, p. 50.

Legality Threshold

It should also be remembered that even publicists who insist on the usefulness of economic enforcement actions by regional organizations often do not insist on their unconditional legality. Attempts by regional organizations to get at least *post facto* support for economic measures from the UN Security Council,[282] despite their alleged right to impose non-military sanctions without its authorization, clearly testify to the opposite.

Another method used by those who seek to get around the limitation of art. 53 is the manipulation of the very notion of "enforcement." As noted above, the need for authorization concerns only activity which would itself violate international law.[283] Any non-military action that constitutes normal intercourse in interstate relations (and a broad range of economic and diplomatic means do, *e.g.*, a breaking of diplomatic relations or the termination or non-prolongation of trade agreements),[284] or whose illegality is excluded on other grounds, *e.g.*, in the course of countermeasures or due to the consent of the "target" state, cannot be qualified as "enforcement."[285] In other words, Security Council authorization cannot be requested for acts which are by themselves legal under general international law. Despite the opinion of the ILC on the necessity to distinguish between the aggregate of measures taken by individual states and enforcement measures imposed through institutionalized structures,[286] it is generally agreed in international

---

[282] In the aftermath of ECOWAS sanctions against Sierra Leone, the UN Security Council authorized economic sanctions by Resolution 1132 (1997).

[283] Morrison F.L., "The Role of Regional Organizations in the Enforcement of International Law," *op. cit.*, p. 43; Kewenig W.A., Heini A., *Die Anwendung wirtschaftlicher Zwangsmaßnahmen im Völkerrecht und im internationalen Privatrecht* (Heidelberg: Müller, Juristische Verlag, 1982), p. 11-15.

[284] Weintraub S., ed., *Economic Coercion and U.S. Foreign Policy: Implications of Case Studies from the Johnson Administration* (Boulder: Westview Press, Inc., 1982), p.7; Nincic M., Wallensteen P., ed., *Dilemmas of Economic Coercion: Sanctions in World Politics* (New York: Praeger Publishers, 1983), p. 1.

[285] The question about the legality of such measures is, however, rather complicated and is to be decided in each particular case; *e.g.*, the ICJ in the Military and Paramilitary activity case (1986) was unable to conclude whether US economic measures against Nicaragua (cessation of economic assistance, 90% reduction in the import quota for Nicaragua sugar in 1981, trade embargo imposed in 1983), could be qualified as intervention; see Military and Paramilitary Activities in and against Nicaragua (Nicaragua v. United States of America), Merits, Judgment, *I.C.J. Reports* (The Hague: I.C.J., 1986), p. 126.

[286] Draft Articles on Responsibility of States for Internationally Wrongful Acts, with commentaries, *op. cit.*, p. 137.

law that international organizations may legally take measures which may legally be taken by their member states.[287]

As a result, in practice, most of the doctrinal claims for the excessiveness of UN Security Council authorization for the use of non-military means of pressure concern only those sorts of non-military activity that individual states may legally take.[288] An example is peacekeeping activity conducted with the expressed prior consent of the target state.[289] With due account for the freedom of contracts (the right of states to enter into international obligations), it is widely agreed that regional organizations may apply certain non-military measures to its member states if the measures are foreseen by their constituent documents.[290]

The above, however, definitely does not mean that any and all economic enforcement measures are allowed without authorization of the UN Security Council.[291] References to different purposes, *e.g.*, "*restoration of peace*," as in the case of the Dominican Republic in 1965, instead of enforcement does not change the coercive (forcible) nature of this activity; such a case may not be viewed as a circumstance precluding wrongfulness

---

[287] Kelsen H., *The Law of the United Nations*, *op. cit.*, p. 724; Walter C., "Security Council Control over Regional Action," *op. cit.*, p. 130, 137-138, 191; Frowein J.A., "Reactions by Not Directly Affected States," *op. cit.*, p. 388-389; Wolfrum R., "Der Beitrag regionaler Abmachungen zur Friedenssicherung: Möglichkeiten und Grenzen," *Zeitschrift für Ausländisches Öffentliches Recht und Völkerrecht*, 1 (1993), p. 582; de Vries A.W., Hazelzet H., "The EU as a New Actor on the Sanctions Scene," in *International Sanctions: Between Words and Wars in the Global System*, ed. P. Wallensteen, C. Staibano (London/New York: Frank Cass, 2005), p. 98; Geyrhalter B., *Friedenssicherung durch Regionalorganizationen*, *op. cit.*, p. 65; Pernice R., *Die Sicherung des Weltfriedens*, *op. cit.*, p. 112; Frowein J.A., "Zwangsmaßnahmen von Regionalorganizationen," *op. cit.*, p. 66.

[288] Geyrhalter B., *Friedenssicherung durch Regionalorganizationen*, *op. cit.*, p. 61, 65; Frowein J.A., "Legal Consequences for International Law Enforcement in Case of Security Council Inaction," *op. cit.*, p. 122; Walter C., *Vereinte Nationen und Regional Organisationen*, *op. cit.*, p. 220.

[289] See Geyrhalter B., *Friedenssicherung durch Regionalorganizationen*, *op. cit.*, p. 61, 66-74; Pernice R., *Die Sicherung des Weltfriedens*, *op. cit.*, p. 116-117. It is expressly supported that peacekeeping operations, regardless of whether they are military or non-military, cannot be viewed as enforcement if they occur with the consent of the target state (Frowein J.A., "Zwangsmaßnahmen von Regionalorganizationen," *op. cit.*, p. 63).

[290] Walter C., "Security Council Control over Regional Action," *op. cit.*, p. 141-142, 191.

[291] This approach is supported, *e.g.*, by T.L. Friedman (Röling B.V.A., "International Law and the Maintenance of Peace," *Netherlands Yearbook of International Law*, IV (1973), p. 87).

under general international law[292] and therefore does not exempt the activity from the framework of art. 53(1).[293]

Decision Leading to "Enforcement"

As noted above in discussing the power of regional organizations to take enforcement measures, it is relevant whether an enforcement decision has a recommendatory character as opposed to an obligatory one (*e.g.*, the OAS recommendations concerning the embargo and sea blockade against Cuba).[294]

In its much-cited advisory opinion on Certain Expenses of the United Nations, the ICJ clearly asserted that states are not obliged to implement the recommendations of international bodies (in this case, the UN General Assembly) and are also not obliged to bear expenses arising in conjunction with the implementation of these recommendations.[295] This approach has resulted in repeated claims that the mere recommendation by a regional organization to take an enforcement action cannot be considered as a breach of the obligation under art. 53(1) because they have only a moral or political effect.[296]

It shall nevertheless be remembered that if "enforcement" measures cannot be lawfully taken by member states of an international organization, then a prior recommendation of a regional organization will not grant them any legitimacy. States will be held responsible for the breach of their international obligations if they act with or without the recommendation of a regional organization.[297] Moreover, if a recommendation is made by an institutionalized international organization, the organization may be held responsible together with its member states for the direction or control over

---

292 The DARS lists only six circumstances that preclude wrongfulness: consent, countermeasures, self defense, force majeure, distress and necessity (art. 20-25).

293 This view is supported by Pernice R., *Die Sicherung des Weltfriedens*, *op. cit.*, p. 113; Körbs H., *Die Friedensdicherung duech die Vereinten Nationen und Regionalorganizationen*, *op. cit.*, p. 184.

294 Cited by Pernice R., *Die Sicherung des Weltfriedens*, *op. cit.*, p. 100.

295 Certain Expenses of the United Nations, *op. cit.*, p. 162.

296 H. Lauterpacht, D.H.N. Johnson, Alvarez, cited by Pernice R., *Die Sicherung des Weltfriedens*, *op. cit.*, p. 103.

297 Neither decisions or authorizations are viewed as circumstances precluding wrongfulness in the DARS. The responsibility of the state in the above circumstances has also been reaffirmed by the ECHR in Bosphorus Hava Yollari Turizm ve Ticaret AS v. Ireland, European Court of Human Rights, Decision of 13 September 2001 and Judgment of 30 June 2005.

an internationally wrongful act.[298] So in practice, as correctly noted by R. Pernice, unless there are provisions making recommendations obligatory for member states, the recommendations have very little impact on the application of enforcement measures.[299] In view of the issues discussed above, it is believed here that regional organizations may make recommendations to their member states to apply only those coercive measures which the states themselves may legally take when acting unilaterally.

As a result, considering the clear prohibitions on using force and intervening in the domestic affairs of states, and in light of preparatory materials as well as textual and logical interpretations of the UN Charter, it may be concluded that the term "*enforcement action*" in art. 53 may only be viewed in a broad sense. The very fact of the existence of art. 41 in the Charter, providing for the application of non-military measures, nicely illustrates that its drafters did not see these types of measures as natural in interstate relations. Moreover, due to the initial distrust of regional alliances and attempts to subordinate all regional activity to the universal mechanism of collective security, it would be illogical to grant this right to regional organizations without any special provisions of this sort.

Therefore, UN Security Council authorization is required for any (military or non-military) action aimed at applying pressure on a target state, if this action does not constitute part of the normal intercourse in interstate relations or if its illegality is not excluded by circumstances recognized under general international law as excluding wrongfulness of otherwise illegal action.

Neither the UN Charter nor subsequent practice may or should be interpreted as endowing regional organizations with freedom of action in this respect. Chapter VIII imposes very few but rigorous restrictions over their autonomy. Due to the comprehensive nature of the prohibition on the use of force and intervention, any exceptions from them are recognized to be interpreted in the most restrictive way.[300] Declarations on the high legality and the low possibility of abuse on the part of regional organizations as

---

[298] Draft Articles on Responsibility of International Organizations, 2011, art. 15. DARIO contains no reference to the responsibility for recommendations (although this issue has been fiercely debated in the course of Commission's work) and limits itself to cases of decisions and authorizations; see Draft Articles on the Responsibility of International Organizations, 2011, with Commentaries, comment to art. 17.

[299] Pernice R., *Die Sicherung des Weltfriedens*, *op. cit.*, p. 109-110.

[300] Goodrich L.M., Hambro E., *Charter of the United Nations*, *op. cit.*, p. 160; Frowein J.A., Krisch N., "Introduction to Chapter VII," in *The Charter of the United Nations: A Commentary*, 2nd ed., vol. 1, ed. B. Sinna (Munich: Verlag C.H. Beck, 2002), p. 713.

collective entities in comparison to individual states, repeatedly invoked in the legal doctrine,[301] may hardly serve as an excuse for the absence of any legal grounds.

3.2 UN Security Council and "Enforcement" Activity of Regional Organizations

Art. 53, which establishes the legal grounds and rules for enforcement action by regional organizations, is perceived in various ways in the legal doctrine. Some publicists view it as an alternative to the enforcement measures of Chapter VII.[302] Others believe that art. 53 does not widen the enforcement powers of the UN Security Council but rather widens the set of modalities for their use.[303] In particular, D. Sarooshi expressely names the Security Council's authorization of regional organizations to take enforcement action as one of the possible forms of delegation of power under Chapter VII, and insists on the equality of position of the UN members acting individually or through regional arrangements in this area.[304] Illustrating the correctness of the second approach is the wording used by the Security Council itself in its resolutions that sanction, under Chapter VII, states acting individually or through regional organizations.[305] Let us look into the details of the competences of the Security Council and regional organizations in this regard.

UN's Right to "Use" Regional Organizations for Enforcement Action

Art. 53 of the UN Charter provides for the right of the UN Security Council to utilize regional organizations for enforcement action under its authority and establishes an obligation on the part of regional organizations to get authorization from the Council before any enforcement action takes

[301] Geyrhalter B., *Friedenssicherung durch Regionalorganizationen*, *op. cit.*, p. 173.
[302] Körbs H., *Die Friedensdicherung duech die Vereinten Nationen und Regionalorganizationen*, *op. cit.*, p. 180.
[303] Villani U., "The Security Council's Authorization of Enforcement Action by Regional Organizations," *op. cit.*, p. 536.
[304] Sarooshi D., *The United Nations and the Development of Collective Security*, *op. cit.*, p. 248-249.
[305] See, *e.g.*, UN Security Council Resolutions 1031 (1995), 15 December 1995, paras. 14-17, 36; 1247 (1999), 18 August 1999, paras. 10-13; 1575 (2004), 22 November 2004, paras. 10, 14-16; 1785 (2007), 21 November 2007, paras. 10, 14-16; 1948 (2010), 18 November 2010, paras. 10, 14-16; 1973 (2011), 17 March 2011, paras. 4, 8, 15.

place. The Charter, however, sets neither the grounds nor the modalities for this utilization or authorization.

As concerns *non-military enforcement action*, the provision of art. 53(1) of the Charter which states that "*the UN Security Council shall utilize [...] regional arrangements or agencies for enforcement action under its authority*" itself provides sufficient legal grounds and sets forth an obligation of regional organizations to accept this. At the same time, the practical application of this provision may turn rather complicated, especially concerning regional organizations that possess no international legal personality. In this case, some instruction may be found elsewhere in the UN Charter, in particular in Chapter VII.

As follows from art. 41, the Security Council may decide what measures of non-military character are to be applied by the members of the United Nations, and the UN member states are obliged to implement these decisions (art. 25). As a result, regional organizations (regardless of possessing or not possessing international legal personality) are obliged to take non-military enforcement measures upon the decision of the Security Council through the unconditional obligation of their member states in accordance with art. 41.[306]

With respect to *military enforcement action*, however, the situation is more complicated. The provision of art. 53(1) can *per se* scarcely be interpreted as imposing an obligation on regional organizations to provide armed forces for any enforcement action.[307] No indirect obligation of this sort may be deduced from the wording of Chapter VII either. In accordance with art. 42, military measures may only be taken by the UN Security Council itself or by "*air, sea, or land forces of Members of the United Nations.*" States, though, are not obliged to make their military forces available to the Security Council. Any transfer of this sort may only take place on the basis of their free will, implemented in special agreements between the Security Council and UN member states or groups of states (art. 43(3)). Formally, such agreements may also be concluded between the

---

[306] Most publicists, however, insist on the two-step scheme in this case: if regional organizations reject the application of non-military enforcement measures because of the absence of any obligation, these measures are to be taken by their member states (Ress G., Bröhmer J., "Article 53," *op. cit.*, p. 863; Bentwich N., Martin A., *A Commentary on the Charter of the United Nations*, *op. cit.*, p. 113). It is believed here that this gap in legal regulation is one of the reasons why the UN Security Council prefers to authorize states "*acting independently or through regional organizations*" rather than regional organizations directly.

[307] This position is generally recognized in international law; see Wilson G., "Regional Arrangements as Agents of the UN Security Council," *op. cit.*, p. 189.

Security Council and regional organizations, insofar as the latter may be qualified as the "*groups of states*" referred to in art. 43(3).[308]

To date, however, no agreement of this kind (even between the Security Council and individual states) has ever been concluded. As a result, the Security Council *authorizes* rather than *utilizes* so-called "coalitions of the willing,"[309] which may also fall under the criteria of regional organizations on the basis of *ad hoc* agreements.[310]

Competence Constraints

Another question repeatedly dicussed in the international legal doctrine is whether an international organization may possess enforcement capacity in accordance with its constituent documents to be utilized by the UN Security Council. As regional organizations are not required to have effective enforcement mechanisms to be qualified under Chapter VIII, it is very doubtful that the Security Council may utilize them for any action unless they do possess appropriate mechanisms.[311] In theory, it is also sometimes discussed whether such utilization is possible when combined with an *ad hoc* decision of a regional organization under which it consents to establish an enforcement mechanism.[312] In practice, however, one may hardly consider this scheme as the utilization of regional organizations by the Security Council.[313]

Therefore, the question to be answered is a broader one: whether the regional organization must have enforcement powers fixed in its constituent documents to be able to take any enforcement action with the authorization of the Security Council. As follows from the UN Charter and as generally agreed in the legal doctrine, two basic conditions are to be met: (1) the

---

[308] See Ress G., Bröhmer J., "Article 53," *op. cit.*, p. 863; Lind K., *The Revival of Chapter VIII of the UN Charter*, *op. cit.*, p. 141.

[309] See Weiss T.G. *et al.*, *The United Nations and Changing World Politics*, *op. cit.*, p. 23. It basically means that states may agree or disagree to take enforcement measures even with authorization of the UN Security Council. See also Abass A. *Regional Organizations and the Development of Collective Security*, *op. cit.*, p. 68-70.

[310] Bother N., "Peace-keeping," *op. cit.*, p. 684. The same approach is maintained by Frowein J.A., Krisch N., "Article 42," *op. cit.*, p. 756.

[311] See Körbs H., *Die Friedensdicherung duech die Vereinten Nationen und Regionalorganizationen*, *op. cit.*, p. 574-575, 577, 581; Lind K., *The Revival of Chapter VIII of the UN Charter*, *op. cit.*, p. 138.

[312] Wilson G., "Regional Arrangements as Agents of the UN Security Council," *op. cit.,* p. 189; Körbs H., *Die Friedensdicherung duech die Vereinten Nationen und Regionalorganizationen*, *op. cit.*, p. 581.

[313] See Lind K., *The Revival of Chapter VIII of the UN Charter*, *op. cit.*, p. 141.

regional organization must have powers to take enforcement action,[314] and (2) it must consent to take it. The form and wording of these elements have never been specified. Therefore, there is no need for all of the necessary mechanisms to be established in the organization's constituent documents. In the absence of special mechanisms in the constituent documents of regional organizations, they may take enforcement action on an *ad hoc* basis with due authorization from the UN Security Council.

Territorial Constraints

The question of territorial contraints in the activities of regional organizations has already been discussed to some extent in the last chapter. Regarding enforcement action under art. 53, this concerns the powers of the UN Security Council to utilize regional organizations in taking enforcement measures against third states[315] as well as the right of regional organizations to employ enforcement measures against non-members when authorized by the Security Council.[316]

It has often been asserted that regional organizations enjoy absolutely no competence toward third states.[317] In support of this position, one may cite the initial pursuit of states to preserve some degree of autonomy from the Security Council and to bypass the powers of the Security Council to utilize regional organizations for enforcement action either in general or at least beyond their territory,[318] as well as the fact that the establishment of regional organizations does not grant them rights that are not provided for in the UN Charter.[319] This approach, however, seems to be too restrictive and unrealistic. It has mostly sought to limit the "utilizing" powers of the Security Council toward regional organizations.

As noted above, this problem is currently much more theoretical than of practical value. Apparently, in the absence of corresponding standby agreements with regional organizations or even individual states, the UN Security Council's powers of utilization (even indirectly, through the art. 42 mechanism) are close to zero. Moreover, the Security Council takes no steps

---

[314] Pernice R., *Die Sicherung des Weltfriedens*, *op. cit.*, p. 117, 149.

[315] See *ibid.*, p. 118-133; Körbs H., *Die Friedensdicherung duech die Vereinten Nationen und Regionalorganizationen*, *op. cit.*, p. 554-571.

[316] See Pernice R., *Die Sicherung des Weltfriedens*, *op. cit.*, p. 118-133.

[317] *Ibid.*, s. 127, 133; Körbs H., *Die Friedensdicherung duech die Vereinten Nationen und Regionalorganizationen*, *op. cit.*, p. 568.

[318] Positions of Chile, Egypt – *Documents of the UN Conference on International Organization*, vol. III., *op. cit.*, p. 284, 290, 460.

[319] Pernice R., *Die Sicherung des Weltfriedens*, *op. cit.*, p. 147.

even to authorize regional organizations to take any enforcement action and prefers to turn directly to their member states "*acting independently or through international organizations.*"

I will also oppose here those who claim that the UN Security Council owns no right to *authorize* regional organizations to act beyond their territory.[320] The powers of the Security Council to impose non-military sanctions to any state arise from art. 41 and shall be implemented by all members of the United Nations (they are not limited on territorial grounds). Nothing in the UN Charter prohibits the Security Council from authorizing states (including when they act through regional organizations) to take military action under art. 42 in any other state in any part of the world.[321] The same conclusion, *inter alia*, had been reached by the German Constitutional Court in 1994, in deciding that German troops may participate in NATO actions directed at the implementation of UN Security Council resolutions (Adria-, AWACS- und Somalia- Einsätze der Bunderwehr).[322]

3.3 The Need for Authorization to Take Enforcement Measures

Although it is unlikely that the UN Security Council will utilize regional organizations for enforcement activity under its authority in the very near future, the problem of enforcement by regional organizations remains a matter of controversy. Art. 53(1) of the UN Charter expressly states: "*no enforcement action shall be taken under regional arrangements or by regional agencies without the authorization of the Security Council.*" As a result, the need for the UN Security Council authorization is generally agreed.[323]

---

[320] This position is supported, *e.g.*, by U. Beyerlin (Beyerlin U., "Regional Arrangements," *op. cit.*, p. 1043) and J.A. Frowein (Frowein J.A., "Legal Consequences for International Law Enforcement in Case of Security Council Inaction," *op. cit.*, p. 122). The opposite position is maintained by K. Lind (Lind K., *The Revival of Chapter VIII of the UN Charter*, *op. cit.*, p. 139).

[321] Lind K., *The Revival of Chapter VIII of the UN Charter*, *op. cit.*, p. 139. The same approach is supported by Sarooshi D., *The United Nations and the Development of Collective Security*, *op. cit.*, p. 250.

[322] Cited by Sarooshi D., *The United Nations and the Development of Collective Security*, *op. cit.*, p. 251.

[323] *Documents of the UN Conference on International Organization*, vol. III., *op. cit.*, p. 215; Wilson G., "Regional Arrangements as Agents of the UN Security Council," *op. cit.*, p. 184; Abass A. *Regional Organizations and the Development of Collective Security*, *op. cit.*, p. 52-53; Walter C., "Security Council Control over Regional Action," *op. cit.*, p. 134, 141; Report of the UN Secretary-General (S/2008/18), *op. cit.*, para. 10; Sobakin V.K., *Collective Security*

Yet already at the San Francisco conference, some states advocated for regional organizations to have greater autonomy: *e.g.*, Latin American states stood up for a special privileged position for the OAS;[324] Colombia claimed that "effective" regional organizations need no authorization for enforcement action;[325] Austria asserted that authorization is not necessary in the case of UN Security Council inaction;[326] France claimed it is not needed when the right to take enforcement action is already set forth by the constituent documents of the organization;[327] and Venezuela sought validity for *post facto* confirmation instead of authorization.[328] Remarkably, however, none of these proposals were accepted.

Repeated attempts to bypass the unconditional requirement for Security Council authorization may be observed throughout the whole period of the UN's existence. For example, the "Uniting for Peace" resolution of the General Assembly (377(V) of 3 November 1950) initiated debates on the right of this organ to authorize enforcement activity in the case of Security Council inaction.[329] Other publicists and politicians have questioned the proper time, form and wording of the Security Council's authorization,[330]

– *A Guarantee of Peaceful Coexistence*, *op. cit.*, p. 353; Frowein J.A., "Reactions by Not Directly Affected States," *op. cit.*, p. 387; Pernice R., *Die Sicherung des Weltfriedens*, *op. cit.*, p. 133; Akehurst M., "Enforcement Action of Regional Organizations," *op. cit.*, p. 182. N. Bentwich and A. Martin even assert that apart from self-defense, states are not allowed to take any enforcement (including non-military) measures without authorization of the UN Security Council (Bentwich N., Martin A., *A Commentary on the Charter of the United Nations*, *op. cit.*, p. 93); It is notable that peacekeeping activity as exercised upon the agreement of the states/parties involved cannot be viewed as an enforcement activity, although it is sometimes advanced as such in the legal doctrine (Korkelia K., "The CIS Peace-Keeping Operations in the Context of International Legal Order," p. 11.

[324] Colombia, Mexico, Chile, Paraguay – *Documents of the UN Conference on International Organization*, vol. I., *op. cit.*, p. 364; 371; *Documents of the UN Conference on International Organization*, vol. III., *op. cit.*, p. 187, 283, 347, 441. See also Beyerlin U., "Regional Arrangements," *op. cit.*, p. 1041.

[325] Colombia – *Documents of the UN Conference on International Organization*, vol. I., *op. cit.*, p. 364.

[326] *Documents of the UN Conference on International Organization*, vol. XII., *op. cit.*, p. 766.

[327] L. Miker, cited by Ress G., Bröhmer J., "Article 53," *op. cit.*, p. 866.

[328] *Documents of the UN Conference on International Organization*, vol. III., *op. cit.*, p. 215-216. For histories, see Körbs H., *Die Friedensdicherung duech die Vereinten Nationen und Regionalorganizationen*, *op. cit.*, p. 472.

[329] *Ibid.*, p. 540-554.

[330] Although the UN's founders viewed enforcement action as any sort of enforcement, attempts have been made to confine "enforcement action" under art. 53 to exclusively military action, so that non-military action would need no authorization; see, *e.g.*, Abass A. *Regional Organizations and the Development of Collective Security*, *op. cit.*, p. 43, 45, 46, 49; Walter C., "Security Council Control over Regional Action," *op. cit.*, p. 142; Farer T., "Political and Economic Coercion in Contemporary International Law," *op. cit.*, p. 407; Frowein J.A., "Legal Consequences for International Law Enforcement in Case of Security Council

although it is commonly agreed that the concretely expressed prior authorization of the Security Council is necessary and sufficient for regional organizations to take enforcement actions.[331]

Timing of Authorization

The idea of having the possibility of *post facto* authorization developed in the context of the sluggishness and repeated inactivity of the UN Security Council.[332] Despite this, the Security Council has never adopted any resolution expressly authorizing, approving or endorsing *post facto* activity of states or regional organizations. As a result, it has been repeatedly asserted that *post facto* authorization does not necessarily have to be clear and expressed. It was supposed that the Security Council's support of activity already taken by regional organizations,[333] or even the absence of condemnation,[334] are by themselves sufficient.

Inaction," *op. cit.*, p. 121. The opposite opinion is expressed by Akehurst M., "Enforcement Action of Regional Organizations," *op. cit.*, p. 186; Kelsen H., *The Law of the United Nations*, *op. cit.*, p. 724. Some authors claim the possibility of *post facto* or implied sanction, *e.g.*, L. Miker, Z. Wolter, cited by Ress G., Bröhmer J., "Article 53," *op. cit.*, p. 864. See also Abass A. *Regional Organizations and the Development of Collective Security*, *op. cit.*, p. 53-54.

[331] Beyerlin U., "Regional Arrangements," *op. cit.*, p. 1042; Wilson G., "Regional Arrangements as Agents of the UN Security Council," *op. cit.*, p. 187-188, 190. The need to turn to the UN Security Council for authorization in cases of serious threat to international peace and security is stressed also in the conclusions of the High Panel on Threats, Challenges and Change; see *A More Secure World*, *op. cit.*, p. 63, paras. 188-191; Walter C., "Security Council Control over Regional Action," *op. cit.*, p. 177-179; Lind K., *The Revival of Chapter VIII of the UN Charter*, *op. cit.*, p. 151; Eide A., "Peace-keeping and Enforcement by Regional Organizations," *op. cit.*, p. 129; Akehurst M., "Enforcement Action of Regional Organizations," *op. cit.*, p. 214; Frowein J.A., "Zwangsmaßnahmen von Regionalorganizationen," *op. cit.*, p. 64; Sarooshi D., *The United Nations and the Development of Collective Security*, *op. cit.*, p. 249.

[332] *A More Secure World*, *op. cit.*, p. 85, para. 272(a); Müllerson R., "Jus ad Bellum: Plus ça change (le Monde) plus c'est la même chose (le droit)?," *Journal of Conflict and Security Law*, 7(2) (2002), p. 155. See also Ress G., Bröhmer J., "Article 53," *op. cit.*, p. 864. It is sometimes maintained that *post facto* authorization may be useful to guarantee the rapidness of action; see Walter C., "Security Council Control over Regional Action," *op. cit.*, p. 180; Murdock J.O., "Collective Security Distinguished from Intervention," *op. cit.*, p. 500.

[333] Abass A. *Regional Organizations and the Development of Collective Security*, *op. cit.*, p. 54-55; Karns M.P., Mingst K.A., *International Organizations*, *op. cit.*, p. 350.

[334] Abass A. *Regional Organizations and the Development of Collective Security*, *op. cit.*, p. 53-54. L.C. Meeker has maintained that in the case of UN Security Council inaction no authorization is necessary at all (Meeker L.C., "Defensive Quarantine and the Law," *American Journal of International Law*, 57(3) (1963), p. 515). For the opposite view, see Akehurst M., "Enforcement Action of Regional Organizations," *op. cit.*, p. 219.

Formally, it may be assumed that art. 53(1) does not contain the word "*prior.*" At the same time, the clear prohibition on taking any enforcement action without the authorization of the UN Security Council makes any action not authorized in advance *ab initio* illegal. Moreover, *post facto* authorization undoubtedly undermines the possibility of Security Council control over regional action;[335] naturally, this was not the purpose of Chapter VIII.

That is why I will join here those who believe that neither of the above acts can be considered as an authorization, although they still possess certain legal effects. In particular, these acts may demonstrate the Security Council's approach toward the activity of regional organizations, assess the legality or illegality of actions,[336] and, depending on the wording, may be viewed as an authorization for future action.

It should also be taken into account that the so called *"support" or "welcome" of the UN Security Council to the activity of regional organizations* does not concern their operations in general. The wording of its resolutions is rather conservative and cautious (the Security Council "*welcomes,*"[337] "*takes into account,*"[338] "*notes with satisfaction*"[339] and "*expresses appreciation*"[340] rather than "*authorizes*") and concerns only particular acts or activities (deployment of an EU monitoring mission;[341] EU international efforts;[342] EU decision to provide a police mission in Bosnia and Herzegovina;[343] deployment of EU police forces;[344] NATO decision to

[335] Körbs H., *Die Friedensdicherung duech die Vereinten Nationen und Regionalorganizationen*, *op. cit.*, p. 537.
[336] Abass A. *Regional Organizations and the Development of Collective Security*, *op. cit.*, p. 56; Ress G., Bröhmer J., "Article 53," *op. cit.*, p. 864-865; Alvarez J.E., *International Organizations as Law-Makers* (New York: Oxford University Press, 2005), p. 188-189; Frowein J.A., "Zwangsmaßnahmen von Regionalorganizationen," *op. cit.*, p. 65.
[337] UN Security Council Resolutions 786 (1992), 10 November 1992; 913 (1994), 22 April 1994; 943 (1994), 23 September 1994, *etc.*
[338] UN Security Council Resolutions 798 (1992), 18 December 1992, preamble; 1575 (2004), *op. cit.*, preamble.
[339] UN Security Council Resolutions 934 (1994), 30 June 1994, para. 2; 1575 (2004), *op. cit.*, para. 21; 1845 (2008), 20 November 2008, para. 21; 1895 (2009), 18 November 2009, para. 20.
[340] UN Security Council Resolutions 942 (1994), 23 September 1994, preamble; 1022 (1995), 22 November 1995, para. 9; 1247 (1999), *op. cit.*, preamble; 1305 (2000), 21 June 2000, preamble; 1357 (2001), 21 June 2001, preamble; 1423 (2002), 12 July 2002, preamble; 1551 (2004), 9 July 2004, preamble; 1575 (2004), *op. cit.*, preamble; 1639 (2005), 21 November 2005, preamble; 1722 (2006), 21 November 2006, preamble; 1785 (2007), *op. cit.*, preamble, paras. 9, 11; 1895 (2009), *op. cit.*, preamble; 1948 (2010), *op. cit.*, preamble.
[341] UN Security Council Resolution 786 (1992), *op. cit.*
[342] UN Security Council Resolutions 913 (1994), *op. cit.*; 943 (1994), *op. cit.*
[343] UN Security Council Resolution 1423 (2002), *op. cit.*, para. 20.

terminate KFOR operations in Bosnia and Herzegovina;[345] NATO's decision to continue its presence in Bosnia and Herzegovina;[346] contribution of the CIS international forces;[347] efforts of the OSCE, EU, NATO;[348] *etc.*).

An _absence of condemnation_ hardly demonstrates the UN Security Council's approach to a situation, although already in early cases (1960s) the view was promoted that any regional action is legal unless the Security Council decides that it is illegal.[349] The absence of condemnation is often a result of a disagreement among Security Council members and a threat by veto-holding powers rather than an illustration of any consent on the topic, and therefore (as correctly noted by A. Frowein[350]) it can never amount to authorization.

Form and Wording of Authorization

Another approach in practice and doctrine to get around the requirement of UN Security Council authorization is formed by claims that it is not necessary for an authorization to be explicit. As noted by K. Lind, the possibility of implicit, retroactive, tacit or general authorization is often discussed.[351]

*_Implicit authorization_* merits little mention, as far as no-one can clearly say what it looks like. It may be formally discussed as an authorization "*gathered by implication or necessary deduction from the*

---

344 UN Security Council Resolutions 1575 (2004), *op. cit.*, para. 21; 1845 (2008), *op. cit.*, para. 21; 1895 (2009), *op. cit.*, para. 20.

345 UN Security Council Resolution 1575 (2004), *op. cit.*, para 11.

346 UN Security Council Resolution 1722 (2006), *op. cit.*, para 11.

347 UN Security Council Resolutions 1150 (1998), 30 January 1998, preamble; 1187 (1998), 30 July 1998, preamble; 1225 (1999), 28 January 1999, preamble; 1255 (1999), 30 July 1999, preamble; 1287 (2000), 31 January 2000, preamble; 1311 (2000), 28 July 2000, preamble; 1339 (2001), 31 January 2001, preamble; 1364 (2001), 31 July 2001, preamble; 1393 (2002), 31 January 2002, preamble; 1427 (2002), 29 July 2002, preamble; 1462 (2003), 30 January 2003, preamble; 1524 (2004), 30 January 2004, preamble; 1554 (2004), 29 July 2004, preamble; 1582 (2005), 28 January 2005, preamble; 1615 (2005), 29 July 2005, preamble.

348 UN Security Council resolution 1371 (2001), 26 September 2001, preamble, para. 4.

349 Cited by Eide A., "Peace-keeping and Enforcement by Regional Organizations," *op. cit.*, p. 129.

350 Frowein J.A., "Legal Consequences for International Law Enforcement in Case of Security Council Inaction," *op. cit.*, p. 119.

351 Lind K., *The Revival of Chapter VIII of the UN Charter*, *op. cit.*, p. 143. See also Walter C., *Vereinte Nationen und Regional Organisationen*, *op. cit.*, p. 291-310. C. Walter also discussed the possibility of subsidiary authorizations through the UN General Assembly (*ibid.*, p. 317-318).

circumstances, the general language or a conduct of the parties,"[352] although all these factors are too vague and have nothing to do with the UN Charter.

General authorization concerns authorization which is interpreted broadly without specifying the particular situation.[353] After having huge problems with this, the Security Council currently seeks to formulate its sanctions in the narrowest possible way.

Tacit authorization is usually interpreted as the absence of condemnation (discussed above).

Before deciding on the sufficiency of measures cited, it is necessary to pay some attention to the *wording of the UN Security Council's resolutions*, as this is the material constantly cited and interpreted by states and regional organizations for the justification of their activity. It should be accepted that the wording of the resolution provides an assessment of the legality of the planned or ongoing action.[354] It is believed here, however, that any interpretation must conform to the general rules of interpretation, taking due account of the context and ongoing practice of the Security Council, as well as of the UN's purposes and principles. In particular, it should be taken into account that any use of enforcement measures constitutes an exception from the principles of international law. Therefore, authorizations by the UN Security Council should be interpreted in the narrowest possible way.

It is generally noted that the UN Charter provides for no special wording for authorization.[355] The approach, scope and formulas of authorization have changed over the course of time. When the Security Council decides on the application of enforcement measures, it "*authorizes*"[356] or "*calls upon*"[357] states to apply "*all necessary measures*" or "*all measures [...] as may be necessary*"[358] (wording used until the end of the 1990s) or specific measures (during the last 10-15 years). It is remarkable that due to repeated attempts to interpret UN Security Council resolutions broadly to please national or regional interests, the Council makes all possible efforts to restrict this freedom by establishing the specific

---

352 Lind K., The *Revival of Chapter VIII of the UN Charter, op. cit.,* p. 143. See also Ress G., Bröhmer J., "Article 53," *op. cit.*, p. 866.

353 Lind K., *The Revival of Chapter VIII of the UN Charter, op. cit.*, p. 143.

354 Walter C., "Security Council Control over Regional Action," *op. cit.*, p. 184.

355 Lind K., *The Revival of Chapter VIII of the UN Charter, op. cit.*, p. 143.

356 UN Security Council Resolutions 678 (1990), 29 November 1990; 940 (1994), *op. cit.*

357 UN Security Council Resolutions 665 (1990), 25 August 1990; 875 (1993), 16 October 1993; 794 (1992), 3 December 1992, para. 16; 1785 (2007), *op. cit.*, paras. 14-16; 1845 (2008), *op. cit.*, paras. 14-16; 1857 (2008), 22 December 2008, para. 15.

358 UN Security Council Resolutions 161 (1961), *op. cit.*, para. 1; 875 (1993), *op. cit.*, para. 1.

purpose to be achieved,[359] making reference to the purposes of earlier resolutions,[360] establishing the purposes and tasks of operations,[361] authorizing the application of specific measures,[362] setting time constraints[363] and by other means.

The very idea of implicit, tacit or general authorization is not one that receives broad support in the international legal doctrine.[364] It has no grounding in the UN Charter and undermines the Security Council's primary responsibility in the sphere.[365] Indeed, the wording of Security Council resolutions serves to illustration this.

Sanctions by Regional Organizations

The uncertainty associated with all of the notions considered in this section is also intrinsic in the term "*sanctions*,"[366] which may be characterized as the most controversial of them. Besides its use in international law, the term is often employed in politics, criminal law and even everyday life, and is applied to diverse types and categories of measures taken by entirely different subjects.

---

[359] UN Security Council Resolutions 1838 (2008), 7 October 2008, para.3; 1856 (2008), 22 December 2008, paras. 14-16; 1863 (2009), 16 January 2009, para. 2.

[360] *E.g.*, Resolution 875 (1993) is aimed at securing fulfillment of Resolutions 841 (1993) and 873 (1993); Resolution 1203 (1998) is aimed at securing fulfillment of Resuolutions 1160 (1998) and 1199 (1998).

[361] UN Security Council Resolutions 1856 (2008), *op. cit.*, paras. 3-5; 1863 (2009), *op. cit.*, para. 6.

[362] UN Security Council Resolution 1856 (2008), *op. cit.*

[363] UN Security Council Resolutions 1572 (2004), 15 November 2004, paras. 7-10; 1845 (2008), *op. cit.*, paras. 10-11.

[364] The application of enforcement measures with reference to implied sanctions of the UN Security Council has been condemned, *e.g.*, by Gowlland-Debbas V., "The Limits of Unilateral Enforcement of Community Objectives in the Framework of UN Peace Maintenance," *European Journal of International Law*, 11(2) (2000), p. 373; Malanczuk P., *Humanitarian Intervention and the Legitimacy of the Use of Force* (The Hague: Het Spinhuis, 1993), p. 17-19; Müllerson R., "Jus ad Bellum," *op. cit.*, p. 175; Byers M., "Terrorism, the Use of Force and International Law after 11 September 2001," *op. cit.*, p. 402; Orakhelashvili A., "The Impact of Peremptory Norms," *op. cit.*, p. 63-64; Körbs H., *Die Friedensdicherung duech die Vereinten Nationen und Regionalorganizationen*, *op. cit.*, p. 538.

[365] See also Lind K., *The Revival of Chapter VIII of the UN Charter*, *op. cit.*, p. 156; see also Frowein J.A., "Legal Consequences for International Law Enforcement in Case of Security Council Inaction," *op. cit.*, p. 119.

[366] Draft Articles on Responsibility of States for Internationally Wrongful Acts, with commentaries, *op. cit.*, 128.

Even in international law, sanctions may be viewed as a power (possibility) to ensure the law,[367] an analog of responsibility for internationally wrongful acts,[368] punishment,[369] a complex of enforcement measures applied to a deliquent state,[370] a method to make someone comply,[371] negative consequences in the case of violation,[372] measures of protection of the international legal order,[373] measures not involving the use of armed force in order to maintain or restore international peace and security,[374] or a means of implementation of international responsibility.[375]

---

[367] Sparrow G., *Sanctions* (London: Knightly Vernon Ltd., 1972), p. 11-12.

[368] Kovalev A.A., Chernichenko S.V., ed., *International Law*, *op. cit.*, p. 237-238.

[369] Abass A. *Regional Organizations and the Development of Collective Security*, *op. cit.*, 49; Thakur R., *The United Nations, Peace and Security*, *op. cit.*, p. 135. This approach is, however, disputed by the UN Secretary-General in the Supplement to the Agenda for Peace, *op. cit.*, para. 66; although the punitive nature of sanctions has been rejected by most states – see UN Security Council Report, 4128th Meeting, 17 April 2000, S/PV.4128; Galtung J., "On the Effects of International Economic Sanctions," in *Dilemmas of Economic Coercion: Sanctions in World Politics*, ed. M. Nincic, P. Wallensteen, (New York: Praeger Publishers, 1983), p. 19.

[370] Ignatenko G.V., Tiunov O.I., ed., *International Law*, *op. cit.*, p. 202.; Kalamkarjan R.A., Migachev, Y.I., *International Law*, *op. cit.*, p. 182; Шибаева Е.А., "Международные организации в системе международно-правового регулирования" [Shibaeva E.A., "International Organizations in the System of International Legal Regulation"], *Soviet Yearbook of International Law*, 1978 (Moscow: Nauka, 1980), p. 214-224; Grünfeld F., "The Effectiveness of United Nations Economic Sanctions," in *United Nations Sanctions: Effectiveness and Effects, Especially in the Field of Human Rights: A Multidisciplinary Approach,* ed. W.J. van Genugten, (Antwerp: Intersentia, 1999), p. 115.

[371] Galtung J., "On the Effects of International Economic Sanctions," *op. cit.*, p. 19; Ronzitti N., "The Report of the High-Level Panel on Threats, Challenges and Change, the Use of Force and the Reform of the United Nations," *Italian Yearbook of International Law*, XIV (2004), (Leiden/Boston: Martinus Nijhoff Publishers, 2005), p. 11.

[372] Cited by Лукашук И.И., *Право международной ответственности* [Lukashuk I.I., *Law of International Responsibility*] (Moscow: Walters Kluwer, 2004), p. 309; Нешатаева Т.Н., *Международно-правовые санкции специализированных учреждений ООН* [Neshataeva T.N., *International Legal Sanctions of the UN Specialized Agencies*], extended abstract of PhD dissertation (Moscow: Moscow State University, 1985), p. 9, 12, 14.

[373] Neshataeva T.N., *International Legal Sanctions of the UN Specialized Agencies*, *op. cit.*, p. 17.

[374] Supplement to the Agenda for Peace, *op. cit.* The same approach was taken by states that participated in the discussion of the problem in the UN Security Council (UN Security Council Report, 17 April 2000, S/PV.4128, *op. cit.*).

[375] Lukashuk I.I., *Law of International Responsibility*, *op. cit.*, p. 306, 308; The same approach is supported by G.I. Tunkin, N.A. Ushakov, P. Kuris, cited by Нешатаева Т.Н., "Понятие санкций международных организаций" [Neshataeva T.N., "The Notion of Sanctions of International Organizations"], *Jurisprudence*, 6 (1984), p. 94; Abass A. *Regional Organizations and the Development of Collective Security*, *op. cit.*, 49, 51.

Formally, sanctions may be applied by any subjects of international law,[376] as confirmed by the ILC in the commentary to the DARS.[377] In practice, however, this term usually relates to measures taken by international organizations and imposed through their institutional structures,[378] primarily to their member states.

The right of international organizations to apply enforcement measures set forth in their constituent and other documents to their member states for violations of procedural and substantive norms is not disputed in the international legal doctrine.[379] In exceptional cases (the violation of *erga omnes* norms), some authors consent that international organizations may impose sanctions against third states.[380] In accordance with art. 39 of the UN Charter, the Security Council may decide on the measures to be taken (*e.g.*, applying sanctions) if it determines the existence of any threat to the peace, breach of the peace or act of aggression (that is, when it acts in accordance

---

376 See Kovalev A.A., Chernichenko S.V., ed., *International Law*, *op. cit.*, p. 229; Lukashuk I.I., *Law of International Responsibility*, *op. cit.*, p. 318; Nincic M., Wallensteen P., ed., *Dilemmas of Economic Coercion*, *op. cit.*

377 Draft Articles on Responsibility of States for Internationally Wrongful Acts, with commentaries, *op. cit.*, p. 128. It should also be noted that the term "sanctions" is not used either in the the UN Charter or in DARIO.

378 For example, Y.M. Kolosov views as sanctions only measures applied by the UN Security Council; see Kolosov Y.M., Krivchikova, E.S., ed., *International Law*, *op. cit.*, p. 293; Lukashuk I.I., *Law of International Responsibility*, *op. cit.*, p. 317. P.V. Chikov demonstrates the same approach for military sanctions – Чиков П.В., *Военные санкции в международном праве* [Chikov P.V., *Military Sanctions in International Law*], extended abstract of PhD dissertation (Kazan: Kazan State University, 2003), p. 9-10, 15.

379 Commentary to art. 21 of DARIO stipulates that sanctions which international organizations may apply to their member states are legal and cannot be equated to countermeasures (Responsibility of International Organizations, 2011: Draft Text with Commentaries Thereto, p. 98). See also Lukashuk I.I., *Law of International Responsibility*, *op. cit.*, p. 321; Shibaeva E.A., "International Organizations in the System of International Legal Regulation," *op. cit.*, p. 214-224; Kalamkarjan R.A., Migachev, Y.I., *International Law*, *op. cit.*, p. 182-183; Neshataeva T.N., *International Legal Sanctions of the UN Specialized Agencies*, *op. cit.*, p. 10, 19-20; Walter C., "Security Council Control over Regional Action," *op. cit.*, p. 141-142; Frowein J.A., "Reactions by Not Directly Affected States," *op. cit.*, p. 388-389; Lind K., *The Revival of Chapter VIII of the UN Charter*, *op. cit.*, p. 205.

380 Lukashuk I.I., *Law of International Responsibility*, *op. cit.*, p. 321-322; Neshataeva T.N., *International Legal Sanctions of the UN Specialized Agencies*, *op. cit.*, p. 10, 19-20. It is sometimes advocated that sanctions against third states do not fall under art. 53 and as such do not require authorization; see Lind K., *The Revival of Chapter VIII of the UN Charter*, *op. cit.*, p. 109. He acknowledges, however, that general international law is more restrictive toward sanctions against third states than toward sanctions against member states.

with Chapter VII); this may also include situations when no breach of international law has taken place.[381]

It may thus be concluded that sanctions by international organizations are enforcement measures that are applied by an organization to a delinquent state for the breach of its international obligations within its international responsibilities, even (as concerns sanctions imposed by the UN Security Council) irrespective of violations of international law aimed at restoring or maintaining international peace and security.

No general agreement may be found as regards the scope of the sanctions that international organizations may apply. In the application of sanctions towards third states, their range may be limited to acts not prohibited by international law (retorsion, unfriendly legal acts or countermeasures[382]) or, *vice versa*, to coercive measures that fall between (but do not include) diplomatic efforts and military enforcement.[383] In the special meeting of the UN Security Council on 17 April 2000, most states emphasized the exceptional nature of sanctions (notably Bangladesh, France, Ukraine, Tunisia, Russia) as well as the need for the authorization of the UN Security Council (France, China, Malaysia, Russia).[384]

It thus follows that the notion of sanctions by regional organizations is broader than their enforcement action in accordance with Chapter VIII. An international organization may apply sanctions to its members in accordance with the organization's constituent and other documents if the member breaches procedural and substantive norms, but with due regard to the limitations of the UN Charter.

As concerns any other situation (the application of sanctions to third states or the application of coercive means not provided for by constituent or other documents to member states), the sanctions should conform to the rules and limitations of art. 53, that is, they are to be applied with the explicit prior authorization of the UN Security Council, or include measures not prohibited by international law when applied by individual member states of an organization.

---

[381] See Frowein J.A., Krisch N., "Introduction to Chapter VII," *op. cit.*, p. 707; Frowein J.A., Krisch N., "Article 39," in *The Charter of the United Nations: A Commentary*, 2nd ed., vol. 1, ed. B. Simma, (Munich: Verlag C.H. Beck, 2002), p. 721. The UN Security Council, *e.g.*, has recognized that threats to international peace and security can exist in the case of civil conflict (Resolution 161 (1961), *op. cit.*); antidemocratic governance (Resolution 221 (1966), *op. cit.*); destabilization of a situation by refugee flows (Resolution 812 (1993), *op. cit.*); and trade of weapons in the course of civil conflict (Resolution 775 (1992), *op. cit.*).

[382] Lind K., *The Revival of Chapter VIII of the UN Charter*, *op. cit.*, p. 197.

[383] UN Security Council Report, 17 April 2000, S/PV.4128, *op. cit.*

[384] *Ibid.*

Despite a general enthusiasm about the role of sanctions by the UN Security Council and regional organizations as a means for the maintenance of international peace and security, there can hardly be found any comprehensive study that demonstrates or establishes their efficacy.[385] On the contrary, low efficacy and superfluous humanitarian impact on populations from comprehensive sanctions or even simply economic sanctions is now generally agreed.[386] As a result, recent years have been characterized by attempts to move from comprehensive sanctions applied to states toward targeted sanctions applied against non-state actors and aimed at minimizing the negative effects of the former.[387] Non-state actors are not expressly mentioned in the UN Charter and remain one of the most controversial issues in the sphere of maintenance of international peace and security.

3.4 Targeted Sanctions of Regional Organizations

The matter of targeted sanctions by regional organizations, as opposed to the targeted sanctions by the UN Security Council,[388] is nearly ignored in the international legal doctrine. European authors mostly care about the enhancement of efficacy as well as the mechanisms for implementation of these sanctions,[389] or consider traditional forms of activity

---

[385] The same position is supported by R. Thakur, who notes that sanctions mostly serve the interests of major powers (Thakur R., *The United Nations, Peace and Security*, *op. cit.*, p. 136-137).

[386] UN Security Council Report, 17 April 2000, S/PV.4128, *op. cit.*

[387] Thakur R., *The United Nations, Peace and Security*, *op. cit.*, p. 151.

[388] Beisdes the legal doctrine, this issue has been considered in detail within the Interlaken process (1998-2001), Switzerland (Interlaken Process: Smart Sanctions – Targeted Sanctions); Bonn-Berlin Process: 1999-2001, Germany; Stockholm Process (2001-2002), Sweden. See also Orakhelashvili A., "The Impact of Peremptory Norms," *op. cit.*, p. 59-88; Arnold R., "Human Rights in Times of Terrorism," *Zeitschrift für Ausländisches Öffentliches Recht und Völkerrecht*, 66 (2006), p. 297-319; Reinisch A., "Developing Human Rights and Humanitarian Law of the Security Council for the Imposition of Economic Sanctions," *American Journal of International Law*, 95 (2001), p. 851-872; Biersteker T.J., "Targeted Sanctions and Individual Human Rights," *International Journal*, 65 (2009-2010), p. 99-118.

[389] Wallensteen, P. Stainbano C., ed., *International Sanctions: Between Words and Wars in the Global System* (London: Frank Cass, 2005); *Targeted Financial Sanctions: A Manual for Design and Implementation.* Contributions from the Interlaken Process (Institute for International Studies, 2001); Brzoska M., ed., *Design and Implementation of Arms Embargoes and Travel and Aviation Related Sanctions: Results of the Bonn-Berlin Process* (Bonn, BICC, 2001).

of international organizations,[390] omitting problems relating to qualification, status and legal regime. Particular issues arise when sanctions are applied to promote the respect for human rights. As Italian author N. Ranzitti observes, "*targeted sanctions [...] are difficult to apply or at best do not work.*"[391]

Targeted Sanctions of the UN Security Council

Targeted sanctions against non-state actors were initially applied in 1992-1993 by the UN Security Council against the Party of Democratic Kampuchea in Cambodia (Resolution 792 (1992) of 30 November 1992), UNITA in Angola (Resolution 864 (1993) of 15 September 1993), and individuals in Haiti (Resolution 841 (1993) of 16 June 1993, paras. 5-8). Since 1994, the Security Council has preferred to impose sanctions against particular individuals and organizations[392] instead of comprehensive sanctions against states.[393]

Targeted sanctions have been imposed in the course of the struggle against international terrorism[394] (259 individuals and 69 organizations);[395] on situations in Ethiopia, Eritrea and Somalia – Resolution 1844 (2008)[396] (12 individuals);[397] Iraq – Resolution 1518 (2003)[398] (89 individuals and 208 organizations);[399] Liberia – Resolution 1521 (2003)[400] (45 individuals with limits on freedom of movement;[401] 23 individuals and 31 organizations with assets frozen);[402] DRC – Resolution 1533 (2004)[403] (24 individuals and 6

---

[390] Abass A. *Regional Organizations and the Development of Collective Security*, *op. cit.*; Akehurst M., "Enforcement Action of Regional Organizations," *op. cit.*; Frowein J.A., "Zwangsmaßnahmen von Regionalorganizationen," *op. cit.*

[391] Ronzitti N., "The Report of the High-Level Panel on Threats, Challenges and Change," *op. cit.*, p. 11.

[392] Staibano C., "Trends in UN Sanctions: From ad hoc Practice to Institutional Capacity Building," in *International Sanctions: Between Words and Wars in the Global System*, ed. P. Wallensteen, C. Staibano, (London/New York: Frank Cass, 2005), p. 48.

[393] *Ibid.*, p. 47.

[394] UN Security Council Resolution 1267 (1999), 15 October 1999. The sanctions regime is developed in Resolutions 1333 (2000); 1390 (2002); 1455 (2003); 1526 (2004); 1617 (2005); 1735 (2006); 1737 (2006); 1822 (2008); 1904 (2009); 1989 (2011).

[395] Consolidated List, Resolution 1267.

[396] The sanctions regime is developed in Resolutions 751 (1992); 1356 (2001); 1725 (2006); 1744 (2007); 1772 (2007); 1846 (2008); 1851 (2008).

[397] Consolidated List, Resolution 1844.

[398] See also Resolutions 661 (1990), 6 August 1990; 1483 (2003), 22 May 2003.

[399] Consolidated List, Resolution 1518, Individuals; Consolidated List, Resolution 1518, Entities.

[400] The sanctions regime is developed in Resolutions 1532 (2004); 1683 (2006); 1903 (2009).

[401] Consolidated List, Resolution 1521.

[402] Consolidated List, Resolution 1521, 1532.

organizations);[404] Côte d'Ivoire – Resolution 1572 (2004)[405] (8 individuals);[406] Sudan – Resolution 1591 (2005)[407] (4 individuals);[408] DPRK – Resolution 1718 (2006)[409] (5 individuals and 8 organizations);[410] Iran – Resolution 1737 (2006)[411] (45 individuals and 86 organizations);[412] Libya – Resolution 1970 (2011) (5 individuals with travel bans; 15 individuals and 2 entities with assets frozen);[413] Taliban – Resolution 1988 (2011) (129 individuals).[414] At the time of writing, targeted sanctions imposed by the UN Security Council are in effect against about 650 individuals and 400 organizations.

Targeted sanctions usually include the following types of measures:

- Freezing assets and other economic resources, such as property, directly or indirectly controlled by individuals and organizations included on the list (*Resolutions 1267 (1999), §4(b); 1844 (2008), §3; 1572 (2004), §12; 1483 (2003), §23; 1591 (2005), §3g; 1970 (2011), §17; 1737 (2006), §12; 1904 (2009), §1(a)*);
- Prohibiting entry into the territory of states or transit through their territory; aviation restrictions (*Resolutions 1904 (2009), §1(b)*; *1844 (2008), §1; 1572 (2004), §10; 1483 (2003), §19; 1591 (2005), §3f; 1970 (2011), §15; 1737 (2006), §12*);
- Prevention of the direct or indirect supply, sale or transfer of weapons and military equipment; the direct or indirect supply of technical assistance or training, financial or other assistance, including investment, brokering or other financial services, related to military activities or to the supply, sale, transfer, manufacture, maintenance or use of weapons and military

---

403 The sanctions regime is developed in Resolutions 1533 (2004); 1596 (2005); 1649 (2005); 1698 (2006); 1768 (2007); 1771 (2007); 1799 (2008); 1807(2008); 1857 (2008), *op. cit.*; 1896 (2009); 1952 (2010).

404 Consolidated List, Resolution 1533.

405 The sanctions regime is developed in Resolutions 1584 (2005); 1643 (2005).

406 Consolidated List, Resolution 1572.

407 Strengthened by Resolution 1945 (2010).

408 Consolidated List, Resolution 1591.

409 The sanctions regime is developed in Resolution 1874 (2009).

410 Consolidated List, Resolution 1718.

411 The sanctions regime is developed in Resolutions 1737 (2006), *op. cit.*; 1747 (2007); 1803 (2008); 1929 (2010).

412 Consolidated List, Resolution 1737.

413 Consolidated List, Resolution 1970.

414 The list of individuals and entities established pursuant to Security Council Resolution 1988 (2011).

equipment *(Resolutions 1844 (2008), §7; 1518 (2003); 1904 (2009), §1(c))*.[415]

In the international doctrine, targeted sanctions are divided into two main groups: (1) those aimed at imposing pressure on the leaders/administration of a country without impacting its general population, in order to change policies of the state; and (2) those taken in the pursuit of isolating particular actors (companies, insurgent groups, criminal networks), aimed at restricting their access to natural and financial resources.[416]

It is believed here, however, that these groups are too imprecise. For example, the UN Security Council imposes targeted sanctions over different categories of actors:

- Organizations and insurgency movements whose activities threaten international peace and security (*PDK in Cambodia (Resolution 792 (1992) of 30 November 1992); UNITA in Angola (Resolution 864 (1993) of 15 September 1993); Al Qaeda (Resolution 1267 (1999)*);
- Other organizations concerned with activities threatening international peace and security, or controlled by individuals involved in these activities;
- Individuals suspected of involvement in terrorist acts and other international crimes (*Resolution 1267 (1999)*);
- State officials involved in nuclear programs;
- Individuals in possession of certain knowledge and skills, in particular pertaining to nuclear energy (*Resolutions 1718 (2006), 1737 (2006), 1747 (2007), 1803 (2008)*);
- State officials suspected of being involved in the commission of international crimes (*Resolution 1970(2011)*).

---

[415] Basic targeted sanctions usually include financial sanctions, arms embargoes, visa and entrance bans (see Ward C.A., "The Counter-Terrorism Committee: Its Relevance for Implementing Targeted Sanctions," in *International Sanctions: Between Words and Wars in the Global System*, ed. P. Wallensteen, C. Staibano, (London/New York: Frank Cass, 2005), p. 168; Resolution 1597 (2008) PACE United Nations Security Council and European Union Blacklists, paras. 9-12; *Targeted Financial Sanctions*, *op. cit.*; *Design and Implementation of Arms Embargoes and Travel and Aviation Related Sanctions*, *op. cit.*

[416] Eriksson M., "EU Sanctions: Three Cases of Targeted Sanctions," in *International Sanctions: Between Words and Wars in the Global System,* ed. P. Wallensteen, C. Staibano, (London/New York: Frank Cass, 2005), p. 108.

It should be noted, however, that the very nature of targeted sanctions (even when decided by the UN Security Council) is rather ambiguous, full of controversy and disposed to abuse. As they are aimed against individuals and non-state entities, they are often positioned as punishment.[417] It is maintained here, however, that this approach is fallacious because neither the UN Security Council nor any other organizations are allotted judicial functions.[418] At the same time, the Security Council is viewed as as the last resort in problems involving the maintenance of international peace and security, and is more and more often considered to own, *inter alia*, quasi-judicial functions.[419]

The power of the Security Council to impose targeted sanctions against non-state actors, although not directly mentioned in art. 41 of the UN Charter, is not disputed in state practice or in the legal doctrine.[420] Neither the list of non-military measures nor the scope of respondent actors in art. 41 is exhaustive, which endows the Security Council with substantial freedom of action. As a result, similar to its use of other non-military sanctions, the Security Council, acting under Chapter VII, may impose targeted sanctions if it determines the existence of any threat to the peace, breach of the peace, or act of aggression.[421]

It is not the purpose here to consider in detail the legality of targeted sanctions of the Security Council, although legality and credibility are generally recognized to be inalienable prerequisites for their effectiveness.[422] However, with due account for extraordinary powers of the Council, it is still obliged to act in conformity with the purposes and principles of the United Nations (UN Charter, art. 24(2)) as well as peremptory norms of

---

[417] In 2000 the UN Secretary-General, in his Address to the International Rescue Committee, expressly announced: "*If we want to punish, let us punish the guilty*" (Address to International Rescue Committee on the humanitarian impact of economic sanctions, UN Secretary-General, press release, SG/SM/7625, 15 November 2000). See also The Experience of the United Nations in Administering Arms Embargoes and Travel Sanctions, in Smart Sanctions, the Next Step: Arms Embargoes and Travel Sanctions, Second Expert Seminar, Berlin, 3-5 December 2000.

[418] Supplement to an Agenda for Peace, *op. cit.*, para. 66. The same approach is maintained by Grünfeld F., "The Effectiveness of United Nations Economic Sanctions," *op. cit.*, p. 117-118.

[419] Farral J.M., *United Nations Sanctions and the Rule of Law*, *op. cit.*, p. 17; Alvarez J.E., *International Organizations as Law-Makers*, *op. cit.*, p. 188-189.

[420] See Frowein J.A., Krisch N., "Introduction to Chapter VII," *op. cit.*, p. 710.

[421] See, *e.g.*, model resolutions of the UN Security Council regarding targeted sanctions, in *Design and Implementation of Arms Embargoes and Travel and Aviation Related Sanctions*, *op. cit.*, p. 26, 40, 49, 64, 73, 85.

[422] UN Security Council Report, 17 April 2000, S/PV.4128, *op. cit.*

international law.[423] The obligations to "*reaffirm faith in fundamental human rights*" and to promote and encourage "*respect for human rights and for fundamental freedoms for all*" are expressly set forth as purposes and principles of the United Nations in the preamble and art. 1(3) of the Charter.[424]

Unfortunately, at present, the Security Council is still unable to guarantee minimal standards of human rights, even those which are to be applied in emergency situations, and this has been repeatedly condemned in theory and practice of international organizations.[425] The same problems and sometimes even more serious ones are faced by regional organizations applying targeted sanctions to entities and individuals.

EU Targeted Sanctions (Characteristics)

The history of sanctions applied by the European Union can be traced back to 1965, when UN sanctions against Rhodesia had been jointly implemented by member states of the European Economic Community.[426] Today, sanctions are viewed as an important tool of the external policy of the EU and its member states.[427] The EU's system of targeted sanctions is the most developed of all that exist at present.[428]

The circumstances, procedures and forms of the EU's targeted sanctions as well as the mechanisms for their implementation are regulated

---

[423] A variety of arguments are cited on this point. It is generally agreed that the UN's founders could not endow it with competences (to breach *jus cogens* norms) they did not posses, or were willing to set the United Nations above the law (Orakhelashvili A., *Peremptory Norms in International Law*, *op. cit.*, p. 425, 432; Doehring K., "Unlawful Resolutions of the Security Council," *op. cit.*, p. 92-93; Orakhelashvili A., "The Impact of Peremptory Norms," *op. cit.*, p. 60-62; Farral J.M., *United Nations Sanctions and the Rule of Law*, *op. cit.*, p. 21).

[424] On this issue, see Bianchi A., "Assessing the Effectiveness of the UN Security Council's Anti-terrorism Measures: The Quest for Legitimacy and Cohesion," *European Journal of International Law*, 17(5) (2007), p. 886; Orakhelashvili A., "The Impact of Peremptory Norms," *op. cit.*, p. 67; Orakhelashvili A., *Peremptory Norms in International Law*, *op. cit.*, p. 429.

[425] Resolution 1597 (2008) PACE, *op. cit.*, para. 6; United Nations Security Council and European Union Blacklists, PACE doc. 11454, 16 November 2007: Explanatory Memorandum, paras. 86-95. See also Kadi v. Council and Commission, ECJ Case T 315/01 of 21 September 2005, para. 230; Yusuf and al Barakaat International Foundation v. Council and Commission, CFI Case T306/01, 21 September 2005, para. 281.

[426] Kreutz J., *Hard Measures by a Soft Power? Sanctions Policy of the European Union.* Paper 45, Bonn International Center for Conversation (Bonn: Bonn International Center for Conversation, 2005), p. 8-13.

[427] de Vries A.W., Hazelzet H., "The EU as a New Actor on the Sanctions Scene," *op. cit.*, p. 103.

[428] Restrictive measures (sanctions) in force, European Commission List as of 17 April 2012.

by the Guidelines on Implementation and Evaluation of Restrictive Measures (Sanctions) in the Framework of the EU Common Foreign and Security Policy, of 2 December 2005[429] (hereafter, EU Guidelines), and EU Best Practices for the Effective Implementation of Restrictive Measures, of 24 April 2008[430] (hereafter, EU Best Practices), *etc.*

The types of EU sanctions conform to those of the United Nations and include arms embargoes, embargoes over dual-use (civilian and military) goods and some other specific types of exports and imports; visa, admission and flight bans; the freezing of funds and economic resources (Guidelines, para. 15, part. III; Basic Principles of the Use of Restrictive Measures (hereafter, Principles), para. 6);[431] diplomatic sanctions; boycotts of sport and cultural events; and the suspension of cooperation with third states.[432]

Targeted sanctions (restrictive measures) are imposed within the framework of the EU common external and security policy (Guidelines, para. 7) on the basis of regulations, decisions and common positions adopted by the Council (TFEU, art. 215,[433] Guidelines, para. 7). They may be aimed against a target country, part of the country, its government, non-state entities or individuals (TFEU, art. 215; Guidelines, paras. 2, 4, 7). Targeted sanctions against states and governments seek to bring about changes in their policy or activity (Guidelines, para. 4). Sanctions against individuals (persons responsible, high-ranking officials) may be imposed to change either a policy or activity of a state (Guidelines, paras. 14, 18; Council Decision 2010/639/CFSP, art. 2(1c))[434] or their own activity (*e.g.*, Council Decision 2010/639/CFSP, art. 2(1d)). Depending on the type of sanctions, they are implemented either by states (arms embargoes, admission bans) or the European Union (trade and financial sanctions, flight bans).[435]

---

[429] Guidelines on Implementation and Evaluation of Restrictive Measures (Sanctions) in the Framework of the EU Common Foreign and Security Policy, 2 December 2005.

[430] Update of the EU Best Practices for the Effective Implementation of Restrictive Measures, EU Council 8666/1/08 rev. 1, 24 April 2008.

[431] Basic Principles of the Use of Restrictive Measures (Sanctions), 10198/1/04 Rev. 1, 7 June 2004.

[432] Kreutz J., *Hard Measures by a Soft Power?*, *op. cit.*, p. 5-6.

[433] Treaty on the Functioning of the European Union, *Official Journal of the European Union*, 51 (2008), p. 47-200.

[434] Council Decision 2010/639/CFSP, 25 October 2010, concerning Restrictive Measures against Certain Officials of Belarus.

[435] Kreutz J., *Hard Measures by a Soft Power?*, *op. cit.*, p. 6-7; de Vries A.W., Hazelzet H., "The EU as a New Actor on the Sanctions Scene," *op. cit.*, p. 96-97; Eriksson M., "EU Sanctions: Three Cases of Targeted Sanctions," *op. cit.*, p. 109.

It should also be taken into account that EU restrictive measures are not homogeneous. They may be aimed toward the struggle against international terrorism;[436] the proliferation of weapons of mass destruction;[437] the elimination of a threat to international peace and security;[438] or the promotion and protection of human rights, democracy, the rule of law and good governance.[439] That is why it seems necessary to divide them here into several groups depending on their purposes and on the legal grounds for their adoption (see Principles, paras. 1, 4):[440]

(1) *Measures to implement (support) sanctions of the UN Security Council* mostly concern joint implementation by the EU member states of their obligations under art. 41 of the UN Charter.[441] These measures are

---

[436] Measures against Afghanistan – Council Decision 2011/486/CFSP; Council Implementing Decisions 2011/639/CFSP, 2011/698/CFSP; Council Regulation (EU) No 753/2011; Council Implementing Regulations (EU) No 968/2011, No 1049/2011. See also measures against Eritrea, terrorist groups – Restrictive measures (sanctions) in force, *op. cit.*

[437] Iran – Council Decision 2010/413/CFSP; Council Decisions 2010/644/CFSP, 2011/299/CFSP, 2011/783/CFSP, 2012/35/CFSP; Council Regulation (EU) No 961/2010; Council Implementing Regulations (EU) No 503/2011, No 1245/2011, No 54/2012.See also measures against DPRK – Restrictive measures (sanctions) in force, *op. cit.*

[438] Bosnia and Herzegovina – Council Decision 2011/173/CFSP, 21 March 2011; Common Position 1997/193/CFSP; Congo – Council Decision 2010/788/CFSP; Council Implementing Decisions 2011/699/CFSP, 2011/848/CFSP; Council Regulations (EC) No 889/2005, No 1377/2007, No 666/2008, No 1183/2005, No 1791/2006; Commission Implementing Regulation (EU) No 1097/2011, No 7/2012. See also measures against Cote d'Ivoire, Haiti, Lebanon, Somalia, South Sudan, Sudan, Zimbabwe – see "Restrictive measures (sanctions) in force, *op. cit.*

[439] Kreutz J., *Hard Measures by a Soft Power?*, *op. cit.*, p. 4, 14; de Vries A.W., Hazelzet H., "The EU as a New Actor on the Sanctions Scene," *op. cit.*, p. 95, 98; Eriksson M., "EU Sanctions: Three Cases of Targeted Sanctions," *op. cit.*, p. 109. See also measures against Belarus – Council Decisions 2010/639/CFSP, *op. cit.*, 2011/69/CFSP, 2011/357/CFSP, 2011/666/CFSP, 2012/36/CFSP, 23 January 2012; Council Implementing Decisions 2011/174/CFSP, 2011/301/CFSP, 2011/847/CFSP, 2012/126/CFSP; Council Regulations (EC) No 765/2006, No 646/2008, No 84/2011, No 588/2011, No 999/2011; Council Implementing Regulations (EU) No 271/2011, 505/2011, No 1000/2011, No 1320/2011, No 114/2012; China – Declaration of European Council, Madrid, 27.6.1989; Egypt – misappropriation of Egyptian state funds – Council Decision 2011/172/CFSP, 21 March 2011; Council Regulation (EU) No 270/2011, as well as measures against Burma, Syria, Tunisia, Yugoslavia – Restrictive measures (sanctions) in force, *op. cit.*

[440] See also Kreutz J., *Hard Measures by a Soft Power?*, *op. cit.*, p. 4, 14; de Vries A.W., Hazelzet H., "The EU as a New Actor on the Sanctions Scene," *op. cit.*, p. 96-99; Eriksson M., "EU Sanctions: Three Cases of Targeted Sanctions," *op. cit.*, p. 109.

[441] Measures against Afghanistan – Council Decision 2011/486/CFSP; Council Implementing Decisions 2011/639/CFSP, 2011/698/CFSP, ; Council Regulation (EU) No 753/2011; Council Implementing Regulations (EU) No 968/2011, No 1049/2011; Congo – Council Decision 2010/788/CFSP; Council Implementing Decisions 2011/699/CFSP, 2011/848/CFSP; Council Regulations (EC) No 889/2005, No 1377/2007, No 666/2008, No 1183/2005, No 1791/2006; Commission Implementing Regulations (EU) No 1097/2011, No 7/2012. See also measures

taken on the basis of the corresponding resolution of the UN Security Council and are implemented in the prescribed form against the entities and individuals listed by the Security Council.

(2) *Independent EU sanctions aimed at the struggle against international terrorism, the proliferation of weapons of mass destruction or the maintenance of international peace and security.*[442] This group includes measures which are generally based on resolutions/sanctions/condemnation by the Security Council but go beyond it as concerns the forms of measures or lists of subjects. Due to their nature, these measures are not legitimized by the Security Council and need to be carefully examined as concerns their legality in each situation. At the same time, as far as they are definitely concerned with the maintenance of international peace and security, they fall under art. 53 of the UN Charter and are subject to the restrictions of Chapter VIII.

(3) *Independent EU sanctions aimed at the promotion and protection of human rights, democracy, the rule of law and good governance.*[443] Human rights violations may be viewed as threatening international peace and security only when we speak about mass violations of fundamental human rights that shock the conscience of mankind.[444] In theory, such situations would be brought to the UN Security Council for consideration, and rules of any sanctions it approves would apply. This group of EU sanctions, however, concerns the opposite situation – the absence of a Security Council resolution or even its recognition of the situation as threatening international peace and security.

Measures taken by regional organizations and aimed at the promotion and protection of human rights, democracy, good governance and the rule of law are not aimed at the maintenance of international peace and security, and as such do not fall under the coverage of Chapter VIII of the UN Charter.[445] As a result, an organization can escape from even that

---

against Côte d'Ivoire, Eritrea, Haiti, Iraq, DPRK, Lebanon, Liberia, Libya, Somalia, South Sudan, Sudan, terrorist groups, Yugoslavia – Restrictive measures (sanctions) in force, *op. cit.*

[442] Côte d'Ivoire – measures against persons not listed in the UN Security Council resolutions – Council Decisions 2010/801/CFSP, 2011/18/CFSP; Council Regulation (EU) No 25/2011. See also measures against Lybia, Moldova, terrorist groups – Restrictive measures (sanctions) in force, *op. cit.*

[443] Measures against Belarus, China, Egypt, Iran, Burma, Tunisia. As concerns the promotion of sanctions of the UN Security Council, see measures against Syria – Restrictive measures (sanctions) in force, *op. cit.*

[444] UN Security Council Resolutions 775 (1992), *op. cit.*; 929 (1994), *op. cit.*; 940 (1994), *op. cit.*

[445] See de Vries A.W., Hazelzet H., "The EU as a New Actor on the Sanctions Scene," *op. cit.*, p. 95, 98.

minimal control the UN Charter imposes through Chapter VIII. Formally, the EU is not obliged to obtain authorization of the UN Security Council in accordance with art. 53(1) or even to inform it on the measures taken according to art. 54. It should however, be noted that the aforementioned situations are rather exceptional.[446] As demonstrated above, the EU mostly imposes sanctions in situations qualified by the UN Security Council as threatening international peace and security. At the same time, the absence of legal regulation on this point cannot be interpreted as providing for arbitrary behavior by regional organizations in this sphere. In any case, they are subject to the provisions of the UN Charter, including its purposes and principles as well as obligations arising from the Charter in accordance with art. 103.

It may hereby be concluded that regardless of qualification under Chapter VIII of the UN Charter, regional organizations may apply enforcement measures over third states, their individuals or their entities only with the authorization of the UN Security Council except for measures that may be legally taken by their member states[447] – that is, measures not violating the obligations of member states or those whose wrongfulness is precluded under international law.

Targeted Sanctions as Acts Not Prohibited by International Law

A variety of acts not involving the use of force but imposing some preassure on states are legal under international law. For example, a state may freely decide on visa matters and is not obliged to give reasons for a refusal. It may decline a request for agrément, claim the head of a diplomatic mission *persona non grata* or members of staff as unacceptable at any moment without having to explain its decision (Vienna Convention on Diplomatic Relations, art. 4(2), 9(1)). A state also has the choice of maintaining or suspending economic relations with others (including those relating to trade in arms, dual-use goods, ammunition, etc.).

The obligation of the European Union and of its member states to act in accordance with the purposes and principles of the United Nations, with obligations arising from the UN Charter and with other international

---

[446] Restrictive measures (sanctions) in force, *op. cit.*

[447] Kelsen H., *The Law of the United Nations*, *op. cit.*, p. 724; Walter C., "Security Council Control over Regional Action," *op. cit.*, p. 130, 137-138; Frowein J.A., "Reactions by Not Directly Affected States," *op. cit.*, p. 388-389; Wolfrum R., "Der Beitrag regionaler Abmachungen zur Friedenssicherung," *op. cit.*, p. 582; de Vries A.W., Hazelzet H., "The EU as a New Actor on the Sanctions Scene," *op. cit.*, p. 98; Lind K., *The Revival of Chapter VIII of the UN Charter*, *op. cit.*, p. 197.

obligations following from the UN Charter and the principle *pacta sunt servanda*, is expressly recognized by the EU member states (TEU, art. 3(5); Principles, para. 3; Guidelines, paras. 9, 11), CJEU decisions[448] and the legal doctrine.[449]

As a result, before any measures (including targeted sanctions) are imposed by the EU, it is obliged to make sure that no international obligation of any of its member states is broken. This rule concerns all sorts of obligations, not only those arising in conjunction with limitations imposed by sanctions (for example, regarding freedom of movement or economic rights). In the economic sphere, for example, it relates to obligations arising from trade, economic and financial treaties (including those within the GATT/WTO framework), agreements and customs regarding immunities of states and their property. And, taking due account of the very targets of targeted sanctions (non-state entities and individuals), it concerns obligations in the sphere of human rights protection (TEU, art. 6(2); Principles, para. 7; Guidelines, para. 9,10, 17).[450]

There are no limitations concerning the territorial or quantitative scope of obligations: they may be multilateral, bilateral or even unilateral. Any state whose property, entities or nationals have been targeted by measures taken by an international organization may demand the termination of the breach and invoke the responsibility of a violator if the measures applied by the organization run counter to the obligations of any single member state toward the targeted state. Other members of a regional organization, or the organization itself (as long as no obligation toward the targeted state is broken) may only take retaliatory measures not prohibited by international law, *e.g.*, claiming the same number of diplomatic agents *persona non-grata* or unacceptable, refusing to issue visas to nationals of these states, suspending economic relations.

When applying targeted sanctions that primarily infringe the rights of individuals and non-state entities, special attention is to be paid to obligations in the sphere of promotion and protection of human rights and the rule of law. EU documents contain rather developed provisions of this sort. Besides the aforementioned obligation to implement sanctions in

---

[448] Joined cases C-402/05 P and C-415/05 P, Kadi and Al Barakaat International Foundation v. Council of the European Union and Commission of the European Union, paras. 6, 92.

[449] de Vries A.W., Hazelzet H., "The EU as a New Actor on the Sanctions Scene," *op. cit.*, p. 102.

[450] It is remarkable that the European Commission itself protested against the effects of US extraterritorial measures infringing the rights and interests of EU natural and legal persons and claimed them to be contrary to international law; see Council Regulation (EC) No 2271/96, 22 November 1996; Joint Action 96/668/CFSP of 22 November 1996.

accordance with the international obligations of member states, including obligations to promote and protect human rights and the rule of law, they provide for:

- The need to adopt and implement sanctions in accordance with the purposes and principles of the United Nations (Principles, para. 1) and obligations under the UN Charter (Principles, para. 4);
- The obligation to define precisely the objective of sanctions as well as criteria upon which individuals are subjected to them (Guidelines, paras. 5, 18; Principles, para. 9) and to lift sanctions as soon as the objectives are met (Principles, para. 9);
- The possibility for the sanctions' legality to be appealed to the CJEU (TFEU, art. 275);
- The obligation to develop mechanisms for humanitarian exceptions from the sanctions regime (Guidelines, paras. 24, 68)[451] in order to prevent improper application of the sanctions (Practices, paras. 6-9, 22).

Theoretically, these principles cover the whole spectrum of human rights and are able to guarantee these rights when targeted sanctions are imposed (if it is ensured that the sanctions do not violate the obligations of any EU member state). However, the reality, as repeatedly acknowledged in the legal doctrine, is unfortunately not that optimistic.

In particular, the EU bans on admission are recognized to violate the right to freedom of movement (ECHR, art. 2;[452] ICCPR, art. 12[453]),[454] the right to privacy and family life (ICCPR, art. 17; ECHR, art. 8), and the right

---

[451] As a subtle step in this direction, provisions on humanitarian exeptions are introduced in most of the Council's decisions and regulations (see, *e.g.*, Council Regulation 765/2006, 18 May 2006, art. 3(a); Council Decision 2010/639/CFSP, *op. cit.*, para. 6). Moreover, in late 2011 special notice was taken by the Council in explaining the possibility for individuals subjected to restrictive measures to apply to "*competent authorities of relevant Member states*" – see Restrictive measures (sanctions) in force, *op. cit.*

[452] Convention for the Protection of Human Rights and Fundamental Freedoms, 4 November 1950, *European Convention on Human Rights, COETS*, 5, p. 5-32.

[453] International Covenant on Civil and Political Rights, 16 December 1966.

[454] It is believed here that provisions of art. 13 of ICCPR ("*An alien lawfully in the territory of a State Party to the present Covenant may be expelled therefrom only in pursuance of a decision reached in accordance with law and shall, except where compelling reasons of national security otherwise require, be allowed to submit the reasons against his expulsion and to have his case reviewed by, and be represented for the purpose before, the competent authority or a person or persons especially designated by the competent authority*") may analogously be applied.

to life, when access to medical help is urgent (ICCPR, art. 6; ECHR, art. 2).[455] Financial sanctions are viewed as violating the rights to privacy, family life and property (ECHR, art. 8; Protocol 4, art. 1).[456] An arms embargo – property rights.[457] Sanctions against journalists concerning anything said or written by them – the right to hold opinions and freedom of expression (ECHR, art. 10; ICCPR, art. 19). The introduction of targeted sanctions in general – the right to a fair trial, to a fair hearing, to effective remedy, to protection by law, procedural guarantees (ECHR, art. 6, 13, 14;[458] ICCPR, art. 14(2), 26), the right to be informed promptly on the nature and cause of the accusation, to defend oneself (ECHR, art. 6(3)) and to protection of reputation (Zollman v. Great Britain;[459] ICCPR, art. 17).[460]

The above problems are well grounded. Despite the stated readiness of the EU and its member states to fulfill their international obligations, including those in the sphere of human rights, procedural rights and guarantees are not observed in the course of applying targeted sanctions. In particular, despite the obligation to review regularly the lists of sanctioned individuals (at least once every six months) in accordance with art. 1(6) of the EU Common Position 2001/931/CFSP[461] and the possibility to apply for de-listing,[462] reviews take place rather seldomly – once every several years. Art. 275 of the TFEU provides for the possibility to appeal the legality of applying restrictive measures to natural and legal persons to the CJEU.[463] In practice, this is limited to the right of states to bring to the attention of the

[455] Cameron I., "Protecting Legal Rights: On the (In)security of Targeted Sanctions," in *International Sanctions: Between Words and Wars in the Global System*, ed. P. Wallensteen, C. Staibano (London/New York: Frank Cass, 2005), p. 184-185.

[456] See, *e.g.*, Report of the Special Rapporteur on the Promotion and Protection of Human Rights and Fundamental Freedoms while Countering Terrorism, Martin Scheinin (A/HRC/4/26), 29 January 2007, paras. 38-41.

[457] Cameron I., "Protecting Legal Rights," *op. cit.*, p. 185-186.

[458] Obligation to observe these rights is stressed in the PACE documents, e.g., Resolution 1597 (2008) PACE, *op. cit.*, para. 5.1.

[459] Zollman v. Great Britain, Application no. 62902/00 of 27 November 2003. Accessed 15 October 2011.

[460] See also Cameron I., "Protecting Legal Rights," *op. cit.*, p. 186.

[461] Council Common Position of 29 December 2001 on the Application of Specific Measures to Combat Terrorism 2001.931.CFSP.

[462] Update of the EU Best Practices, *op. cit.*

[463] See Resolution 1597 (2008) PACE, *op. cit.*, paras. 54-63, 79-85. At the time of writing, the CJEU had considered about 20 cases involving the application of targeted sanctions. Only two of them (the Mojahedines case and Maria Sison case) concerned the application of EU autonomous sanctions (Mojahedines du people d'Iran, Case T-228/02, Judgment of 12 December 2006; Jose Maria Sison v. Council of the EU, Case T-47/03, Judgment of 11 July 2007). None of the cases involved the application of targeted sanctions with the aim of ensuring human rights, democracy and the rule of law.

Court measures taken against their nationals or legal persons,[464] or the submission of written objections by a person (Mojahedines case, para. 69). Individuals are deprived of any possibility to be heard both before and after restrictions are imposed.[465]

In addition, the EU often prevents individuals from exercising procedural rights, referring to the administrative rather than criminal nature of restrictions (Mojahedines, para. 77). I would, however, disagree with the last assumption. The wording of the EU acts that impose restrictive measures "*for ...[something]*" clearly demonstrates a punitive purpose and turns it into punishment.[466] Moreover, in the majority of cases, restrictive measures are applied to individuals expressly accused of the commission of serious crimes ("*who are responsible for*," in the wording of EU documents), *e.g.*, "*severe human rights violations*," "*crackdown on civil society*,"[467] undermining "*the sovereignty, territorial integrity, constitutional order and international personality*" of ... state,[468] "*harbouring, financing, facilitating, supporting, organizing, training or inciting individuals or groups to perpetrate acts of violence or terrorist acts against other States or their citizens in the region*."[469] Thus, the only conclusion one can reach is that EU targeted sanctions tend to substitute for criminal punishment. The EU instruments claim people guilty and impose punishment without criminal investigations, hearings or the possibility of appeal. Beyond any doubt, this violates the presumption of innocence as well as other procedural guarantees that become even more important due to the seriousness of the accusations.

Some other persons – "*natural and legal persons, bodies and entities associated with them*,"[470] "*persons or entities benefitting from or supporting the ... regime*,"[471] persons responsible for "*undermining ... agreement*"[472] or "*misappropriation of ... state funds*"[473] – are sanctioned and, as concerns the

---

[464] Kadi v. Council and Commission, *op. cit.*, paras. 261-291; Yusuf and al Barakaat International Foundation, *op. cit.*, paras. 309-346.
[465] "Resolution 1597 (2008) PACE, *op. cit.*, para. 9; United Nations Security Council and European Union Blacklists, PACE doc. 11454, *op. cit.*, paras. 87-90.
[466] See, *e.g.*, Bianchi A., "Assessing the Effectiveness of the UN Security Council's Anti-terrorism Measures," *op. cit.*, p. 905; Herik L. van den, "The Security Council's Targeted Sanctions Regimes: In Need of Better Protection of the Individual," *Leiden Journal of International Law*, 20 (2007), p. 798.
[467] Council Decision 2010/639/CFSP, *op. cit.*, art. 1(1).
[468] Council Decision 2011/173/CFSP, *op. cit.*, art. 1(1a).
[469] Council Decision 2010/127/CFSP, 1 March 2010, art. 3.
[470] Council Decision 2010/639/CFSP, *op. cit.*, art. 2; Council Decision 2011/172/CFSP, *op. cit.*, art. 1(1).
[471] Council Decision 2012/36/CFSP, *op. cit.*, art. 1(2).
[472] Council Decision 2011/173/CFSP, *op. cit.*, art. 1(1c).
[473] Council Decision 2011/172/CFSP, *op. cit.*, art. 1(1).

consequences, punished for acts which are not qualified as crimes under the legislation of either their own or any other state. This results in the violation of the right not to be held guilty for any offense that did not constitute an offense at the moment of its commission (ICCPR, art. 15(1); ECHR, art. 7(1)).

None of these violations may be justified through reference to the emergent and extraordinary character of the situation. In the modern world, the rights of particular individuals may only be restricted in accordance with a court's decision taken in compliance with procedural rules. Any other limitations may take place only in a time of public emergency, the existence of which is officially proclaimed (ICCPR, art. 4; ECHR, art. 15).

The latter limitations, however, as stipulated by the ICHR in General Comments No. 29, must be expressly prescribed by national law and have a minimal, proportionate, necessary and non-discriminatory character (paras. 2, 4-5).[474] In accordance with art. 4 of the ICCPR, no derogation is allowed from the right to life (art. 6), freedom from torture (art. 7) or slavery (art. 8(1, 2)), prohibition of imprisonment on grounds of an inability to fulfill contractual obligations (art. 11), prohibition of punishment for offenses that are not viewed as crimes at the moment of their commission (*nullum crimen*) (art. 15), right to recognition of personality (art. 16), or freedom of thought, conscience and religion (art. 18). The ECHR limits this list to the first four freedoms.

I will indeed insist that such lists included in international instruments are not exhaustive. They should also include all procedural guarantees – in particular the right to due process (ICCPR, art. 14(2-7); ECHR, art. 6, 13, 14), the inalienable nature of which is broadly recognized by human rights institutions (General Comments No. 29, para. 16), legal scholars[475] and international treaties (Principles of Nurnberg Tribunal, principle V;[476] Fourth Geneva Convention, 1949, art. 72-73, 146(4);[477] Third Geneva Convention, 1949, art. 105-108, 129(4);[478] Additional Protocol I,

---

[474] General Comment No. 29: Article 4: Derogations during a State of Emergency (CCPR/C/21/Rev.1/Add.11), in *General Comments and Recommendations*, vol. I, 4th ed. (Lund, 2003).

[475] Arnold R., "Human Rights in Times of Terrorism," *op. cit.*, p. 305; *Handbook on Criminal Justice and Responses to Terrorism*, Criminal Justice Handbook Series (New York: United Nations, 2009), p. 40-41.

[476] Principles of Nurnberg Tribunal, 1950.

[477] Convention (IV) relative to the Protection of Civilian Persons in Time of War, Geneva, 12 August 1949.

[478] Convention (III) relative to the Treatment of Prisoners of War, Geneva, 12 August 1949.

1977, art. 75;[479] Additional Protocol II, 1977, art. 6).[480] Breaching this right is qualified in time of war as a serious violation of international humanitarian law (Fourth Geneva Convention, art. 147; Additional Protocol I, art. 85(4e)).

All of the above rights, including the right to due process, are therefore inalienable. They constitute basic standards of promotion and protection of human rights, are of interest to the international community as a whole (*erga omnes*) and have a peremptory character (*jus cogens*).[481] As such, they occupy the supreme position in the international legal system and are obligatory for all subjects of international law (including regional organizations and even the UN Security Council) in all situations.[482] Acts of any of these organizations (including resolutions of the Security Council) are to conform with *jus cogens* norms, including in the sphere of human rights. Otherwise, applying analogously the provisions of art. 53 of the Vienna Convention on the Law of Treaties ("*A treaty is void if [...] it conflicts with a peremptory norm of general international law*"), they will be void from the moment of their adoption.[483]

---

[479] Protocol Additional to the Geneva Conventions of 12 August 1949, and relating to the Protection of Victims of International Armed Conflicts, 8 June 1977.

[480] Protocol Additional to the Geneva Conventions of 12 August 1949, and relating to the Protection of Victims of Non-International Armed Conflicts, 8 June 1977.

[481] Barcelona Traction, Light and Power Company, Ltd., *I.C.J. Reports 1970* (The Hague: I.C.J., 1970), p. 32; International Status of South-West Africa, Advisory Opinion, *I.C.J. Reports 1950* (The Hague: I.C.J., 1950), p. 133; Interpretation of Peace Treaties, Advisory Opinion, *I.C.J. Reports 1950* (The Hague, I.C.J., 1950), p. 77; Kadi v. Council and Commission, *op. cit.*, paras. 226-232; Yusuf and al Barakaat International Foundation, *op. cit.*, paras. 277-283.

[482] Bianchi A., "Assessing the Effectiveness of the UN Security Council's Anti-terrorism Measures," *op. cit.*, p. 886; Reinisch A., "Developing Human Rights and Humanitarian Law of the Security Council," *op. cit.*, p. 858-859; Cannizaro E., "A Machiavellian Moment? The UN Security Council and the Rule of Law," *International Organizations Law Review*, 3 (2006), p. 207-215.

[483] Herik L. van den, "The Security Council's Targeted Sanctions Regimes," *op. cit.*, p. 801; Doehring K., "Unlawful Resolutions of the Security Council," *op. cit.*, p. 98; Orakhelashvili A., *Peremptory Norms in International Law*, *op. cit.*, p. 423, 465-469; Бекяшева К.А., Отв. ред., *Международное публичное право*: *Учебник* [Bekjashev K.A., ed., *International Public Law: Textbook*] (Moscow: Prospect, 1999), p. 66-67; Case Concerning Armed Activities on the Territory of the Congo (Democratic Republic of the Congo v. Rwanda), Judgment of 3 February 2006, Separate Opinion of Judge Dugard, *I.C.J. Reports 2006* (The Hague: I.C.J., 2006), p. 88-89, para. 8; Case Concerning the Application of the Genocide Convention (Bosnia and Herzegovina v. Yugoslavia), Order of 13 September 1993 on the Request for the Indication of Further Provisional Measures, Separate Opinion of Judge Lauterpacht, *I.C.J. Reports 1993*, (The Hague: I.C.J., 1993), p. 440, para. 100; Cassese A., "Ex Iniuria ius oritus: Are we Moving Toward International Legitimation of Forcible Humanitarian Countermeasures in the World Community?" *European Journal of*

Due to the superior character of these rights, there can be no grounds for limiting them with respect to individuals through reference to public benefit or interest[484] (as formally recognized both in international and national law – ICCPR, art. 12(3); ECHR, art. 8(2), 9(2), 10(2), 11(2), protocol 1, art.1 – as well as by legal scholars).[485] As concerns other infringed rights, it is maintained here that the very idea of violating human rights in order to promote and protect human rights or achieve some other public good in situations not prescribed by international law is invalid. It would result in establishing exceptions from exceptions, which is hardly logical from the point of view of international law or that of the rule of law.[486] It is also notable that unilateral coercive measures and legislation taken under the banner of promoting and protecting human rights have also been condemned by UN human rights bodies as being contrary to international law and the UN Charter by infringing human rights.[487]

It may thus be concluded that EU targeted sanctions in their existing form, even in the absence of other international treaties concluded between the EU/EU member states and target states, violate at the very least obligations emerging from universal and regional instruments in the sphere of human rights. Some of these rights (right to life, procedural guarantees, prohibition of punishment for offenses that are not viewed as crimes at the moment of their commission) have peremptory character. Acts taken by EU institutions in breach of these rights (in general, all resolutions introducing targeted sanctions more or less violate them) are thus void from the moment of their adoption.

International Law, 10(1) (1999), p. 26; Conte A., *Handbook on Human Rights Compliance While Countering Terrorism* (Washington: Center on Global Counterterrorism Cooperation, 2008), p. 3, 7; Bianchi A., "Assessing the Effectiveness of the UN Security Council's Anti-terrorism Measures," *op. cit.*, p. 906-909; Kadi v. Council and Commission, *op. cit.*, para. 299; Yusuf and al Barakaat International Foundation, *op. cit.*, para. 248.

484 As S. Chesterman correctly noted, extraordinary emergency powers of the UN Security Council only mean the right of the Council to "*intrude upon the domestic jurisdiction in the time of crisis*" in order to settle emergency situations that arise (Chesterman S., "UNaccontable? The United Nations, Emergency Powers, and the Rule of Law," *Vanderbilt Journal of Transnational Law*, 42(5) (2009), p. 1539.

485 See Doehring K., "Unlawful Resolutions of the Security Council," *op. cit.*, p. 95; Benvenisti E., "The US and the Use of Force: Double-edged Hegemony and Management of Global Emergencies," *European Journal of International Law*, 15 (2004), p. 697-699; Farral J.M., *United Nations Sanctions and the Rule of Law*, *op. cit.*, p. 220.

486 Bianchi A., "Assessing the Effectiveness of the UN Security Council's Anti-terrorism Measures," *op. cit.*, p. 891-892.

487 Commission on Human Rights Resolution 2003/17, "Human rights and Unilateral Coercive Measures," 22 April 2003; Resolution adopted by the Human Rights Council 12/22, "Human Rights and Unilateral Coercive Measures," 2 October 2009; "Human Rights and Unilateral Coercive Measures," draft resolution.

Targeted Sanctions as Applied in the Course of Countermeasures

The right of international organizations to apply countermeasures is not viewed in DARIO as being very broad. Art. 51 provides for the possibility to take countermeasures in the event of a wrongful act by another international organization. As concerns member states, countermeasures may only be taken for the breach of rules of international organizations and only if the possibility to apply countermeasures is provided by these rules (art. 22(3)).[488] DARIO does not recognize the right of international organizations to apply countermeasures to non-members. This situation clearly demonstrates that the idea of international organizations applying sanctions or countermeasures to third states does not enjoy much support in international law. When considering the status and legal grounds for targeted sanctions of international organizations in light of the absence of special applicable rules, it is necessary to rely on the rules regulating countermeasures of states.

In accordance with art. 49(1) of DARS, "*An injured State may only take countermeasures against a State which is responsible for an internationally wrongful act in order to induce that State to comply with its obligations.*"[489] Therefore, sanctions of regional organizations, unlike those of the UN Security Council, may be introduced in the course of countermeasures only in response to the *violation of a specific international obligation by a specific state* and may be directed only *against that state*[490] to induce it to comply with the obligation. The need to act in the framework of countermeasures substantially limits the possibilities of applying targeted sanctions. They may only be applied against individuals immediately responsible for the policy or activity of a state in breach of an international obligation, in order to change that policy or activity. The institution of countermeasures is not applicable to other categories of persons or entities.

---

[488] It should be noted that DARIO distinguishes between sanctions by international organizations toward their members (which are provided for in its documents) and countermeasures – the application of which is restricted; see Comment to art. 22 of DARIO, paras. 3, 6. A special regime of measures applied by an international organization to member states that breach their obligations within the organization has also been recognized by the ILC in the course of work on DARS (Draft Articles on Responsibility of States for Internationally Wrongful Acts, with commentaries, *op. cit.*, comments to art. 50, para. 10.

[489] Draft Articles on Responsibility of States for Internationally Wrongful Acts, 2001, *Yearbook of the International Law Commission*, 2001, vol. II, Part Two (New York/Geneva: United Nations, 2006), p. 43-59. See also The Protection of Human Rights and the Principle of Non-Intervention in Internal Affairs of States. Institut de Droit International, Session in Santiago de Compostela, 1989.

[490] In support, see Geyrhalter B., *Friedenssicherung durch Regionalorganizationen*, *op. cit.*, p. 66.

Another very important point concerns the <u>*subject entitled to apply countermeasures*</u>. In accordance with art. 22, 49(1) of DARS, countermeasures may be taken in relations between the directly injured state and the respondent state.[491] The application of countermeasures by other states (taking place in the context of sanctions by regional organizations) is only allowed as regards so-called "*collective obligations*" to all members of an organization or to the international community as a whole (*erga omnes* obligations) (Vienna Convention on the Law of Treaties, 1969, art. 60(2); DARS, art. 42, 48).[492] As concerns regional organizations of collective security, due to their functions, they may apply sanctions (including targeted sanctions) with the purpose of bringing about an end to a breach and securing guarantees of non-repetition (art. 48(2), 54)[493] regarding obligations toward the international community as a whole.

It should also be considered that despite the importance of protected values as well as proclaimed good intentions, the invocation of responsibility by states other than the directly injured state as concerns *erga omnes* obligations was the most debated issue in the course of work toward DARS. A number of states (China, Japan, *etc.*) called these provisions "revolutionary," referred to the high potential for abuse and demanded to exclude them from the Draft.[494]

The very <u>notion</u> of *erga omnes* obligations is rather broad and uncertain. No precise list of these obligations may be found. It is generally agreed that *erga omnes* obligations are those obligations owed to the

---

[491] Draft Articles on Responsibility of States for Internationally Wrongful Acts, with commentaries, *op. cit.*, comments to art. 22, para. 5. The same approach is taken by international courts and tribunals, *e.g.*, by the R.I.A.A. in the Cysne case (Responsibility of Germany for acts committed subsequent to 31 July 1914 and before Portugal entered into the war, *RIAA*, 1930, vol. II, p. 1056-1057; Case Concerning the Gabčíkovo-Nagymaros Project (Hungary v. Slovakia), Decision of 25 September 1997, *I.C.J. Reports 1997* (The Hague: I.C.J., 1997), p. 55, para. 83.

[492] Frowein J.A., "Reactions by Not Directly Affected States," *op. cit.*, p. 391-404; Geyrhalter B., *Friedenssicherung durch Regionalorganizationen, op. cit.*, p. 65; Wolfrum R., "Der Beitrag regionaler Abmachungen zur Friedenssicherung," *op. cit.*, p. 581.

[493] Wolfrum R., "Der Beitrag regionaler Abmachungen zur Friedenssicherung," *op. cit.*, p. 581; Draft Articles on Responsibility of States for Internationally Wrongful Acts, with commentaries, *op. cit.*, p. 130; Geyrhalter B., *Friedenssicherung durch Regionalorganizationen*, *op. cit.*, p. 147.

[494] Xinmin MA, "Statement on Responsibility of States for Internationally Wrongful Acts," *Chinese Journal of International Law*, 7(2) (2008), p. 565; Tams Ch.J., "All's Well that Ends Well: Comments on the ILC's Articles on State Responsibility," *Zeitschrift für ausländisches öffentliches Recht und Völkerrecht*, 62 (2002), p. 789; Crawford J., *The International Law Commission's Articles on State Responsibility: Introduction, Text and Commentaries* (Cambridge: Cambridge University Press, 2007), p. 302.

international community as a whole.[495] As a result, all states in the international community have an interest in upholding them.[496] They may also be sometimes viewed as any collective obligations in the meaning of art. 42(b) of DARS.[497] The latter opinion, however, is not very popular.

In the modern interdependent world, a broad scope of problems and questions are of obvious interest to the entire international community. The list includes issues of security, environmental protection, terrorism, the proliferation of weapons of mass destruction, the protection of fundamental human rights, desertification, the eradication of poverty and diseases, stable trade, *etc.*[498]

It should be noted that the promotion and protection of fundamental human rights (repeatedly cited by the EU as a ground for autonomous targeted sanctions, as noted above) had already been included in this list in the first part of the 20th century, *e.g.*, by L. Oppenheim and H. Lauterpacht.[499] The same approach was then reaffirmed by the ICJ in the advisory opinions on Interpretation of Peace Treaties (1950)[500] and International Status of South-West Africa (1950),[501] as well as in the Barcelona Traction decision (1970).[502] Later, this idea developed into the concepts of solidarity[503] and the responsibility to protect.[504] Today, the UN

---

[495] Barcelona Traction, Light and Power Company, Ltd., *op. cit.*, p. 32; Vaur-Chaumette A.-L., "The International Community as a Whole," in *The Law of International Responsibility*, ed. J. Crawford, A. Pellet, S. Olleson, (Oxford: Oxford University Press, 2010), p. 1024-1025; General Comment No. 31, The Nature of the General Legal Obligation Imposed by States Parties by the Covenant, 24 March 2004, para. 2.

[496] Simma B., "Does the UN Charter Provide an Adequate Legal Basis for Individual or Collective Responses to Violations of Obligations Erga Omnes?" in *The Future of International Law Enforcement: New Scenarios – New Law?*, ed. J. Delbruck (Berlin: Dunker and Humblot, 1993), p. 126-127.

[497] Obligations erga omnes in international law: Resolution of the Institut de Droit International, 2005 Krakow, art. 1.

[498] Draft Articles on Responsibility of States for Internationally Wrongful Acts, with commentaries, *op. cit.*, p. 126.

[499] Cited by Frowein J.A., "Reactions by Not Directly Affected States," *op. cit.*, p. 407-408.

[500] Interpretation of Peace Treaties, *op. cit.*, p. 77.

[501] International Status of South-West Africa, *op. cit.*, p. 133.

[502] Barcelona Traction, Light and Power Company, Ltd., *op. cit.*, p. 32.

[503] Simma B., "From Bilateralism to Community Interest in International Law," *Recueil des Cours/Collected Courses of the Hague Academy of International Law*, 250 (1994), (The Hague: Martinus Nijhoff Publishers, 1994), p. 217-384; Wolfrum R., Kojima C., ed., *Solidarity: A Structural Principle of International Law* (Heidelberg: Springer, 2010); Brunnée J., "International Law and Collective Concerns: Reflections on the Responsibility to Protect," in *Law of the Sea, Environmental Law and Settlement of Disputes,* ed. T.M. Ndiaye, R. Wolfrum, (Leiden/Boston: Martinus Nijhoff Publishers, 2007), p. 35-51.

[504] Wellens K., "Theoretical Aspects of the Implementation Processes: General Observations," in *Public Interest Rules of International Law: Towards Effective*

HRC insists that measures taken to ensure compliance with these obligations shall not be "*regarded as an unfriendly act*" and shall "*be considered as a reflection of legitimate community interest*" (General comment 31, para. 2).[505]

It is maintained here, however, that owing to the high potential for abuse,[506] the scope of *erga omnes* obligations for the purpose of application of countermeasures by states not directly affected is considerably narrower.[507] That is why I will join those publicists who believe that for the purposes of responsibility the lists of *jus cogens* norms and *erga omnes* obligations are nearly identical.[508]

Therefore, states (and, intermediately, regional organizations) not directly injured may only apply countermeasures in the case of a serious breach of obligations arising under peremptory norms of general international law as defined in art. 40-41 of DARS. The list of these is rather narrow. The ICJ identifies them as serious violations of the right to self-determination,[509] international humanitarian law[510] and fundamental human rights.[511] We may add here situations threatening international peace and security. Due to the extreme danger constituted by these situations to international peace and security, the UN Security Council is named by the

---

Implementation, ed. T. Komori, K. Wellens, (Farnham: Ashgate Publishing Ltd, 2009), p. 15-52.

[505] General Comment No. 31, *op. cit.*, para. 2.

[506] B. Simma emphasizes the high possibility of abuse regarding human rights protection because these obligations are owned towards individuals – Simma B., "Does the UN Charter Provide an Adequate Legal Basis," *op. cit.*, p. 134.

[507] *E.g.*, British author N.J. Calamita was able to conclude that obligations arising from the breach of the Non-Proliferation Treaty injure all member states only upon very careful and detailed consideration; see Calamita N.J., "Sanctions, Countermeasures, and the Iranian Nuclear Issue," *Vanderbilt Journal of Transnational Law*, 42(5) (2009), p. 1421-1428.

[508] Vaur-Chaumette A.-L., "The International Community as a Whole," *op. cit.*, p. 1026; Brunnée J., "International Law and Collective Concerns," *op. cit.*, p. 37-38; Kovalev A.A., Chernichenko S.V., ed., *International Law*, *op. cit.*, p. 239; Cassese A., "The Character of the Violated Obligation," in *The Law of International Responsibility*, ed. J. Crawford, A. Pellet, S. Olleson, (Oxford: Oxford University Press, 2010), p. 418; Simma B., "Does the UN Charter Provide an Adequate Legal Basis," *op. cit.*, p. 133.

[509] Draft Articles on Responsibility of States for Internationally Wrongful Acts, with commentaries, *op. cit.*, p. 113; Crawford J., *The International Law Commission's Articles on State Responsibility*, *op. cit.*, p. 277-279; Barcelona Traction, Light and Power Company, Ltd., *op. cit.*, paras. 34-35; East Timor (Portugal v. Australia), Judgment, *I.C.J. Reports 1995*, (The Hague: I.C.J., 1995), p. 102, para. 29; Fourth Report on State Responsibility, *op. cit.*, p. 30-31.

[510] Legal Consequences of the Construction of a Wall in the Occupied Palestinian Territory, Advisory Opinion, *I.C.J. Reports 2004*, (The Hague: I.C.J., 2004), p. 172, 199, paras. 88, 155.

[511] Interpretation of Peace Treaties, *op. cit.*, p. 77; International Status of South-West Africa, *op. cit.*, p. 133; Barcelona Traction, Light and Power Company, Ltd., *op. cit.*, p. 32.

ILC special rapporteur[512] as well as other legal publicists[513] as the most appropriate (the only) organ endowed with powers to act.

This approach, however, does not seem solidly grounded. International law currently contains no provisions that prohibit states and regional organizations from taking countermeasures and, intermediately, sanctions, in response to breaches of *jus cogens* norms of international law. In the face of the repeated inaction of the Security Council, these measures may often be the only applicable means. As concerns violations of human rights, only those involving mass systematic and outrageous[514] violations of fundamental human rights (human rights of *jus cogens* character) are eligible for international protection.[515] Therefore, the powers of regional organizations in the sphere of targeted sanctions, including the composition of lists, should be interpreted in the narrowest possible way, a position that is also maintained by, *inter alia*, the CJEU.[516]

It should also be taken into account that <u>*the right of states to apply countermeasures is not unlimited*</u>. Countermeasures shall generally be limited to the "*non-performance for the time being of international obligations of the State taking the measures towards the responsible State*" (DARS, art. 49),[517] proportionate with the injury suffered (DARS, art. 51), taken with due account for the requirements of humanity and the rules of good faith[518] and implemented in accordance with the rules of art. 52 of DARS.

---

[512] Vaur-Chaumette A.-L., "The International Community as a Whole," *op. cit.*, p. 1026.
[513] Simma B., "Does the UN Charter Provide an Adequate Legal Basis," *op. cit.*, p. 136.
[514] Crawford J., *The International Law Commission's Articles on State Responsibility*, *op. cit.*, p. 133; Brunnée J., "International Law and Collective Concerns," *op. cit.*, p. 49. The same level of human rights violations is often cited as a sufficient ground for humanitarian intervention (sanctions with the use of military force); see Geyrhalter B., *Friedenssicherung durch Regionalorganizationen*, *op. cit.*, p. 134-135.
[515] The Protection of Human Rights and the Principle of Non-Intervention, *op. cit.*, art. 2; Interpretation of Peace Treaties, *op. cit.*, p. 77; International Status of South-West Africa, *op. cit.*, p. 133; Barcelona Traction, Light and Power Company, Ltd., *op. cit.*, p. 32; Kadi v. Council and Commission, *op. cit.*, paras. 226-232; Yusuf and al Barakaat International Foundation, *op. cit.*, paras. 277-283.
[516] Joined Cases C-57/09, C-101/09, Judgment of the Court (Grand Chamber) of 9 November 2010.
[517] Even so, B. Geyrhalter, *e.g.*, claims it is possible that economic sanctions may be applied to states responsible for mass violations of fundamental human rights; see Geyrhalter B., *Friedenssicherung durch Regionalorganizationen*, *op. cit.*, p. 66.
[518] See Naulilaa Portuguese Colonies Case, 1928, *UNRIAA*, vol. II, p. 1026; Draft Articles on Responsibility of States for Internationally Wrongful Acts, with commentaries, *op. cit.*, p.132, comments to art. 50, para. 6.

Art. 50(1) lists obligations which cannot be affected by countermeasures. They are:

(a) the obligation to refrain from the threat or use of force as embodied in the Charter of the United Nations;

(b) obligations for the protection of fundamental human rights;

(c) obligations of a humanitarian character prohibiting reprisals;

(d) other obligations under peremptory norms of general international law.

It is believed here that special attention should be paid to the limitation listed in para. b – the prohibition on affecting *fundamental* human rights. It is rather important that measures allowed by international law cannot violate any human rights, but measures applied in the course of countermeasures are restrained only by fundamental human rights. It is advocated here, however, that in the absence of a state of emergency (when a situation is not evaluated by the UN Security Council), the exceptional and temporary character of admissible limitations of fundamental human rights[519] and the orientation of countermeasures toward restoring the fulfillment of international obligations, the prohibition on affecting fundamental human rights in the course of countermeasures should cover the broader category of rights than those which may be viewed as grounds for applying countermeasures to third states. Moreover, art. 50(1b) prohibits violations of the rights of every individual, rather than only mass systematic and outrageous violations.

This can be illustrated by the practice of international organizations. EU documents expressly view as "*fundamental*" a broader scope of rights, including procedural rights and the right to effective remedy, and provide for guaranteeing them (TEU, art. 2.; Guidelines, paras. 9, 10, 17). The Parliamentary Assembly of the Council of Europe supports the view that for the credibility of targeted sanctions, the following guarantees (at least) are to be provided to a person who is the object of sanctions:

- to be notified promptly and fully informed of the charges held against himself or herself, and of the decision taken and the reasons for that decision;
- to enjoy the fundamental right to be heard and to be able to defend himself or herself;

[519] General Comment No. 29, *op. cit.*, para. 2.

- to be able to have the decision affecting his or her rights speedily reviewed by an independent, impartial body with a view to modifying or annulling it;
- to be compensated for any violation of his or her rights.[520]

The obligation to guarantee these rights does not depend on qualification of these measures within the state or international organizations. Therefore, the aforementioned references by EU institutions to the administrative character of restrictive measures[521] do not waive this obligation. Moreover, the recognition of the possible deviation from human rights standards in order to ensure the promotion and protection of human rights, democracy, the rule of law and good governance hardly appears logical.[522]

This all brings me to the conclusion that instituting countermeasures provides very narrow grounds for the application of targeted sanctions to individuals and non-state entities of third states, because of the very limited purpose (to restore the fulfillment of international obligations by states), the targets (states), the grounds (violations of obligations owned by the international community as a whole), the requirements of proportionality and humanity, and the prohibition on violating the fundamental human rights of every affected human being.

3.5 Treaty-based Intervention

The last decade has witnessed a regeneration of so-called "treaty-based intervention," which includes (in its current form) attempts by regional organizations to take military and other measures to their member states on the basis of provisions in their constituent and other documents (see, *e.g.*, Constitutive Act of the African Union, art. 4(h);[523] Protocol on Amendment to the Constitutive Act of the African Union of 11 July 2003;[524] Protocol Relating to the Mechanism for Conflict Prevention, Management, Resolution, Peacekeeping and Security (ECOWAS) of 10 December 1999,

[520] Resolution 1597 (2008) PACE, *op. cit.*, para. 5.1.
[521] Mojahedines du people d'Iran," *op. cit.*, para. 77.
[522] S. Chesterman makes a special note that "*the irony that lawless means are being used to promote law*" is rarely noticed (Chesterman S., "UNaccontable?" *op. cit.*, p. 1517.
[523] Constitutive Act of the African Union, 11 July 2000.
[524] Protocol on Amendment to the Constitutive Act of the African Union, 11 July 2003.

art. 25;[525] Kampala Convention for the Protection and Assistance of Internally Displaced Persons, 2009).[526] None of these documents provides for the need to have UN Security Council authorization in accordance with art. 53 of the UN Charter.

Intervention by invitation and treaty-based intervention used to be rather popular in the practice of states[527] under the view that the prohibition on the use of force as a *jus cogens* norm in combination with art. 2(4) and 103 of the UN Charter do not prohibit treaties inviting foreign military forces as such.[528] Formally, this argument may hardly be rejected. States are not precluded from providing their territory for foreign military bases, or from inviting foreign troops for maneuvers or collective self-defense.

In the classical period of international law, provisions on the possibility of intervention under certain conditions had been set forth, *e.g.*, in the Küçük Kaynarca Peace Treaty between the Russian Empire and the Osman Empire (1774); the Treaty of Bucharest (Russian Empire and Osman Empire, 1812); the Vienna Peace Treaty (1815); US treaties with Mexico (1853), Cuba (1903), Panama (1903), the Dominican Republic (1915) and Nicaragua (1915); the Treaty of Versailles (1919); the USSR treaty with Persia (1921); and the Treaty of Guarantee between Cyprus, Greece, Turkey and the United Kingdom (1930).[529] In the period since the UN's founding, the USSR cited consent of the government when it invaded Hungary (1956), Czechoslovakia (1968) and Afghanistan (1979); the US did likewise when it intervened militarily in Lebanon (1958), the Dominican Republic (1965), Grenada (1983) and Afghanistan (2001). The same justification was invoked in the course of British operations in Jordan in 1958, Belgian action in Congo in 1964, US anti-terrorist operations in the Philippines in 2002, *etc.*[530]

---

[525] Protocol Relating to the Mechanism for Conflict Prevention, *op. cit.* See also Abass A., "The New Collective Security Mechanism of ECOWAS: Innovations and Problems," *Journal of Conflict and Security Law*, 5(2) (2000), p. 211-229.

[526] African Union Convention for the Protection and Assistance of Internally Displaced Persons in Africa, 23 October 2009. On this issue, see also Omorogbe E., "The African Union and the United Nations: Conflict or Cooperation?"

[527] See Winfield P.H., "The Grounds of Intervention in International Law," *British Yearbook of International Law*, 5 (1924), p. 149-162; Wippman D., "Treaty-Based Intervention," *op. cit.*, p. 607-687.

[528] Lind K., *The Revival of Chapter VIII of the UN Charter*, *op. cit.*, p. 158.

[529] See Winfield P.H., "The Grounds of Intervention in International Law," *op. cit.*, p. 158-159; Jennings R., Watts A., ed., *Oppenheim's International Law*, 9th ed., vol.1. Peace. Introduction and Part 1 (Harlow: Longman, 1992), p. 446; Wippman D., "Treaty-Based Intervention," *op. cit.*, p. 202-203; Lind K., *The Revival of Chapter VIII of the UN Charter*, *op. cit.*, p. 158-161.

[530] See, *e.g.*, Wippman D., "Treaty-Based Intervention," *op. cit.*, p. 620-621.

Odd as it may seem, this topic is not very popular in the international legal doctrine. There are hardly any works devoted to it directly.[531] Some aspects are considered in publications on the principle of non-intervention in the domestic affairs of states[532] and on assessing the legality of specific situations[533] or documents.[534]

Intervention by Invitation (Consent-based Intervention)

It is generally recognized in international law that "*valid consent by a state to a commission of a given act by another State precludes the wrongfulness of that act in relation to the former State to the extent that the act remains within the limits of that consent*" (DARS, art. 20; DARIO, art. 20). The same approach was taken by the ICJ in the Certain Expenses[535] and Military and Paramilitary Activity[536] cases as well as in the legal doctrine.[537] The absence of consent is a necessary criterion for a state to be in violation of the principles of non-use of force and non-intervention in the domestic affairs of states.[538] Currently, this issue is mostly discussed as regards consent to peacekeeping operations.[539]

---

[531] Wippman D., "Treaty-Based Intervention," *op. cit.*, p. 613; Zotiades G.B. *Intervention by Treaty Right: Its Legality in Present Day International Law* (Nicosia: Geka Press, 1965).

[532] Winfield P.H., "The Grounds of Intervention in International Law," *op. cit.*, p. 158-159; Jennings R., Watts A., ed., *Oppenheim's International Law, op. cit.*, p. 446; Jamnerjad M., Wood M., "The Principle of Non-Intervention," *Leiden Journal of International Law*, 22(2) (2009), p. 345-381.

[533] Henkin L., "The Invasion in Panama," *op. cit.*, p. 309; Omorogbe E., "The African Union and the United Nations," *op. cit.*

[534] Reisman M.W., "Termination of the USSR's Treaty Right of Intervention in Iran," *op. cit.*, p. 150-153; Abass A. *Regional Organizations and the Development of Collective Security, op. cit.*, p. 164-167.

[535] Certain Expenses of the United Nations, *op. cit.*, p. 162.

[536] Military and Paramilitary Activities in and against Nicaragua, 1986, *op. cit.*, p. 126, para. 246.

[537] Kunig P., "Intervention, Prohibition of," para. 29; Nolte G., "Intervention by Invitation," paras. 1-6, 11; Jamnerjad M., Wood M., "The Principle of Non-Intervention," *op. cit.*, p. 378; Simma B., ed., *The Charter of the United Nations: A Commentary, op. cit.*, p. 50; Zwanenburg M., "Regional Organizations and the Maintenance of International Peace and Security: Three Recent Regional African Peace Operations," *Journal of Conflict & Security Law*, 11(3) (2006), p. 505-506; Henkin L., "The Invasion in Panama," *op. cit.*, p. 299.

[538] Пирадов А.С., Старушенко Г.Б., "Принцип невмешательства в современном международном праве" [Piradov A.S., Starushenko G.B., "The Principle of Non-Intervention in Modern International Law"], *Soviet Yearbook of International Law*, 1958 (Moscow: USSR Academy of Sciences, 1959), p. 248; Skakunov E.I., *Self-Defense in International Law, op. cit.*, p. 15; Waldock C.H.M., "The Regulation of the Use of Force," *op. cit.*, p. 461; Simma B., ed., *The Charter of the United Nations: A Commentary, op. cit.*, p. 50; Rajan M.S., *United Nations and Domestic Jurisdiction, op. cit.*, p. 9; Henkin L., *How Nations*

Despite the apparent simplicity and clarity of the matter, it is not that obvious in practice.[540] Every case of consent-based intervention provokes active debates on its legality.[541] Let us look at the basic characteristics of a valid consent.

The wording or art. 20 of DARS and DARIO – "*valid consent by a State to a commission of a given act by another State (international organization) precludes the wrongfulness of that act in relation to the former State (international organization) to the extent that the act remains within the limits of that consent*" – provides for the need in any given case to establish that (1) state consent is given, (2) the consent is valid, and (3) the act remains within the limits of this consent.

Consent is given. The fact that consent is given by a state for the commission of certain acts should result from the wording of the consent.[542] It is to be clearly established and may be given both verbally or in written form, *ad hoc* or in advance – or also in the form of an international treaty.[543] No presumption of consent may be established on the basis that it had been requested but no negative answer was received.[544]

Consent *should identify the acts that may be committed*. In reality, the scope of these acts is rather disputable. In particular, it is not that clear whether consent may be given to an act that would otherwise be in breach of peremptory norms of general international law.

Formally, the answer is obvious. The Vienna Convention on the Law of Treaties stipulates that provisions being in conflict with *jus cogens* norms are void (art. 53, 64). In comments to art. 26 of DARS and DARIO, it is further maintained that "*circumstances precluding wrongfulness in chapter*

Behave: Law and Foreign Policy, 2nd ed., (New York: Columbia University Press, 1979), p. 153; Malanczuk P., *Humanitarian Intervention*, *op. cit.*, p. 5; Geyrhalter B., *Friedenssicherung durch Regionalorganizationen*, *op. cit.*, p. 67; Frowein J.A., "Zwangsmaßnahmen von Regionalorganizationen," *op. cit.*, p. 63.

539 See Geyrhalter B., *Friedenssicherung durch Regionalorganizationen*, *op. cit.*, p. 66-74; Pernice R., *Die Sicherung des Weltfriedens*, *op. cit.*, p. 116-117. It is asserted that peacekeeping operations, regardless of their military or non-military form, cannot be viewed as enforcement if they occur with the consent of the target state (Frowein J.A., "Zwangsmaßnahmen von Regionalorganizationen," *op. cit.*, p. 63).

540 Jamnerjad M., Wood M., "The Principle of Non-Intervention," *op. cit.*, p. 378.

541 Wippman D., "Treaty-Based Intervention," *op. cit.*, p. 621.

542 Draft Articles on Responsibility of States for Internationally Wrongful Acts, with commentaries, *op. cit.*, comments to art. 20, para. 3.

543 Kunig P., "Intervention, Prohibition of." *op. cit.*, para. 29; Nolte G., "Intervention by Invitation," *op. cit.*, para. 24.

544 Draft Articles on Responsibility of States for Internationally Wrongful Acts, with commentaries, *op. cit.*, comments to art. 20, paras. 4, 6.

V of Part One do not authorize or excuse any derogation from a peremptory norm of general international law."[545] At the same time, these provisions shall not be interpreted unequivocally. It is usually rather difficult to decide whether any breach of peremptory norms of general international law has taken place. The absoluteness of the above prohibition may, in the extreme, result in the prohibition against concluding any international treaty because a state, by doing it, limits its domestic jurisdiction. In reality, however, a state is free to conclude international treaties, to sell, lease or otherwise pass a part of its territory to another state, to unite with another state or to admit foreign troops to its territory for some lawful purposes.[546]

Consent is valid. Valid consent should be freely given (without the application of pressure on a state or its agent) by the agent representing a state who is authorized to give consent in a given case,[547] in advance of the act or when it is occurring[548] (consent given after the act is only a waiver to invoke responsibility for a committed act).[549]

A government representing a state should be effective both at the moment when it gives consent and at the time the act (which otherwise would be wrongful) is committed.[550] The right of an effective government (as opposed to its opposition)[551] to invite foreign troops is usually recognized in the legal doctrine.[552] In recent years, it has sometimes been asserted that the effectivenes of the government is not sufficient, and that the government should also be recognized by other states and claim its adherence to democracy and the rule of law.[553] These criteria are, however, too loose. They are often politically motivated and conditioned.

It is, however, maintained here that the invitation of a government to have foreign troops enter the country to suppress opposition in a civil conflict may hardly be legal, although corresponding practice is rather

---

[545] *Ibid.*, comments to art. 26, paras. 4, 6.

[546] See *ibid.*, comments to art. 26, para. 6.

[547] *Ibid.*, comments to art. 20, paras. 4, 5.

[548] *Ibid.*, comments to art. 20, para. 3; Kunig P., "Intervention, Prohibition of." *op. cit.*, para.29.

[549] *Ibid.*, comments to art. 45(a), paras. 2, 3.

[550] Walter C., "Security Council Control over Regional Action," *op. cit.*, p. 146-147.

[551] Military and Paramilitary Activities in and against Nicaragua, 1986, *op. cit.*, p. 126; Geyrhalter B., *Friedenssicherung durch Regionalorganizationen*, *op. cit.*, p. 71.

[552] Jamnerjad M., Wood M., "The Principle of Non-Intervention," *op. cit.*, p. 378; Kunig P., "Intervention, Prohibition of." *op. cit.*, para. 29.

[553] Nolte G., "Intervention by Invitation," *op. cit.*, para. 17; Zwanenburg M., "Regional Organizations and the Maintenance of International Peace and Security," *op. cit.*, p. 504; Geyrhalter B., *Friedenssicherung durch Regionalorganizationen*, *op. cit.*, p. 72.

representative.[554] The very fact of civil war may demonstrate that a government is not supported by the majority of the population and is, therefore, inffective.[555] Moreover, military intervention in a civil conflict upon the consent/invitation of one of the parties contradicts general principles and norms of international law (see Additional Protocol II (1977), art. 3).[556] It thus follows that foreign involvement in such situations may only be legal when it takes place upon the decision of the UN Security Council or with the consent of both parties in the conflict. In recent years, it has usually been given in agreements on the peaceful settlement of conflicts or on peacekeeping operations[557] in which regional organizations are appointed as guarantors of their observance (*e.g.*, NATO as concerns the Dayton agreement,[558] ECOWAS with the Cotonou agreement).[559]

Treaty-based Intervention

As noted above, the consent of a state to the commission of a certain act may be given, *inter alia*, in written form, including in an international treaty. Formally, in every treaty states consent to cede part of their powers in exchange for certain benefits.

Traditionally, the notion of treaty-based intervention has very little to do with the law of international treaties. It is mostly invoked to justify military intervention[560] committed by members of a corresponding treaty to another member if certain circumstances occur.[561] The content of these treaties may be different. Historically, there have been treaties on guaranteeing certain dynasties, forms of governance, territorial integrity and

[554] G. Nolte notes that even in traditional international law there was no customary norm providing for the legality of military intervention in a state with civil conflict, even upon the invitation of its government (Nolte G., "Intervention by Invitation," *op. cit.*, para. 2). For example, the intervention by the Organization of Eatern Carribean States in Grenada in 1983 upon the invitation of its governor was condemned by the UN Security Council (Official Record, 2389th Meeting, 26 October 1983) and General Assembly (Official Record, 1983, 43rd Plenary Meeting, 2 November 1983), cited by Walter C., "Security Council Control over Regional Action," *op. cit.*, p. 150-152).

[555] In support of this point see also *ibid.*, p. 147; Jennings R., Watts A., ed., *Oppenheim's International Law*, *op. cit.*, p. 437-438.

[556] See also Frowein J.A., Krisch N., "Article 42," *op. cit.*, p. 754.

[557] Neuhold H., "Collective Security after 'Operation Allied Force,'" *op. cit.*, p. 88.

[558] Agreement on the Military Aspects of the Peace Settlement, Annex 1A.

[559] Cotonou Agreement, 25 July 1993, art. 3.

[560] Winfield P.H., "The Grounds of Intervention in International Law," *op. cit.*, p. 150, 155.

[561] It has sometimes been asserted that intervention (including military intervention) is implied in every international treaty as a punishment for the breach of its provisions; see *ibid.*, p. 156.

political independence as well as some specific rights, including neutrality in war.[562]

In the UN's first decades, treaties providing for the possibility of military intervention were not very popular. It is only possible to name the Nicosia Treaty of Guarantee of 16 August (1960)[563] (concerning the status of Cyprus) and the Panama Canal Treaty (1977), art. IV(2), which endows the US with primary responsibility for protection and defense of the Canal.[564] These treaties, however, were seen as violating the principle of non-intervention in the domestic affairs of states. For example, Turkey's invasion of Cyprus in 1974 with reference to art. IV of the Treaty of Guarantee was condemned by the UN Security Council.[565]

A new era of treaties providing for the possibility of outside military action started after the end of the Cold War. This involved the transformation of the mechanism of bilateral cooperation into grounds for the application of military enforcement measures by regional organizations in response to mass violations of human rights, war crimes, genocide, crimes against humanity (including against internally displaced persons) and violations of legitimate order (Constitutive Act of the African Union (2001), art. 4(h); Protocol relating to the Mechanism for Conflict Prevention, Management, Resolution, Peacekeeping and Security, art. 25; Kampala Convention for the Protection and Assistance of Internally Displaced Persons (2009), art. 8), and in response to serious threats to legitimate order (Protocol on Amendment to the Constitutive Act of the African Union 2003, art. 4).[566]

---

562 *Ibid.*, p. 130; Wippman D., "Treaty-Based Intervention," *op. cit.*, p. 613.

563 Treaty of Guarantee, Nicosia, 16 August 1960.

564 Texts of the Panama Canal Treaties with United States Senate Modifications.

565 UN Security Council Resolutions 353 (1974), 20 July 1974; 360 (1974), 16 August 1974. After the change of government in 1974, Cyprus asserted the illegality of the Nicosia Treaty for conflicting with peremptory norms of international law; see Wippman D., "Treaty-Based Intervention," *op. cit.*, p. 644.

566 On the issue see Omorogbe E., "The African Union and the United Nations," *op. cit.*; Wippman D., "Treaty-Based Intervention," *op. cit.*, p. 608-609, 667-684; Farer T.J., "A Paradigm of Legitimate Intervention," in *Enforcing Restraint: Collective Intervention in Internal Conflicts*, ed. L.F. Damrosch, (New York: Council on Foreign Relations Press, 1993), p. 332; Farer T.J., "The United States as Guarantor of Democracy in the Caribbean Basin: Is There a Legal Way?" *Human Rights Quarterly*, 10(1) (1988), p. 161. It should also be noted that the approach of international organizations (including the United Nations) has never been positive; see, *e.g.*, Henkin L., "The Invasion in Panama," *op. cit.*, p. 297; Jennings R., Watts A., ed., *Oppenheim's International Law*, *op. cit.*, p. 446.

It is not disputed that regional organizations may apply internal sanctions against member states for violations of the organizations' rules;[567] at the same time, the application of military measures has specific features.

Theoretical approaches to treaty-based intervention differ significantly. In accordance with one approach – "*freedom of contract*"[568] – states referring to the principle of state sovereignty and freedom to conclude international treaties may limit their domestic jurisdiction as much as they want.[569] According to this approach, acts taken on the basis of treaties do not constitute any intervention or use of force as far as they are advanced by the consent of the target state, which precludes the wrongfulness of these acts.[570] I will however, join here American publicist D. Wippman, who asserts that international law granting states the right to carry out their sovereignty through, *inter alia*, entering into international agreements does not leave this right unlimited. States should act in conformity with peremptory norms of international law and cannot commit acts which violate the rights of other states.[571] As noted above, it is also not that easy to determine whether a breach of *jus cogens* norm has taken place.

A second approach focuses on *jus cogens* norms as fundamental to state sovereignty. According to this approach, any international treaty allowing the possibility of intervention in the domestic affairs of states is void insofar as it breaks peremptory norms of general international law.[572] A state should consent to a specific military operation on its territory by foreign troops immediately before it occurs. Formally, this brings us to the initial point – whether prior treaty-fixed consent to uncertain military action against a state of uncertain character in the indefinite future is valid.

---

[567] Kelsen H., *The Law of the United Nations*, *op. cit.*, p. 724; Walter C., "Security Council Control over Regional Action," *op. cit.*, p. 130, 137-138; Frowein J.A., "Reactions by Not Directly Affected States," *op. cit.*, p. 388-389; Wolfrum R., "Der Beitrag regionaler Abmachungen zur Friedenssicherung," *op. cit.*, p. 582; de Vries A.W., Hazelzet H., "The EU as a New Actor on the Sanctions Scene," *op. cit.*, p. 98.

[568] Wippman D., "Treaty-Based Intervention," *op. cit.*, p. 610.

[569] Jennings R., Watts A., ed., *Oppenheim's International Law*, *op. cit.*, p. 435, 446. Geyrhalter B., *Friedenssicherung durch Regionalorganizationen*, *op. cit.*, p. 75.

[570] Jennings R., Watts A., ed., *Oppenheim's International Law*, *op. cit.*, p. 435, 446; Farer T.J., "The United States as Guarantor of Democracy in the Caribbean Basin," *op. cit.*, p. 161. Some authors assert that ratification of such a treaty already implies that states consent to the application of enforcement measures by an international organization in the event of a breach (Kunig P., "Intervention, Prohibition of." *op. cit.*, para. 29; Nolte G., "Intervention by Invitation," *op. cit.*, para. 24).

[571] Wippman D., "Treaty-Based Intervention," *op. cit.*, p. 618, 621-622.

[572] Reisman M.W., "Termination of the USSR's Treaty Right of Intervention in Iran," *op. cit.*, p. 150-153; Henkin L., "The Invasion in Panama," *op. cit.*, p. 309; Walter C., "Security Council Control over Regional Action," *op. cit.*, p. 141.

Wippman develops a third approach. In his opinion, a treaty providing for the possibility of intervention is not *ipso facto* void. A state may recall the given right to intervene at any moment,[573] but only under the same procedure as it was given.[574] The latter, however may become very problematic, *e.g.*, if a civil conflict starts.

The need to get additional consent besides that fixed in the treaty immediately before a military operation, advocated by K. Lind,[575] annihilates any meaning of the former. It cannot be invoked to preclude the wrongfulness of intervention if no additional consent has been given by a state immediately before military action.

When deciding on the legality of treaty-based intervention, it is necessary to check whether consent given in a treaty corresponds to all of the criteria of validity. Due to the very form of the international treaty, it may not be contested that consent given in a treaty is *explicit*, *expressly given* and *prior*. The treaty-making procedure also guarantees that consent in the treaty is given by the *authorized agent*.

We shall distinguish, however, between consenting to accept some specific international obligations (including the obligation to settle disputes arising from the treaty by designated means; to comply with decisions of international courts and tribunals; and to follow control procedures, which are rather definite and do not threaten sovereignty, political independence or the territorial integrity of a state), and consenting to an obligation to be subjected to an invasion by foreign military troops in the indefinite future, under undetermined circumstances upon the decision of the third entity (the regional organization), although some authors (M. Jamnejad, M. Wood) insist on the identical character of these duties.[576] The latter situation brings back up the question of how the agreed activity corresponds to the peremptory norms of general international law.

I will cite here again art. 20 of DARS, DARIO: "*Valid consent [...] to the commission of a given act [...] precludes the wrongfulness of that act [...].*" The wording of this provision may only be interpreted as setting a requirement of *preciseness* as a prerequisite for the validity of the consent. As a result, consent given in a treaty to an act to be committed in the indefinite future with unclear circumstances, timing and activity necessary for its achievement does not correspond to the criteria of art. 20 of DARS,

---

[573] The same approach is taken by K. Lind (Lind K., *The Revival of Chapter VIII of the UN Charter*, *op. cit.*, p. 161-162).

[574] Wippman D., "Treaty-Based Intervention," *op. cit.*, p. 623, 645-650.

[575] Lind K., *The Revival of Chapter VIII of the UN Charter*, *op. cit.*, p. 162.

[576] Jamnerjad M., Wood M., "The Principle of Non-Intervention," *op. cit.*, p. 378.

DARIO. The credibility of such consent turns even more disputable in light of the vitality of interests under consideration This ambiguity carries, therefore, a high possibility for abuse and subjective assessment.[577] That is why invitation by a government or treaty-based consent are very rarely cited alone as a ground for military action.[578]

Another slippery area concerns the *effectiveness of the government*. To exclude the wrongfulness of military invasion, the government consenting to it must be effective – that is, it must at least enjoy full control over the territory of a state.[579] Meanwhile, an indefinite amount of time will pass between the moment when consent is given and another when a decision about invasion is taken by the regional organization. By the time the latter occurs, the government may have already lost its effectiveness or may not be a government at all. As a result, German professor C. Walters insists, invitation may serve as a ground for military invasion only if the same government stays effective both at the moment when consent is given (when the treaty is signed or ratified) and at the time an invasion takes place.[580] Positions on the sufficiency of the consent given by the effective government regardless of any future action[581] or priority of the will of state at the moment when the treaty is concluded over its will at the moment of invasion[582] may hardly be cited in this case, especially in view of the possible violation of *jus cogens* norms.

It is difficult to imagine that a government committing, *e.g.*, a mass gross violation of fundamental human rights will accede to a treaty providing for the possibility of foreign military intervention, and *vice versa* – that a government acceding to such a treaty will commit such violations. If a serious military conflict or a coup occurs, the government will lose its effictiveness and thus will not conform to the criteria under discussion.[583] Recurrent consent of the government or both sides of a conflict for a specific military operation under specific, already existing circumstances on a specific ground sometimes cited in the legal doctrine[584] deprives the consent expressed in the international treaty of any legal meaning.

---

[577] See Winfield P.H., "The Grounds of Intervention in International Law," *op. cit.*, p. 158.
[578] Walter C., "Security Council Control over Regional Action," *op. cit.*, p. 151-152.
[579] Jennings R., Watts A., ed., *Oppenheim's International Law*, *op. cit.*, p. 437.
[580] Walter C., "Security Council Control over Regional Action," *op. cit.*, p. 150.
[581] Geyrhalter B., *Friedenssicherung durch Regionalorganizationen*, *op. cit.*, p. 72.
[582] Wippman D., "Treaty-Based Intervention," *op. cit.*, p. 630.
[583] This approach was recognized even in traditional international law; see *ibid.*, p. 626-627.
[584] D. Wippman maintains that treaty-based intervention shall conform to international law both at the moment when the treaty was concluded as well as when the military operation takes place (Wippman D., "Treaty-Based Intervention," *op. cit.*, p. 615). The need for contemporaneous consent is also cited by Morrison F.L., "The Role of Regional

Some other arguments against the right of regional organizations to apply military enforcement measures to their member states with reference to an international treaty may be cited. In particular, these acts go counter to principles of international law as *jus cogens* norms as well as provisions of art. 2(4), 53(1) of the UN Charter, which, in accordance with art. 103, enjoy priority over any other international obligations.[585]

I will not focus here on treaties in which the parties to internal conflicts agree to accommodate peacekeeping operations, although these operations are sometimes cited as a specific form of treaty-based intervention.[586] It is generally agreed that these treaties should be signed by all parties to the conflicts, as well as some third states or international organizations. At the same time, as the conflicting parties may very rarely all be viewed as subjects of international law, any agreement between them would likely have a private rather than public law character. Meanwhile, these agreements concern the settlement of specific conflicts in specific situations under specific circumstances, so even by their content they do not enjoy other characteristics and problems that have been under consideration above.

Therefore, even if a peace treaty with a mixed composition of parties provides for the possibility of a state or regional organization to apply military force, *e.g.*, in case of the renewal of armed activities or any breach of obligations by the conflicting parties, this situation will differ drastically from the "classical" treaty providing for the possibility of military intervention because it concerns a specific situation, a specific conflict and specific measures to be taken immediately or in the foreseeable future. In effect, we are dealing here with consent that is very similar to *ad hoc* rather than treaty-based consent.[587]

It may thus be concluded that provisions of the constituent and other documents of regional organizations that authorize them to take military action against a member state in the case of the latter violating its international obligations provide no legal ground for such military action in

---

Organizations in the Enforcement of International Law," *op. cit.*, p. 43; Lind K., *The Revival of Chapter VIII of the UN Charter*, *op. cit.*, p. 162.

585 See also Wippman D., "Treaty-Based Intervention," *op. cit.*, p. 619-620; Henkin L., "The Invasion in Panama," *op. cit.*, p. 309.

586 Wippman D., "Treaty-Based Intervention," *op. cit.*, p. 612, 626-627, 638-639.

587 Even in these cases, one of the parties may annul its consent. *E.g.*, Ch. Taylor, leader of the National Patriotic Front of Liberia, expressed his dissatisfaction at the fact that the treaty endowed international peacekeeping forces with powers to apply enforcement through military measures to guarantee the fulfillment of the peace treaty (cited by Wippman D., "Treaty-Based Intervention," *op. cit.*, p. 634).

the absence of the immediate consent of the state concerned or authorization by the UN Security Council.

Conclusions

Despite its seeming ineffectiveness in the maintenance of international peace and security as well as the apparent inability to use mechanisms of the UN Charter in the application of enforcement actions, the UN Security Council preserves and reaffirms its primary role in the maintenance of international peace and security (UN Security Council Resolutions 1631 (2005), preamble; 1809 (2008), preamble).

Any enforcement action (military or non-military) may only be taken by regional organizations with prior explicit and clear authorization by the Security Council and only within the framework of this authorization. No references to exceptional circumstances, inaction by the Security Council or ambiguity of its authorization constitute a legal ground for enforcement activity.

Enforcement measures in the meaning of art. 53 of the UN Charter do not include measures which may be legally taken by member states of regional organizations or measures whose illegality (when taken by member states) is excluded. Regional organizations may apply these measures in the form of sanctions without authorization of the UN Security Council. Regional organizations may also apply sanctions to its member states for the breach of the organizations' internal rules if such sanctions are set forth in the constituent or other documents of the organization.

When taken as legal "unfriendly" acts, sanctions are obliged to conform to the international obligations of any member state of an international organization. If sanctions breach the obligations of any or some member states, the target state may invoke the responsibility of this state (these states) and request the termination of the violations.

Besides possible violations of some trade, cooperation, economic, financial or other agreements, targeted sanctions in the current form violate a range of human rights guaranteed by universal and regional documents, and as a result they cannot be legally applied by member states of regional organizations or indirectly by these organizations themselves. States whose natural and legal persons are affected by these sanctions may request the termination of these violations and invoke the responsibility of member states of the corresponding regional organizations and/or the organizations themselves.

The application by regional organizations of sanctions that are justified as countermeasures of their member states is based on art. 48 and 54 of DARS. These sanctions should stay within the framework of countermeasures. Therefore, targeted sanctions may be applied only to individuals responsible for a state's violation of its *erga omnes* obligations. They should also be aimed at terminating the violation, be proportionate and not violate fundamental human rights, including procedural guarantees and the right to effective remedy.

Obligations *erga omnes* should be interpreted in the narrowest possible way and include acts of aggression, serious breaches of international humanitarian law and serious mass violations of fundamental human rights. Targeted sanctions may not be applied in the course of countermeasures if the "seriousness" of the violations does not reach the level noted above, or if the sanctions are aimed at changing the activity or behavior of individuals and non-state entities rather than states.

It should also be taken into account that most violated rights, including procedural rights, the right to effective remedy, the right not to be punished for acts which did not constitute crimes at the moment when they were committed, *etc.*, are currently qualified as peremptory norms of general international law. Therefore, acts of regional organizations which are not in conformity with them are void from the moment they are adopted.

As concerns individuals and entities not responsible for the policy of a target state, regional organizations may only take measures that may legally be taken by their member states, that is, diplomatic measures or statements.[588] The alleged rightfulness of freezing assets of nationals and entities of third states with reference to the existence of similar practice[589] has no support or ground in international law.

Targeted sanctions in their existing form thus constitute enforcement measures under art. 53 of the UN Charter, and as such they may be applied with proper authorization of the UN Security Council, although the legality of targeted sanctions even when decided by the Security Council is not that indisputable.

A state, as a basic subject of international law, may exercise its sovereignty in different ways, including the transfer or lease of its territory

---

[588] The Protection of Human Rights and the Principle of Non-Intervention, *op. cit.*, art. 3.

[589] Fourth Report on State Responsibility, *op. cit.*, p. 30-32; Borelli S., Olleson S., "Obligations Relating to Human Rights and Humanitarian Law," *op. cit.*, p. 1180.

and the admission to its territory of foreign military troops. In this situation, however, all criteria of valid consent (effectiveness of the government, validity, expressness, clarity and specificity of the consent) must be fulfilled. This consent precludes the wrongfulness of acts as well as the responsibility of states and regional organizations for consented acts as long as they stay within the limits of the consent. Meanwhile, the scope of the consent should be interpreted in the narrowest possible way so that the possibility of abuse is limited. Consent may be expressed in any form, both orally or written, and, *inter alia*, fixed in an international treaty. This treaty, however, should express its consent to specific acts under specific circumstances in already existing or clearly foreseen situations.

When consent fixed by international treaty transfers to a state, group of states or international organization the right to apply military enforcement measures to the consenting state without the authorization of the UN Security Council or additional consent by the target state in the situations listed in the treaty, this provides no legal ground for such measures and does not preclude the wrongfulness of the acts or the responsibility of the state/group/organization that engages in them.

CHAPTER 4

THE UN SECURITY COUNCIL AND REGIONAL ORGANIZATIONS: DEPENDENCE AND PARTNERSHIP

4.1 UN Security Council Control over Regional Action

In the sphere of maintenance of international peace and security, the UN Charter was primarily drafted to subordinate the activity of regional organizations to the United Nations and to put the former under the control of the UN Security Council. At the same time, the Charter does not provide for exact mechanisms of cooperation between the United Nations and regional organizations and only sets forth some possibilities of control from the side of the UN Security Council.

As discussed in Chapter 3, the wording of the Charter is formulated to ensure the possibility of both preventive and *post facto* control. As concerns preventive control, it is necessary to mention provisions of art. 53(1) stipulating the right of the Security Council to "*utilize, where appropriate, such regional arrangements or agencies for enforcement action under its authority*" as well as the need for prior authorization for any enforcement action.[590] The supreme role of the Security Council follows from art. 54 of the UN Charter as well. It is formulated in such a way ("*The Security Council shall at all times be kept fully informed of activities undertaken or in contemplation under regional arrangements or by regional agencies for the maintenance of international peace and security*") as to grant the Security Council powers not only to intervene in the activities undertaken, to control them and to decide on their legality (*post facto* control), but also to prevent activity it considers unsuitable. The obligation of art. 54 is duplicated and supplemented by the obligation of art. 51 to inform the Security Council immediately upon taking any measures in self-defense.

As noted in the earlier chapters of this book, the establishment of the United Nations as the universal system of collective security with regional organizations as elements of this system, endowing the Security Council with primary responsibility for maintaining international peace and security

[590] See Geyrhalter B., *Friedenssicherung durch Regionalorganizationen*, *op. cit.*, p. 68; Sarooshi D., *The United Nations and the Development of Collective Security*, *op. cit.*, p. 250.

and introducing the general prohibitions on the use of force in international relations and intervening in the domestic affairs of states, demonstrate the subsidiary role of regional organizations in the sphere of maintenance of international peace and security. Regional organizations, however, have preserved their autonomy (and even enjoy priority toward the Security Council) in the sphere of peaceful settlement of international disputes (art. 52(2)) as well as in any other activity "*relating to the maintenance of international peace and security as are appropriate for regional action*" (art. 52(1)), aside from enforcement action in accordance with art. 53(1)). The possibility to act in collective self-defense through regional organizations "*until the Security Council has taken measures necessary to maintain international peace and security*" is also directly provided for in the UN Charter (art. 51).

The Security Council was to keep full control over the application of any enforcement measures (art. 53(1)), and be fully informed about any measures taken in self-defense (art. 51) as well as about any measures taken for, or in contemplation of, the maintenance of international peace and security (art. 54). Despite the priority of regional organizations in the peaceful settlement of international disputes under art. 52(2), the Security Council may take any regional dispute into consideration, although not for settling it but rather to recommend means for its resolution (art. 34, 35(1), 36(1)). It is still often insisted that despite the changes observed in the international arena, the Security Council shall exercise full control over regional action.[591] In reality, however, this control is hardly possible and does not take a form of operational command even as concerns enforcement action.

Regular Mechanisms of Cooperation between the UN and Regional Organizations

Every international organization develops its own rules and practices on cooperation with other actors. The current study provides an overview of the mechanisms and procedures formed within the UN.

During the Cold War, the problem of cooperation between the Security Council and regional organizations was not discussed within the UN. The need for cooperation was first mentioned in UN documents in the

[591] Sarooshi D., *The United Nations and the Development of Collective Security*, *op. cit.*, p. 249.

last decade of the 20th century.[592] On 28 January 1993, the Security Council invited regional organizations to consider methods of enhancing the coordination of their activity with that of the Security Council.[593] In its statement of 3 May 1994, the President of the Council indicated the need to consider, among other factors, when deciding on the establishment of new peacekeeping operations "*whether regional or subregional organizations and arrangements exist and are ready and able to assist in resolving the situation*."[594] The same year, the first high-level meeting between the UN Secretary-General and secretaries-general of regional security organizations took place. Since 2005 they have occurred annually under the coordination of six working groups and a permanent committee that was established in 2004.[595] In 2003 the UN Security Council held the first thematic debates with the participation of selected regional organizations (initially the AU, ECOWAS, EU, LAS, OSCE and OAS; since 2004 the CIS has also been included).[596] The last decade has also been characterized by regular meetings of the Security Council with states and organizations that contribute to specific UN missions.[597] Since 1995 the issue of cooperation with regional organizations has been included in the agendas of various UN institutions, including the Security Council,[598] the Secretary-General[599] and the General Assembly.[600] The latter, besides general issues of cooperation with regional

---

[592] Security Council Report, "The UN and Regional Organizations: Historical Chronology;" Report of the UN Secretary-General (S/2008/18), *op. cit.*, para. 4.

[593] Note by the President of the Security Council (S/25859), 28 May 1993.

[594] Statement by the President of the Security Council, S/PRST/1994/22, 3 May 1994.

[595] Security Council Update Report, 18 September 2006, No. 3, *op. cit.*, p.4; Proposals of the 6th High-Level Meeting. The Electronic Newsletter of the UN University CRIS; Report of the UN Secretary-General (S/2008/18), *op. cit.*, para. 8.

[596] Security Council Update Report, "The United Nations and Regional Organizations," No. 3, 23 March 2007, *op. cit.*

[597] See, *e.g.*, Meeting with countries contributing troops and police to the United Nations Integrated Mission in Timor-Leste – Official Communiqué, 9 February 2012; Meeting with countries contributing troops and police to the United Nations Disengagement Observer Force – Official Communiqué, 12 December 2011; Meeting with countries contributing troops and police to the UN Stabilization Mission in Haiti – Official Communiqué, 14 November 2011; Meeting with countries contributing troops and police to the African Union-United Nations Hybrid Operation in Darfur – Official Communique, 18 July 2011.

[598] See, *e.g.*, UN Security Council Resolutions 1631 (2005), *op. cit.*; 1809 (2008), *op. cit.*; 2033 (2012), *op. cit.*; Statements by the President of the Security Council, S/PRST/2007/42, *op. cit.*; S/PRST/2010/1, *op. cit.*; Security Council Meetings 6256, 13 January 2011 (S/PV.6256); 6306, 4 May 2011 (S/PV.6303); 6702, 12 January 2012 (S/PV.6702).

[599] Supplement to an Agenda for Peace, *op. cit.*; Report of the UN Secretary-General (S/2008/18), *op. cit.*; In Larger Freedom, *op. cit.*, paras. 213-215; Cooperation between the UN and Regional and Other Organizations, *op. cit.*

[600] Declaration on the Enhancement of Cooperation between the United Nations and Regional Arrangements, *op. cit.*

security organizations,[601] pays attention to cooperation with particular organizations.[602]

It shall thus be noted that after the end of the Cold War, the UN sought to intensify its cooperation with regional organizations under Chapter VIII in view of the inadequacy of the UN's own resources and the inability of the Security Council to handle conflicts around the world. Various documents proposed a range of forms and mechanisms of cooperation, including consultations, mutual diplomatic efforts, diplomatic and operational co-deployment, joint operations, financing of regional operations, mutual participation in the activity of coordinating organs, exchanges of information, conclusion of memorandums of understanding, standby agreements or formalized agreements between secretariats, involvement of organizations in the work of the UN Security Council, cooperation with the UN Peace-building Commission, participation in high-level meetings, *etc.*[603]

Practical Mechanisms of Cooperation between the UN and Regional Organizations

Despite these efforts, no comprehensive system has been established and cooperation is still exercised on an *ad hoc* basis.[604] The Security Council, as noted in its report on cooperation between the UN and regional

---

[601] *Ibid.;* Cooperation between the United Nations and Regional and Other Organizations, *op. cit.*; UN General Assembly Resolutions 66/36, 12 January 2012, *op. cit.*; 66/37, 12 January 2012, *op. cit.*; 66/38, 12 January 2012, *op. cit.*.

[602] *E.g.*, cooperation with NATO – UN General Assembly Resolutions 47/10, 28 October 1992, *op. cit.*; 48/19, 16 November 1993; cooperation with the Council of Europe – Resolutions 55/3, 20 October 2000; 56/43, 7 December 2001; 57/156, 16 December 2002; 59/139, 17 February 2005; 61/13, 8 December 2006; 65/130, 24 February 2011; with OSCE – Resolutions 49/13, 15 November 1994; 50/87, 18 December 1995, *op. cit.*; 51/57, 12 December 1996; 52/22, 25 November 1997; 53/85, 7 December 1998; 54/117, 15 December 1999; 55/179, 19 December 2000, *op. cit.*; 56/216, 21 December 2001; 57/298, 20 December 2002; 58/55, 8 December 2003, *op. cit.*; with CSTO – Resolutions 64/256, 2 March 2010, *op. cit.*; 65/122, 13 December 2010, *op. cit.*; with ShCO – Resolutions 64/183, 18 December 2009; 65/124, 13 December 2010.

[603] See Supplement to an Agenda for Peace, *op. cit.*, para. 86; Cooperation between the United Nations and Regional Organizations/Arrangements in a Peacekeeping Environment: Suggested Principles and Mechanisms, March 1999, para. 16; In Larger Freedom, *op. cit.*, paras. 213-215; UN Security Council Resolution 1631 (2005), *op. cit.*, paras 7-8; Proposals of the 6th High-Level Meeting, *op. cit.*; 2005 World Summit Outcome, *op. cit.*, para. 170; Statement by the President of the Security Council, S/PRST/2010/1, *op. cit.*, paras. 6, 7, 9; Report of the UN Secretary-General (S/2008/18), *op. cit.*, paras. 71-76.

[604] Supplement to an Agenda for Peace, *op. cit.*, para. 87; Security Council Update Report, "The United Nations and Regional Organizations," No. 3, 23 March 2007, *op. cit.*

organizations, does not consider the problem in general and still prefers to deal with it on a theoretical abstract level.[605] From a practical standpoint, the Security Council does not utilize regional organizations for its purposes but rather welcomes any activity they take for the maintenance of peace and security in a region.[606] An analysis of Security Council resolutions on European and Central Asian conflicts in the last 20 years provides a good illustration of this point. The Security Council hardly ever refers to Chapter VIII in its resolutions (the only three exceptions were mentioned earlier) and authorizes states (acting individually or through regional organizations) rather than regional organizations directly.[607] Regional organizations are free to decide on their involvement in a conflict.[608] The Security Council takes account of their documents and decisions[609] and adapts the mandate, financing and competences of the UN's missions to those of the regional organizations.[610] Cooperation with or between regional organizations is welcomed but no forms or mechanisms are ever imposed.[611] The Security

---

[605] Security Council Update Report, 18 September 2006, No. 3, *op. cit.*; Security Council Update Report No. 2, "UN Cooperation with Regional and Sub-regional Organizations and Conflict Prevention," 14 April 2008.

[606] See, *e.g.*, UN Security Council Resolutions 1423 (2002), *op. cit.*, para. 20; 1575 (2004), *op. cit.*, para. 11; 1150 (1998), *op. cit.*, preamble; 1187 (1998), *op. cit.*, preamble; 1225 (1999), *op. cit.*, preamble; 1371 (2001), *op. cit.*, preamble.

[607] UN Security Council Resolutions 1031 (1995), *op. cit.*, paras. 14-17, 36; 1247 (1999), *op. cit.*, paras. 10-13; 1575 (2004), *op. cit.*, paras. 10, 14-16; 1785 (2007), *op. cit.*, paras. 10, 14-16; 1948 (2010), *op. cit.*, paras. 10, 14-16; 1973 (2011), *op. cit.*, paras. 4, 8, 15.

[608] UN Security Council Resolutions 1311 (2000), *op. cit.*, preamble; 999 (1995), 16 June 1995, preamble; 937 (1994), 21 July 1994, preamble; 1427 (2002), *op. cit.*, preamble.

[609] UN Security Council Resolutions 937 (1994), *op. cit.*, preamble; 959 (1994), 19 November 1994, preamble; 1551 (2004), *op. cit.*, preamble. This also includes documents and decisions that concern particular situations – *e.g.*, Resolutions 1575 (2004), *op. cit.*, preamble; 1639 (2005), *op. cit.*, preamble; 1722 (2006), 21 November 2006, preamble; 1895 (2009), *op. cit.*, preamble; 999 (1995), preamble; 1036 (1996), 12 January 1996, preamble; 1065 (1996), 12 July 1996, preamble, para. 12; 1255 (1999), *op. cit.*, preamble; 1287 (2000), *op. cit.*, preamble; 1339 (2001), *op. cit.*, preamble; 1393 (2002), *op. cit.*, preamble; 1462 (2003), *op. cit.*, preamble; 1524 (2004), *op. cit.*, preamble; 1554 (2004), *op. cit.*, preamble; 1582 (2005), *op. cit.*, preamble; 1615 (2005), *op. cit.*, preamble.

[610] UN Security Council Resolutions 993 (1995), 12 May 1995, para. 2; 1036 (1996), *op. cit.*, para. 11; 1255 (1999), *op. cit.*, para. 12; 1287 (2000), *op. cit.*, para. 11; 1311 (2000), *op. cit.*, para. 13; 1364 (2001), *op. cit.*, para. 20; 1393 (2002), *op. cit.*, para. 17; 1462 (2003), *op. cit.*, para. 20; 1524 (2004), *op. cit.*, para. 29; 1554 (2004), *op. cit.*, para. 28; 1582 (2005), *op. cit.*, para. 31; 1615 (2005), *op. cit.*, para. 33; 1666 (2006), 31 March 2006, para. 11.

[611] UN Security Council Resolutions 1206 (1998), 12 November 1998, preamble; 1240 (1999), 15 May 1999, preamble; 1274 (1999), 12 November 1999, preamble; 937 (1994), *op. cit.*, preamble; 999 (1995), preamble, para. 13; 1030 (1995), 14 December 1995, preamble, para. 13; 1061 (1996), 14 June 1996, preamble; 1089 (1996), 13 December 1996, preamble; 1036 (1996), *op. cit.*, preamble; 1065 (1996), *op. cit.*, preamble; 1225 (1999), *op. cit.*, preamble; 1255 (1999), *op. cit.*, preamble; 1287 (2000), *op. cit.*, preamble; 1311 (2000), *op. cit.*, preamble; 1666 (2006), *op. cit.*, preamble; 1808 (2008), 15 April 2008, preamble; 1339

Council does not even require regional organizations to submit information on their activity in accordance with art. 54 of the UN Charter. This obligation is transferred to states[612] or to the UN Secretary-General.[613]

It could thus be concluded that since the end of the Cold War, the Security Council has appeared unable to stay in command of regional action. It preserves some control over the legality of actions taken by regional organizations and ensures minimal security standards for their in-field personnel,[614] while the latter are encouraged to take on the burden of practical action. All of this has resulted in a situation in which the Security Council is not viewed as a key player in the security area and its authority is recognized to be limited to a moral one.[615]

The system of relations between the UN Security Council and regional organizations has moved from one of pure subsidiarity to one that involves a combination of subsidiarity (Security Council control over regional action) and complementarity[616] (distribution of tasks in view of the UN system proving unable to handle alone all problems in the sphere of maintenance of international peace and security). The Security Council is viewed more and more often as a control body demonstrating political support, coordination and technical assistance.[617] Even in UN documents, regional organizations are viewed as partners rather than supplements.[618] The

---

(2001), *op. cit.*, preamble; 1393 (2002), *op. cit.*, preamble; 1462 (2003), *op. cit.*, preamble; 1524 (2004), *op. cit.*, preamble; 1554 (2004), *op. cit.*, preamble; 1582 (2005), *op. cit.*, preamble; 1615 (2005), *op. cit.*, preamble.

612 *E.g.*, UN Security Council Resolutions 787 (1992), *op. cit.*, para. 14; 816 (1993), *op. cit.*, para. 7; 1031 (1995), *op. cit.*, para. 25; 1247 (1999), *op. cit.*, para. 18; 1305 (2000), *op. cit.*, para. 18; 1575 (2004), *op. cit.*, para. 18; 1639 (2005), *op. cit.*, para. 18; 1722 (2006), *op. cit.*, para. 18; 1845 (2008), *op. cit.*, para. 18; 1895 (2009), *op. cit.*, para. 18; 1948 (2010), *op. cit.*, para. 18; 1174 (1998), 15 June 1998, para. 18.

613 UN Security Council Resolutions 934 (1994), *op. cit.*, para. 4; 1808 (2008), *op. cit.*, para. 15; 822 (1993), 30 April 1993, para. 4; 853 (1993), 29 July 1993, para. 13.

614 UN Security Council Resolutions 1174 (1998), *op. cit.*, paras. 15-16; 1247 (1999), *op. cit.*, para. 15; 1551 (2004), *op. cit.*, para. 17; 1575 (2004), *op. cit.*, para. 17; 1785 (2007), *op. cit.*, para. 17; 1895 (2009), *op. cit.*, para. 17; 1206 (1998), *op. cit.*, para. 7; 1274 (1999), *op. cit.*, para. 8; 1167 (1998), 14 May 1998, para. 6; 993 (1995), *op. cit.*, preamble, para. 8; 1036 (1996), *op. cit.*, para. 8; 1339 (2001), *op. cit.*, para. 12; 1393 (2002), *op. cit.*, para. 14; 1427 (2002), *op. cit.*, para. 16; 1524 (2004), *op. cit.*, paras. 26, 27; 1582 (2005), *op. cit.*, para. 28; 1615 (2005), *op. cit.*, paras. 28-30; 1808 (2008), *op. cit.*, para. 14.

615 Alagappa M., "Regional Arrangements, the UN and International Security," *op. cit.*, p. 22.

616 The need for complementary roles is underlined in, *e.g.*, In Larger Freedom, *op. cit.*, para. 213; UN Security Council Resolutions 1631 (2005), *op. cit.*, preamble; 1809 (2008), *op. cit.*, para. 1; 2033 (2012), *op. cit.*

617 See Statement by the President of the Security Council, S/PRST/2007/42, *op. cit.*

618 Report of the UN Secretary-General (S/2008/18), *op. cit.*, paras. 8, 11; UN Security Council Resolution 2033 (2012), *op. cit.*, preamble, para. 5. The same approach is generally expressed by states in the course of discussions within the UN; see Security Council Meeting

Security Council even talks about "*regional-global partnership*."[619] At the same time, regional efforts are viewed as a part of the UN mechanism[620] with an invariable accent on the Security Council's primary responsibility for the maintenance of international peace and security.[621]

Cooperation between Regional Organizations

In the course of analyzing the collective security model, it is also necessary to consider "horizontal" cooperation – that is, cooperation between regional organizations in activities aimed at maintaining international peace and security, the need for which is repeatedly acknowledged by the UN Security Council[622] (for systems of organizations involved in the maintenance of international peace and security in the European and European-Central Asian areas, see Annexes 2 and 3).

An examination of this should not be limited to analyzing the cooperation of regional organizations in the same region. On the contrary, practice demonstrates that organizations from different regions more and more often take part in operations in and beyond the borders of their members. As the result, there is an urgent need to develop mechanisms or at least simple algorithms of cooperation between participating organizations, at least in the course of ongoing operations.[623]

In reality, however, despite the Security Council's acceptance and welcome of cooperation and coordination between regional organizations, it has never imposed or even proposed any form or mechanism, even in the course of active operations under its control. As a result, every international organization develops its own rules and practices of cooperation with other actors. Practical cooperation between organizations is rather poor. Due to the

6702, *op. cit.*. M. Karns notes four different forms of interaction: the delegation of powers by the UN Security Council, purely regional initiatives, partnerships and non-collaboration (Karns M.P., "The Challenges of Maintaining Peace and Security in the 21st Century: The United Nations and Regional Organizations," in *The United Nations: Past, Present and Future: Proceedings of the 2007 Francis Marion University UN Symposium*, ed. S Kaufman, A. Warters (New York: Nova Science Publishers Inc., 2009), p. 125-129).

619 Report of the UN Secretary-General (S/2008/18), *op. cit.*, para. 11.

620 UN Security Council Resolutions 1631 (2005), *op. cit.*, preamble; 2033 (2012), *op. cit.*, para. 1.

621 See UN Security Council Resolutions 1631 (2005), *op. cit.*, preamble; 1809 (2008), *op. cit.*, preamble; 2033 (2012), *op. cit.*, preamble; Statement by the President of the Security Council, S/PRST/2007/42, *op. cit.* See also Wilson G., "Regional Arrangements as Agents of the UN Security Council," *op. cit.*, p. 183.

622 UN Security Council Resolution 2033 (2012), *op. cit.*, preamble, para. 3.

623 On the definition of prior tasks of specific regional organizations, see Wilson G., "Regional Arrangements as Agents of the UN Security Council," *op. cit.*, p. 191-201.

existence of the large number of international organizations with concurrent or intersecting membership and similar or associated functions, it often appears that either several organizations or none that are willing to act may be found in every particular case or conflict.

The need to take into account the weaknesses and strengths of the various organizations (both vertically between the UN and regional organizations, and horizontally between regional organizations) as well as the need to distribute tasks and activities on the basis of complementarity[624] are generally acknowledged *pro forma* in the documents of the regional organizations[625] as well as in the legal doctrine.[626] The Russian Federation has even proposed establishing a special body (the European Security Council) for coordinating the positions of international organizations acting in the European area.[627] In reality, as noted in the Report of the UN Secretary-General on cooperation with regional and other organizations in 2010, at least some periodic contacts have been established, although only with the AU, OSCE and EU.[628]

It is thus high time to create stable mechanisms for cooperation and the distribution of tasks and competences between organizations within the same and adjacent regions, as well as algorithms for cooperation between organizations involved in the same conflict. This would preclude the establishment of duplicate functions and mechanisms and the expansion of redundant ones that already exist, each with organizational structures, bureaucratic machinery and corresponding expenses.

---

[624] See India's position in Security Council Meeting 6702, *op. cit.*; Statement by the President of the Security Council, S/PRST/2007/42, *op. cit.*

[625] Security Council Meeting 6257, *op. cit.*; Security Council Meeting 6702, *op. cit.*; UN Security Council Resolution 2033 (2012), *op. cit.*, paras. 7, 14; Security Council Update Report, 14 April 2008, No. 2, *op. cit.*; Report of the UN Secretary-General (S/2008/18), *op. cit.*, para. 71(d).

[626] Weiss T.G. *et al.*, *The United Nations and Changing World Politics*, *op. cit.*, p. 23.

[627] Проект Договора о европейской безопасности [Draft European Security Treaty], *International Security and Control over Armaments. Herald of Diplomatic Academy of the MFA of Russia*, (2010), p. 97-98, para. 4; Андреев М.В., "Современные проблемы обеспечения Евразийской безопасности в контексте выработки нового межгосударственного соглашения" [Andreev M.V., "Contemporary Problems of Ensuring European Security in the Context of the Elaboration of a New Interstate Agreement"], *International Security and Control over Armaments. Herald of the Diplomatic Academy of the MFA of Russia*, (2010), p. 89.

[628] Cooperation between the United Nations and Regional and Other Organizations, *op. cit.*

4.2 Regeneration of the System of Collective Security

It is universally recognized that the UN system is currently in crisis. The voices that speak of its obsolesce and redundancy are clearly heard. At the same time, the rejection of the existing system of maintenance of international peace and security could hardly be expected to result in the establishment of new stable mechanisms in the sphere. The UN Security Council, initially planned to embody the balance of military power[629] between superpowers, is currently more characterized by the word "imbalance."[630] This feature concerns not only the unsatisfactory distribution of permanent positions, but also the formality and lack of feasibility of the Security Council's control functions.

This all brings me to the conclusion that is generally advanced about the need for the UN reform,[631] which has a history dating back to the early 1960s[632] (in particular, the first amendment to the Charter came into force on 31 August 1961). Amendments since then have primarily concerned the number of members of the Security Council and the Economic and Social Council,[633] but have not changed the fundamentals of the United Nations.

It is not advocated here that the whole UN system be dissolved and built anew. On the contrary, I believe that a shift in approach toward the distribution and operational exercise of UN powers and functions without formal amendments to the UN Charter would be sufficient.

Attention is to be paid to two major themes: promoting respect and adherence to the rule of law in the international arena, and functional reform of the UN Security Council.

---

[629] Klabbers J., "The Politics of Institutional Reform," in *United Nations Reform and the New Collective Security*, ed. P.G. Danchin, H. Fisher, (Cambridge: Cambridge University Press, 2010), p. 80-81; Mälksoo L., "Great Powers Then and Now: Security Council Reform and Responses to Threats to Peace and Security," in *United Nations Reform and the New Collective Security,* ed. P.G. Danchin, H. Fisher, (Cambridge: Cambridge University Press, 2010), p. 105.

[630] See Morris J., "UN Security Council Reform: A Counsel for the 21st Century," *Security Dialogue*, 31(3) (2000), p. 266.

[631] Franck T.M. "Collective Security and UN Reform," *op. cit.*, p. 598; Karns M.P., Mingst K.A., *International Organizations*, *op. cit.*, p. 133; Dicke K., "Reform of the United Nations," in *United Nations: Law, Politics and Practice*, ed. R. Wolfrum, (Munich: Verlag C.H. Beck, 1995), p. 1012-1024.

[632] *Ibid.*, p. 1014.

[633] See Charter of the United Nations. Introductory Note.

Promoting Respect and Adherence to the Rule of Law

The very idea of adherence to the rule of law is not new in the international legal doctrine. It is generally agreed to be an inalienable prerequisite of the functioning of the system of collective security.[634] As noted by P.G. Dachin, "*the idea of collective security is premised at some level on the efficacy of the idea of the rule of law in international relations*," based on the autonomy of international legal rules.[635]

It is also obvious that no progress in promoting the rule of law in the sphere of maintenance of international peace and security can ever be achieved without enhancing the legality and credibility of the UN Security Council, which is today widely regarded as having legitimacy problems.[636]

The Security Council does not possess any judicial or norm-creating functions.[637] At the same time, due to its primary responsibility in the sphere of maintenance of international peace and security and the composition of its permanent members, the Council has repeatedly assessed particular situations in the sphere and expressed its approach to them: condemned, welcomed, supported, *etc.* As a result, it has started to be viewed as the last resort in assessing the legality of situations in the international arena[638] (quasi-judicial functions).[639] Its activity and resolutions are viewed as establishing (although indirectly) quasi-rules of behavior for other international actors.[640]

Uncertainty and doubts about the legality and credibility of the Security Council give rise to serious abuse by regional organizations and

---

[634] United Nations Millennium Declaration, A/55/2, 8 September 2000, paras. 7, 9; 2005 World Summit Outcome, *op. cit.*, paras. 11, 119, 134; *A More Secure World*, *op. cit.*, p. 66, para. 204; Nye J.S., *Understanding International Conflicts*, *op. cit.*, p. 83; UN General Assembly Resolution 66/102, 13 January 2012.

[635] Danchin P.G., "Things Fall Apart," *op. cit.*, p. 51-55.

[636] See, *e.g.*, Mälksoo L., "Great Powers Then and Now," *op. cit.*, p. 94.

[637] Каламкарян Р.А., *Кодификация международного права и современный миропорядок* [Kalamkarjan R.A., *Codification of International Law and Contemporary Legal Order*] (Moscow: Science, 2008), p. 112; Bianchi A., "Assessing the Effectiveness of the UN Security Council's Anti-terrorism Measures," *op. cit.*, p. 889; Military and Paramilitary Activities in and against Nicaragua, 1984, *op. cit.*, p. 435.

[638] Alvarez J.E., *International Organizations as Law-Makers*, *op. cit.*, p. 188-189.

[639] *Ibid.*, p.188-189; Farral J.M., *United Nations Sanctions and the Rule of Law*, *op. cit.*, p. 17.

[640] Amerasinghe C.F., *Principles of the Institutional Law of International Organizations*, 2nd ed. (Cambridge: Cambridge University Press, 2005), p. 184-198; Farral J.M., *United Nations Sanctions and the Rule of Law*, *op. cit.*, p. 16-17, 19; Eitel T., "The UN Security Council and its Future Contribution in the Field of International Law," *Max Planck Yearbook of United Nations Law*, 2000, p. 60-61; Klabbers J., "The Politics of Institutional Reform," *op. cit.*, p. 83.

individual states.[641] The control mechanisms of the Security Council, as with any control mechanisms, are only acceptable and effective if they act in accordance with international legal norms.[642] As rightly noted in the Report of the High Panel on Threats, Challenges and Change (2004), legality in the sphere of maintenance of international peace and security may only be achieved through the legality of the UN Security Council itself in conjunction with the establishment of clear principles and standards (para. 83). Consequently, the enhancement of the rule of law in the international arena is not possible without effective control over the UN Security Council[643] – and this creates a big problem.

As opposed to national legal systems, the UN Charter provides for no mechanism for the balance of power. Apparently no body is entitled to judge the legality of acts of the Security Council, or to control or review them,[644] although the need for it – especially as concerns decisions directly affecting private individuals – is generally recognized.[645] As correctly noted by Professor M.W. Reisman, the "primary responsibility" of the UN Security Council for the maintenance of international peace and security confer it with supreme powers, the so-called "*last word*" in the situations listed in art. 39.[646] Despite repeated attempts by international and national courts to decide on the legality of Security Council sanctions (especially as concerns

[641] L. van den Herik correctly notes that divergent state practice may be condemned only if guarantees of fair adjudication are established and followed at the international level; see Herik L. van den, "The Security Council's Targeted Sanctions Regimes," *op. cit.*, p. 802; Abass A. *Regional Organizations and the Development of Collective Security*, *op. cit.*, p. 97; Thakur R., *The United Nations, Peace and Security*, *op. cit.*, p. 345; Brunneé J., "The Security Council and Self-Defence: Which Way to Global Security?" in *The Security Council and the Use of Force: Theory and Reality – the Need for Change*, ed. N. Blokker, N. Schrijver, (Leiden: Martinus Nijhoff Publishers, 2005), p. 114.

[642] See also Валеев Р.М., "Роль контроля в системе международного сотрудничества государств в XXI веке" [Valeev R.M., "The Role of Control in the System of International Cooperation in the XXI Century"], *Russian Yearbook of International Law*, 2001, p. 40.

[643] See Thakur R., *The United Nations, Peace and Security, op. cit.*, p. 346; *A More Secure World*, *op. cit.*, p. 80, para. 249(d).

[644] Already during the drafting of the UN Charter, some proposals were made to establish special control mechanisms, *e.g.*, through the General Assembly; see *Documents of the UN Conference on International Organization*, vol. I., *op. cit.*, p. 202; Frowein J.A., "Reactions by Not Directly Affected States," *op. cit.*, p. 383. It is sometimes maintained that the General Assembly and the ICJ have developed some rudimentary control competences; see Reisman M.W., "The Constitutional Crisis in the United Nations," *American Journal of International Law,* 87(1) (1993), p. 84; Cannizaro E., "A Machiavellian Moment?, *op. cit.*, p. 192.

[645] Cannizaro E., "A Machiavellian Moment?, *op. cit.*, p. 198-199.

[646] Reisman M.W., "The Constitutional Crisis in the United Nations," *op. cit.*, p. 88.

targeted sanctions),[647] these institutions have unanimously determined they have no competence to cancel or change the decisions under consideration. Even the ICJ, in the preliminary objections in the Lockerbie case, preferred not to go too deeply in correlating treaty obligations and decisions of the Security Council (paras. 36-37, 43).[648] Formally, the Council is bound (as noted above) by the purposes and principles of the United Nations, peremptory norms of general international law and UN Charter rules as well as customary rules of international law.[649] In reality, however, no feasible mechanism of control over its activity exists.

Most of the mechanisms proposed in the legal doctrine have only theoretical value. For example, attempts to develop criteria for assessing the legality of Security Council actions[650] do not imply the establishment of a mechanism for their application. The idea that has been asserted the most, the possibility to invalidate an action of the Security Council through a decision taken by an overwhelming majority of UN member states,[651] may hardly be achieved due to the representation of the five major powers in the Council.

The only feasible mechanism may be established by endowing the ICJ with the so called "*role of legalist*" in the international legal system, able to control the legality of the UN Security Council's actions.[652] The ICJ has even been called a potential "*guardian of legality for the international community as a whole, within and without the United Nations.*"[653]

---

[647] Kadi v. Council and Commission, *op. cit.*; Yusuf and al Barakaat International Foundation, *op. cit.*; See also Herik L. van den, "The Security Council's Targeted Sanctions Regimes," *op. cit.*, p. 799.

[648] Case Concerning Questions of Interpretation and Application of the 1971 Montreal Convention Arising from the Aerial Incident at Lockerbie, Judgment of 27 February 1998, Preliminary Objections, *I.C.J. Reports 1998*, (The Hague: I.C.J., 1998), p. 128-131; Reisman M.W., "The Constitutional Crisis in the United Nations," *op. cit.*, p. 87.

[649] O'Connell M.A., "The United Nations Security Council and the Authorization of Force: Renewing the Council through Law Reform," in *The Security Council and the Use of Force: Theory and Reality – A Need for Challenge?*, ed. N. Blokker and N. Schrijver, (Leiden/Boston: Martinus Nijhoff Publishers, 2005), p. 58; Doehring K., "Unlawful Resolutions of the Security Council," *op. cit.*, p. 92-93; Orakhelashvili A., "The Impact of Peremptory Norms," *op. cit.*, p. 60-62; Farral J.M., *United Nations Sanctions and the Rule of Law*, *op. cit.*, p. 21; Orakhelashvili A., *Peremptory Norms in International Law*, *op. cit.*, p. 425.

[650] O'Connell M.A., "The United Nations Security Council," *op. cit.*, p. 58-61.

[651] Abass A. *Regional Organizations and the Development of Collective Security*, *op. cit.*, p. 98.

[652] Kalamkarjan R.A., *Codification of International Law*, *op. cit.*, p. 104.

[653] Case Concerning Questions of Interpretation and Application of the 1971 Montreal Convention Arising from the Aerial Incident at Lockerbie, Separate Opinion of Judge Lachs, *I.C.J. Reports 1992*, (The Hague: I.C.J., 1992), p. 138.

Currently, the ICJ does not posses this function. Moreover, there is no universal approach to the ICJ's involvement. For example, R.A. Kalamkarjan talks about possible parallel or successive consideration of cases[654] that guarantee thorough consideration of disputes in both the legal and political senses[655] but does not entail ICJ control over the activity of the Security Council. E. Cannizzaro mentions that the ICJ may assess incidentally the legality of Security Council resolutions in the course of its dispute settlement functions or when it passes an advisory opinion.[656] His conclusions, however, relate only to incidental reviews in the course of other proceedings and do not involve the establishment of a mechanism for reviewing legality.

It is maintained here that the most effective mechanism for reviewing the legality of UN Security Council resolutions may be organized within the ICJ's advisory jurisdiction. Analogously to regional courts, it may be granted with competences to give advisory opinions on the correspondence of Security Council resolutions to peremptory norms of international law and to the Council's own competence, upon the request of currently authorized subjects as well as states.[657] Resolutions taken in breach of *jus cogens* norms and *ultra vires* would become void from the moment the opinion of the ICJ is issued. The operation of resolutions should not, however, be suspended as soon as a request for an advisory opinion is laid before the ICJ, to prevent possible misuses of this right on the part of affected states.

Functional Reform of the UN Security Council

Proposals on reforming the UN Security Council take different forms and may concern different spheres. For example, R. Thakur insists on the need for enhancing the legality, credibility, trust, efficacy and readiness to assist, the introduction of control mechanisms as well as the maintenance of a geographical balance.[658] Other proposals have concerned the improvement of the decision-making process in the Council, *e.g.*, a prohibition on invoking the veto in certain situations,[659] a prohibition on

---

[654] Kalamkarjan R.A., *Codification of International Law*, *op. cit.*, p. 113.
[655] *Ibid.*, p. 125-126.
[656] Cannizaro E., "A Machiavellian Moment?, *op. cit.*, p. 195-196.
[657] The ICJ and the UN Security Council have already been simultaneously involved in considering the same issues, *e.g.*, Lockerbie case (1998), Hostages case (1980), Corfu Channel case (1946), Nicaragua case (1984, 1986); Genocide case (1993, 1996).
[658] See. Thakur R., *The United Nations, Peace and Security*, *op. cit.*, p. 302-303, 306; *A More Secure World*, *op. cit.*, p. 64, 66, paras. 197, 202.
[659] Franck T.M. "Collective Security and UN Reform," *op. cit.*, p. 609-610.

using the veto at all,[660] a reduction of the number of concurrent permanent members to three,[661] *etc.* Special attention has always been paid to the expansion of the membership of the UN Security Council[662] (structural reform), although the need for both structural and functional changes was recognized by the High-Level Panel on Threats, Challenges and Change.[663]

Remarkably, certain "new" proposals for UN Security Council reform – the limitation of its competences, the elimination of its control over regional actions, an expansion of the Council's membership – had already been discussed and rejected at the San Francisco conference in 1945.[664]

At the same time, the aspiration for structural reform does not seek that much to enhance the Security Council's legality and effectiveness,[665] but rather reflects the aspiration of new superpowers to secure their share in the distribution of military powers and to shield themselves from any application of sanctions against them. Due to this motivation, any attempts to restructure the Security Council (despite the general agreement on the need for its restructuring) are doomed to fail.[666] As a result, functional reform remains the only available means of revitalizing the system of collective security.

Before I start to analize the necessary elements of functional reform of the Security Council, I want to cite the opinion of professor T. Franck, who emphasized that "*the Charter does establish norms, procedures and process for implementing collective security*."[667] I will also agree that the UN Charter has been repeatedly reinterpreted in the course of changes in the international arena, and is able to adapt to the current situation as well.[668] It

---

[660] See Thakur R., *The United Nations, Peace and Security*, *op. cit.*, p. 306-307.

[661] US proposal in the 1950s, cited by Johnson C.H., Niemeyer G., "Collective Security," *op. cit.*, p. 24.

[662] *A More Secure World*, *op. cit.*, p. 80, para. 250; Thakur R., *The United Nations, Peace and Security*, *op. cit.*, p. 303-305; Karns M.P., Mingst K.A., *International Organizations*, *op. cit.*, p. 133-134; Graham K., "Regionalism and Responses to Armed Conflict," *op. cit.*, p. 179-180; Blokker N., "Towards the Second Enlargement of the Security Council? A Comparative Perspective," in *The Security Council and the Use of Force: Theory and Reality – A Need for Challenge?*, ed. N. Blokker and N. Schrijver, (Leiden/Boston: Martinus Nijhoff Publishers, 2005), p. 253-260; Morris J., "UN Security Council Reform," *op. cit.*, p. 272; Klabbers J., "The Politics of Institutional Reform," *op. cit.*, 76-93.

[663] *A More Secure World*, *op. cit.*, p. 80, para. 249.

[664] Sakrasena K.P., *The United Nations and Collective Security*, *op. cit.*, p. 32.

[665] See, *inter alia*, Klabbers J., "The Politics of Institutional Reform," *op. cit.*, p. 84.

[666] Thakur R., *The United Nations, Peace and Security*, *op. cit.*, p. 303.

[667] Franck T.M. "Collective Security and UN Reform," *op. cit.*, p. 598.

[668] As professor T.M. Frank correctly noted, "*when one looks at the system of collective security set out in the 1945 Charter, it is possible to conclude that there is not much wrong with it that could not be fixed by creative reinterpretation of obsolete norms*" (Franck T.M. "Collective Security and UN Reform," *op. cit.*, p. 605-606, 611).

is only necessary to recognize and accept the realities of the 21st century as well as to bring them under the control of the Charter's rules through the reinterpretation of Charter provisions. There is no need to develop detailed rules on coordination and cooperation between the UN and regional organizations and to insert them in the existing UN Charter. One should, however, avoid excessive arbitrariness in its reinterpretation, although sometimes an interpretation may need to be rather broad.[669] It should, in any case, be done with due regard to the purposes and principles of the United Nations, with the principles of subsidiarity[670] and complementarity in mind.

The purpose of Chapter VIII of the UN Charter was to bring regional organizations under the control of the UN Security Council. The UN Charter already recognizes the possibility for *ad hoc* and permanent institutions and arrangements with limited membership to act in the sphere of maintenance of international peace and security at the regional level – and as a result, Chapter VIII affects all entities as far as they are involved in the maintenance of international peace and security. The Charter does not need any improvement, either, with respect to the scope of possible activities of these organizations, as it does not limit their activities to a strict list and it does not prevent organizations with broader competence from being involved in security matters. The obligation to act in accordance with the UN's purposes and principles and specific obligations arising from the UN Charter are among the fundamentals of the current world order and should be unquestionably observed.

The UN Charter clearly provides for the decisive role of the Security Council as concerns the application of enforcement action. And this is the only limitation that preserves the supreme role of the Security Council and allows for its control over the legality of regional action. No action (military or non-military) apart from those which may legally be taken by member states of regional organizations may ever be taken under any conditions without the express clear and prior authorization of the Security Council. At the same time, the primary responsibility of the Security Council for the maintenance of international peace and security does not unequivocally mean it has the responsibility and obligation to take every field action itself.[671]

---

[669] Кирн Р., "Глава VIII Устава ООН: необходимость более широкой интерпретации" [Kirn R., "Chapter VIII of the UN Charter: The Need for Broader Interpretation"], *International Public and Private Law*, 1 (2003), p. 13.

[670] See, *inter alia*, Knight W.A., "Towards a Subsidiarity Model," *op. cit.*, p. 47.

[671] In the report of the High Level Panel it is called a "*redistribution of duties towards controlling and assessment functions of the UN Security Council*" (*A More Secure World*, *op. cit.*, p. 32, para. 81).

In light of the increasing number of contemporary threats and challenges, the Security Council is to keep its authorization, control,[672] supervision and coordination functions, while all (or most) field activity is carried out by regional organizations and individual states.[673] The Security Council will only be operationally involved when regional organizations prove unable to handle a specific situation.[674]

Obligation to Report in Accordance with art. 54 of the UN Charter

In the course of functional reform of the Security Council, special attention should be paid to the reinterpretation of the obligation to inform in accordance with art. 54 of the UN Charter. Art. 54 imposes on regional organizations the obligation to report on "*activities undertaken or in contemplation under regional arrangements or by regional agencies for the maintenance of international peace and security*." Formally, this obligation is still in full force as concerns any act of any regional organization involved in the maintenance of international peace and security.[675]

At the same time, it should be remembered that today many more entities fall under the legal regime of regional organizations in accordance with Chapter VIII, and regional organizations in their turn own much broader competence in the sphere of maintenance of international peace and security than that foreseen in 1945. As a result, M. Akehurst already noted as far back as 1967 that compliance with art. 54 has become "*virtually optional*" because of the difficulty in distinguishing between organizations under Chapter VIII and other regional organizations.[676] It is believed here, however, that this distinction is not of substantial importance. Regardless of whether the competence of an international organization in the security area is primary or secondary, or even if the organization has an *ad hoc* character, the obligation to report under art. 54 should concern its activities that pertain to maintaining international peace and security.

Despite its clearly practical application, the issue of how art. 54 is interpreted is analyzed in the legal doctrine in a simplified way. The aspect

---

[672] Danchin P.G., "Things Fall Apart," *op. cit.*, p. 45.
[673] G. Wilson even calls them "military agents" of the UN Security Council (Wilson G., "Regional Arrangements as Agents of the UN Security Council," *op. cit.*, p. 184). W.A. Knight talks about a "*division of labor*" (Knight W.A., "Towards a Subsidiarity Model," *op. cit.*, p. 32-33; Alagappa M., "Regional Arrangements, the UN and International Security," *op. cit.*, p. 23).
[674] See, e.g., Luck E.C., "Regional Arrangements," *op. cit.*, p. 239.
[675] See, *e.g.*, UN Security Council Resolution 1631 (2005), *op. cit.*, para. 9.
[676] Akehurst M., "Enforcement Action of Regional Organizations," *op. cit.*, p. 183.

that is discussed the most relates to the correlation of the obligation to inform under art. 54 with art. 51.[677] In reality, however, due to the unclear nature of regional organizations and difficulties in establishing which are the responsible actors, the obligation under art. 54 has become nearly declaratory. In its resolutions, the UN Security Council does not even demand that regional organizations submit information on their activity in accordance with art. 54. As noted above, this obligation is transferred to states[678] or to the UN Secretary-General.[679]

The broadening of competences of regional organizations with respect to the maintenance of international peace and security brings even more ambiguity to the matter. The question is whether the obligation to report under art. 54 relates to all types of current activity of regional organizations in the sphere. As analyzed in detail in the first chapter, the very notion of international peace and security has changed drastically over the years. As a result, the system of collective security currently includes, besides the initial pursuit of eliminating international conflicts, prevention and settlement of both international and internal conflicts, prevention of the hypothetical possibility of conflicts through disarmament, control over armaments, confidence- and security-building measures as well as suppression of contemporary threats and challenges (the struggles against international terrorism, proliferation of weapons of mass destruction and transboundary crimes). The functions and activities of regional organizations have expanded correspondingly.

It would thus be naïve, even ridiculous, to expect that regional organizations will report in contemplation of, as well as *post facto*, any single act undertaken, especially when contemplated acts are aimed at preventing the very possibility of conflict or to counter contemporary threats or challenges. I will assume here that the initial purpose of art. 54 was to report on any activity contemplated or undertaken for the settlement of emerging or ongoing international conflicts.

Yet an answer comes from the provisions and logic of the UN Charter as well as current realities. As concerns the application of enforcement measures, the Security Council should be informed before any

---

[677] See, *e.g.*, Walter C., *Vereinte Nationen und Regional Organisationen*, *op. cit.*, p. 346-353.
[678] *E.g.*, UN Security Council Resolutions 787 (1992), *op. cit.*, para. 14; 816 (1993), *op. cit.*, para. 7; 1031 (1995), *op. cit.*, para. 25; 1247 (1999), *op. cit.*, para. 18; 1305 (2000), *op. cit.*, para. 18; 1575 (2004), *op. cit.*, para. 18; 1639 (2005), *op. cit.*, para. 18; 1722 (2006), *op. cit.*, para. 18; 1845 (2008), *op. cit.*, para. 18; 1895 (2009), *op. cit.*, para. 18; 1948 (2010), *op. cit.*, para. 18; 1174 (1998), *op. cit.*, para. 18.
[679] UN Security Council Resolutions 934 (1994), *op. cit.*, para. 4; 1808 (2008), *op. cit.*, para. 15; 822 (1993), *op. cit.*, para. 4; 853 (1993), *op. cit.*, para. 13.

action is taken insofar as no action is possible without its authorization. Regional organizations are also to keep the Security Council informed about the activity, process and progress of authorized enforcement actions. They are not, however, obliged to inform about activity which may legally be taken by its member states.

As concerns non-enforcement activity taken for the prevention or settlement of international and internal conflicts, regional organizations are obliged to to report on planned or undertaken measures. At the same time, as far as they enjoy priority in the sphere, there is no need to send information on any act. It may be transferred to the UN Security Council periodically (the period is, however, to be agreed) or at least before every discussion of the problem within the Security Council.

Any other activity (prevention of the very possibility of conflicts, struggles against contemporary threats and challenges) is to be reported regularly in the course of discussions about corresponding issues in the Security Council, in high-level meetings with representatives of regional organizations or through specially established institutionalized structures. This turns out to be not that complicated, given that *ad hoc* organizations are very rarely established for involvement in such activity.

Conclusions

In the current interdependent world, no organization (even the United Nations) is able to guarantee international peace and security when acting alone. Moreover, the UN Security Council is practically unable to organize, undertake and control all operations in all parts of the world and, besides that, to take measures to prevent the very possibility of conflicts in the future and confront contemporary threats and challenges, especially in the absence of permanent UN forces.

On the other hand, regional organizations are currently willing to assume a substantial burden of responsibilities in this sphere. Some of them possess sufficient financial, military and technical resources. Moreover, there are usually several organizations with concurrent or similar membership and competences acting in the same region.

It is thus necessary to recognize that the initial subsidiarity mechanism of relations between the UN Security Council and regional organizations is already very outdated. Due to the great number of existing regional organizations, current relations in the sphere should be viewed in their complexity in both the vertical (UN/regional organizations) and horizontal (between regional organizations) planes.

Relations between the UN and regional organizations should be established on the principles of subsidiarity and complementarity through the recognition of regional organizations' autonomy in areas not involving the use of enforcement action, leaving to the Security Council the authorizing (as concerns enforcement activity) and controlling functions (although not operational control). This would also eliminate most of the problems that could arise with the strict interpretation of the art. 54 obligation to inform.

There is also an urgent need to develop and deepen stable mechanisms of cooperation between the UN and regional organizations as well as create algorithms of cooperation in cases of emergency. Existing *ad hoc* cooperation or even periodical meetings with representatives of regional organizations are not sufficient.

Cooperation between regional organizations needs to be developed with a view toward the complementarity principle. There is no need to establish identical functions and competences in every organization as far as they may easily complement each other in the course of activity. Certain stable schemes should be established for cooperation between organizations acting in the same area, and mechanisms should be developed for cases of *ad hoc* involvement in specific conflicts.

The UN Charter, due to its flexible nature, still provides a sufficient framework for the activity of regional organizations in the maintenance of international peace and security. At the same time, there is an obvious need for "functional" reform of the UN Security Council, notably to enhance the legality and credibility of its actions. Official recognition of the greater autonomy of regional organizations in the sphere of maintenance of international peace and security, strict observance of and respect for the Security Council's powers as regards enforcement activity, and adherence by the Security Council to the rule of law are the only means able to guarantee the stable functioning of the system of collective security and to prevent anarchy in international relations. The ICJ may play an important role as a guarantor of legality at the international arena.

CHAPTER 5

COLLECTIVE SECURITY IN THE POST-SOVIET REGION

Besides the Commonwealth of Independent States,[680] the so-called "newly emerged" states that were previously part of the Soviet Union participate in a range of other organizations involved in maintaining international peace and security.[681]

5.1 Overview and Qualification

It is maintained here that all of the organizations considered in this chapter – the OSCE, CIS and CSTO – are regional organizations under Chapter VIII.

Membership. The OSCE, CIS and CSTO are organizations with limited membership, although none of them is restricted only to a geographic region.

Purposes. The OSCE was established as a forum for the discussion of urgent matters in the sphere of international security (Helsinki Final Act, 1975), and is currently involved in different dimensions of security activities in the region.

The CIS, founded immediately after the disintegration of the Soviet Union, was not aimed exclusively or even primarily at the maintenance of international peace and security, although peaceful settlement of disputes, disarmament and the maintenance of international peace and security were

---

[680] Currently 11 former republics of the Soviet Union participate in the CIS: Armenia, Azerbaijan, Belarus, Kazakhstan, Kyrgyzstan, Moldova, Russian Federation, Tajikistan, Turkmenistan, Ukraine, Uzbekistan (CIS Member States).

[681] All of the former Soviet republics are members of the UN (United Nations Members) and the OSCE (OSCE members). Seven of them (Armenia, Belarus, Kazakhstan, Kyrgyzstan, Russian Federation, Tajikistan, Uzbekistan) are members of the CSTO (CSTO members), although in June 2012 Uzbekistan informed the CSTO Secretariat of its decision to suspend its membership. Five of them (Kazakhstan, Kyrgyzstan, Russian Federation, Tajikistan, Uzbekistan) are members of the ShCO (ShCO members).

included in the purposes of the organization (CIS Statute, art. 2)[682] and evaluated in parts III-IV of the Statute[683] and in later documents.[684]

The CSTO originated in the Treaty of Collective Security concluded on 15 May 1992 by six CIS member states as a self-defense pact within the CIS system (TCS, art. 1(1), 4). In 2003, after the CSTO Charter came into force, the TCS system separated from the CIS and re-formed into an independent international organization (CSTO Charter, art. 1). The CSTO is aimed at the enhancement of peace, regional security and stability, and at the collective defense of the independence, territorial integrity and sovereignty of member states (CSTO Charter, art. 3). The TCS had already set forth the purpose "*to establish [a] regional system of collective security*" (art. 1(3)) that was developed in subsequent documents.[685]

Adherence to the UN's purposes and principles. All organizations under consideration here have expressed their adherence to the UN's purposes and principles[686] as well as to their obligations under the UN

---

682 Устав Содружества Независимых государств [CIS Statute], 22 January 1993, *Sodruzhestvo* (1993, 1).

683 According to art. 11 of the CIS Statute, member states are to coordinate their policies regarding security, disarmament, control over armaments and the building of armed forces. The maintenance of regional peace and security may also be ensured through the use of military forces and collective peace-maintenance forces, including in peacekeeping operations (art. 11-12).

684 Концепция дальнейшего развития Содружества независимых государств. План реализации Концепции [Concept of the Future Development of the Commonwealth of Independent States, Plan of Actions], Decision of the CIS CHS of 5 October 2007, *Electronic Legal Database Konsul'tant Plus. Technologiia 3000*, paras. 2.2, 2.3, 4.6.

685 This was reaffirmed and developed in the CSTO Charter, art. 7; О модели региональной системы коллективной безопасности [On the Model of the Regional System of Collective Security], Decision of the Collective Security Council, 24 May 2000, *Electronic Legal Database Konsul'tant Plus. Technologiia 3000*; Декларация государств-членов ОДКБ о совершенствовании и усилении эффективности деятельности ОДКБ [Declaration of the CSTO Members on the Improvement and Enhancement of Effectiveness of CSTO Activity], 23 June 2006, *Electronic Legal Database Konsul'tant Plus. Technologiia 3000.*

686 CIS – Соглашение о создании Содружества Независимых Государств [Agreement on the Establishment of the Commonwealth of Independent States], 8 December 1991, *Sodruzhestvo,* (1992, 1), preamble; CIS Statute, *op. cit.*, preamble; Меморандум о поддержании мира и безопасности в СНГ [Memorandum on the Maintenance of Peace and Stability in the CIS], 10 February 1995, *Sodruzhestvo,* (1995, 1), preamble; Концепция согласованной пограничной политики государств-участников СНГ [Concept of the Coordinated Border Policy of the CIS Member States], confirmed by the CIS CHS decision of 26 August 2005, *Electronic Legal Database Konsul'tant Plus. Technologiia 3000*, part I. CSTO – TCS, *op. cit.*, art. 1(1); CSTO Charter, *op. cit.*, preamble, art. 4; Концепция формирования и функционирования миротворческого механизма ОДКБ [Concept of Formation and Functioning of the CSTO Peacekeeping Mechanism], 18 June 2004, *Electronic Legal Database Konsul'tant Plus. Technologiia 3000*, para. 1.

Charter and UN Security Council resolutions.[687] Furthermore, the CSCE Declaration on Principles Guiding Relations between Participating States[688] explained and developed principles that were set forth in the UN Charter and the Declaration on Principles of International Law, Friendly Relations and Co-Operation among States in Accordance with the Charter of the United Nations (General Assembly Resolution 2625 (XXV) of 24 October 1970).

Qualification. The OSCE and CIS qualified themselves as regional organizations under Chapter VIII in their documents.[689] The CSTO documents do not refer to Chapter VIII. Nevertheless, the CSTO was initially established as a regional organization of collective security (CSTO Charter, art.1). Furthermore, recent CSTO documents claim that the system of collective security has been established within the organization.[690] All of these organizations have been treated by UN organs as falling under Chapter VIII. The UN General Assembly has granted them observer status,[691] considers cooperation with them within its agenda[692] and notes their activity as regional agencies in accordance with Chapter VIII.[693]

---

[687] CSTO Charter, *op. cit.*, preamble; TCS, *op. cit.* (with Protocol of 10 December 2010), art. 6(2); Agreement on the Order of Formation and Functioning of Forces, *op. cit.*, preamble.

[688] Helsinki Final Act, 1 August 1975.

[689] Helsinki Summit Declaration 1992, *op. cit.*, para. 25, Helsinki Decision III, para.19; Helsinki Decision IV, para.2; Charter for European Security 1999, *op. cit.*, para. 7; Astana Commemorative Declaration, *op. cit.*, para. 6; see also Evers F., Kahl M., Zellner W., *The Culture of Dialogue*, *op. cit.*, p. 53; CIS – Концепция предотвращения и урегулирования конфликтов на территории государств-участников СНГ [Concept of the Prevention and Settlement of Conflicts on the Territory of CIS Member States (Concept 1996)], confirmed by the CIS CHS Decision of 19 January 1996, *Sodruzhestvo* (1996, 1), para. 2; Заявление глав государств СНГ [Statement on the CIS CHS], 15 April 1994, *Sodruzhestvo*, (1994, 1); О парламентском контроле за военной организацией государства [On Parliamentary Control over the Military Organization of the State], model law adopted 24 November 2001, *Information Bulletin "CIS Interparliamentary Assembly,"* 28 (2002). art. 8(1); Об участии государств-участников СНГ в миротворческих операциях [On Participation of the CIS Member States in Peacekeeping Operations], model law adopted 17 April 2004, *Information Bulletin "CIS Interparliamentary Assembly,"* 34 (2004), art. 3.

[690] Agreement on the Establishment of the System of Management of Forces, *op. cit.*, preamble, art. 3; Agreement on the Order of Formation and Functioning of Forces, *op. cit.*, preamble.

[691] OSCE – UN General Assembly Resolution 48/5, 13 October 1993; CIS – Resolution 48/237, 24 March 1994; CSTO – Resolution 59/50, 2 December 2004.

[692] With OSCE – UN General Assembly Resolutions 50/87, 18 December 1995, *op. cit.*; 51/57, 12 December 1996, *op. cit.*; 52/22, 25 November 1997, *op. cit.*; 53/85, 7 December 1998, *op. cit.*; 54/117, 15 December 1999, *op. cit.*; 55/179, 19 December 2000, *op. cit.*; 56/216, 21 December 2001, *op. cit.*; 57/298, 20 December 2002, *op. cit.*; 58/55, 8 December 2003, *op. cit.*, *etc.*; with CSTO – Resolutions 64/256, 19 May 2009, *op. cit.*; 65/122, 13 December 2010, *op. cit.*

[693] CSTO – UN General Assembly Resolution 64/256, 19 May 2009, *op. cit.*

To be able to decide on the existence of, or prospects for, a system of collective security in the CIS region, it is necessary to have an overview of the functions and competences of relevant regional organizations as well as their involvement in conflicts in the area.

5.2 Obligation to Report in Accordance with art. 54 of the UN Charter

OCSE Activity

The OSCE represents a very broad vision of security. Its activity besides that in the politico-military field involves efforts in the economic, environmental and human realms, which undoubtedly also have some effect in conflict prevention.[694] The OSCE also follows a broad approach to the politico-military dimension of security itself with respect to the three key areas identified earlier. For example, the OSCE Concept of Comprehensive and Cooperative Security (2009) provides for the need to cooperate in risk reduction and early warning, small arms and light weapons, action against terrorism, border security and management, police matters and security aspects related to inter-ethnic tensions.[695] It is repeatedly maintained in the legal doctrine that the OSCE focuses on the prevention of conflicts. It is even sometimes called a "low-intensity" organization.[696]

An emphasis has been placed on measures aimed at the *elimination or minimization of the very possibility of even a hypothetical conflict*, including disarmament, arms control and CSBMs.[697] The development of the system began with the Helsinki Final Act (1975)[698] and continued through

---

[694] See in particular OSCE Mechanisms and Procedures, Vienna, 8 June 2004; *OSCE Mechanisms and Procedures – Summary/Compedium* (SEC.GAL/121/08), 20 June 2008, (Vienna: OSCE, 2011).

[695] OSCE Concept of Comprehensive and Cooperative Security: An Overview of Major Milestones (SEC.GAL/100/09), 17 June 2009, p. 3-18. For an analysis of the OSCE commitment and activities, see Evers F., Kahl M., Zellner W., *The Culture of Dialogue*, *op. cit.*, p. 7-25; Lisbon Declaration on a Common and Comprehensive Security Model for Europe for the Twenty-first Century, 1996; Charter for European Security 1999, *op. cit.*; Corfu Informal Meeting, *op. cit.*; *OSCE Handbook 2007* (Vienna: OSCE, 2007), p. 10-12, 80-87.

[696] Kirn R., "Chapter VIII of the UN Charter," *op. cit.*, p. 12-13.

[697] Charter for European Security 1999, *op. cit.*, para. 28; Astana Commemorative Declaration, *op. cit.*, para. 8.

[698] Helsinki Final Act, 1 August 1975, *op. cit.*, Part II.

the Stockholm document (1986)[699] and a set of Vienna documents (1990, 1992, 1994 and 1999)[700] with regard to CSBM, and a series of OSCE decisions as well as treaties concluded under the OSCE umbrella and concerned with disarmament and arms control.[701] The OSCE system of disarmament, arms control and CSBMs is often claimed to "*establish an outstanding level of military transparency, to which no other part of the world ever comes close.*"[702]

Another group of OSCE mechanisms and procedures includes those aimed at *prevention and settlement of a particular conflict*: early warning and preventive action,[703] mechanisms for consultation and cooperation with regard to emergency situations,[704] disarmament,[705] mechanisms for the peaceful settlement of international disputes,[706] fostering the OSCE's role as

---

[699] Document of the Stockholm Conference on Confidence- and Security-Building Measures and Disarmament in Europe, Convened in Accordance with the Relevant Provisions of the Concluding Document of the Madrid Meeting of the Conference on Security and Co-operation in Europe of 19 September 1986.

[700] Vienna Document of Negotiations on Confidence- and Security Building Measures, 16 November 1999. For the development of CSBMs within the OSCE see Lachowski Z., *Confidence and Security Building Measures in the New Europe*, SIPRI Research Report No. 18 (New York: OUP, 2004).

[701] *E.g.*, Treaty on Conventional Armed Forces in Europe, 19 November 1990; Treaty on Open Skies, 24 March 1992; OSCE Document on Small Arms and Light Weapons, 24 November 2000; OSCE Principles on the Control of Brokering in Small Arms and Light Weapons, Decision No.8/04, 24 November 2004. For a comprehensive list, see OSCE Concept of Comprehensive and Cooperative Security, *op. cit.*, p. 12-15

[702] Evers F., Kahl M., Zellner W., *The Culture of Dialogue*, *op. cit.*, p. 21.

[703] Helsinki Summit Declaration 1992, *op. cit.*, Chapter III; OSCE Stabilizing Measures for Localized Crisis Situations, 25 November 1993; CSCE and the New Europe – Our Security is Indivisible. Ministerial Declaration of 1 December 1993, chapter II, para. 1-3.

[704] Annex 2 to the Summary of Conclusions of the First CSCE Council of Ministers, Berlin, 1991.

[705] Although this mechanism is rather modestly mentioned in the Compendium of OSCE Mechanisms and Procedures, OSCE documents provide a wide spectrum of measures aimed at confidence- and security-building as regards the transfer of conventional weapons; see Principles Governing Conventional Arms Transfers, 25 November 1993, Annex III; light weapons and small arms – OSCE Document on Small Arms and Light Weapons, 24 November 2000; non-proliferation issues – OSCE Document on Stockpiles of Conventional Ammunition, 19 November 2003; land mines – Convention on the Prohibition of the Use, Stockpiling, Production and Transfer of Anti-personnel Mines and on their Destruction, 1997, with Protocol II. For a detailed analysis, see Lachowski Z., *Confidence and Security Building Measures in the New Europe*, *op. cit.*, p, 101-105; 115-127.

[706] Principles for Dispute Settlement and Provisions for a CSCE Procedure for Peaceful Settlement of Disputes, Valletta, 1991; Convention on Conciliation and Arbitration within the CSCE, 1992.

a forum for political dialogue[707] and stabilizing measures for localized crisis situations.[708] Most of these measures are exercised through field activities,[709] which, however, have never been traditional peacekeeping missions.[710] Field operations may vary from representations in the field via mediation efforts to projects outsourced to other entities.[711] The Istanbul Summit established rapid expert assistance and cooperation teams to respond quickly to demands for assistance and for large civilian field operations (Charter of European Security, 1999, paras. 1, 42). Neither the enforcement mechanism nor the establishment of permanent military forces has ever been included in the OSCE documents.

The OSCE takes certain steps to be able _to face threats which do not originate from state behavior_: terrorism, organized crime, illegal migration, the proliferation of weapons of mass destruction, cyber-threats and illicit trafficking in small arms and light weapons, drugs and human beings (see, *e.g.*, Astana Declaration 2010, para. 9).

The OSCE's competences and success in the _peaceful settlement of disputes_ are rather confusing. Despite repeated attempts to establish an effective mechanism of international dispute settlement, neither the Valetta Mechanism of 1992 nor the OSCE Court of Conciliation and Arbitration, despite its wide (unlimited) competence,[712] including, *inter alia*, issues of international security of a non-legal nature,[713] have ever been used by the OSCE states, despite the initial enthusiasm about their possible role in dispute settlement in the region.[714] And (as sometimes maintained in the

---

[707] The basic principles in this area are set forth by Fostering the Role of the OSCE as a Forum for a Political Dialogue, Decision No. 3 of the 9th Bucharest Ministerial Council, 4 December 2001.

[708] OSCE Stabilizing Measures for Localized Crisis Situations, *op. cit.*

[709] Currently 17 missions and other field activities are in operation (What is OSCE? Factsheet).

[710] Para. 38 of the Charter for European Security 1999 (*op. cit.*) describes the tasks of field operations as "providing assistance and advice or formulating recommendations in areas agreed by the OSCE and the host country; observing compliance with OSCE commitments and providing advice or recommendations for improved compliance; assisting in the organization and monitoring of elections; providing support for the primacy of law and democratic institutions and for the maintenance and restoration of law and order; helping to create conditions for negotiation or other measures that could facilitate the peaceful settlement of conflicts; verifying and/or assisting in fulfilling agreements on the peaceful settlement of conflicts; providing support in the rehabilitation and reconstruction of various aspects of society." See also Evers F., Kahl M., Zellner W., *The Culture of Dialogue*, *op. cit.*, p. 22.

[711] *Ibid.*, p. 56-57.

[712] Convention on Conciliation and Arbitration within the CSCE, *op. cit.*, art.1.

[713] Jacobi S., "The OSCE Court: An Overview," *Leiden Journal of International Law*, 10(2) (1997), p. 287, 289-291.

[714] *Ibid.*, p. 294.

legal doctrine) they are not likely to be used, especially in the sphere of maintenance of international peace and security.[715] By contrast, the OSCE's mediation efforts have often demonstrated good results (including in the CIS area);[716] *e.g.*, the OSCE was a mediator in the "5+2" negotiations in the Moldova conflict,[717] and it took part in the functioning of the incidents prevention and response mechanism and assisted with the organization of meetings in Geneva concerning Georgia, even after the cancellation of its mission in the country.[718]

The OSCE's involvement in the CIS area has not focused on the political-military dimension. Its attention has been primarily directed toward the democratization of societies, state- and institution-building, promotion and protection of human rights, reform and training of police, development of economic and environmental objectives, amendment of legislation, assistance in organizing and observing elections, strengthening border security, and combating terrorism and drug trafficking (*e.g.*, through offices in Belarus, Ukraine, Azerbaijan, Armenia, Turkmenistan, Kazakhstan, Kyrgyzstan, Tajikistan and Uzbekistan).[719]

Additionally, in conflict situations, the OSCE has facilitated the achievement of lasting political settlements and national reconciliation (Tajikistan, Georgia, Nagorno-Karabakh) as well as the peaceful settlement of disputes through negotiation, good offices, mediation, country visits, fact-finding and reconnaissance (Moldova, Georgia, Nagorno-Karabakh). It has gathered and provided information on regional situations (Moldova, Georgia); encouraged the implementation of concluded agreements and commitments, *e.g.*, on the withdrawal of foreign troops (Moldova, Georgia); acted as a guarantor of peace agreements (*e.g.*, the Tajik Peace Agreement of 1997); and ensured transparency of the implementation of commitments through border, cease-fire line and other types of monitoring operations (Georgia, Nagorno-Karabakh).[720] The need for peacekeeping forces under

---

[715] Schneider P., Müller-Wort T.-J.A., *The Court of Conciliation and Arbitration within OSCE*: Working Methods, Procedures and Composition. CORE Working paper 16 (Hamburg: CORE, 2007), p. 7-8.

[716] Rotfeld, A.D., "Does the OSCE Have a Future?" *OSCE Yearbook 2003*, 9 (2003), p. 37.

[717] *OSCE Annual Report 2009* (Vienna: OSCE, 2010), p. 15.

[718] *Ibid.*, p. 14.

[719] *OSCE Handbook*, *op. cit.*, p. 54-55, 58, 61, 64-65, 67, 68-69, 70-71, 72-73, 74-75; Also see Reeve R., "The OSCE Mission to Georgia – Activities in 2004," *OSCE Yearbook, 2004*, 10 (2005), p. 155-161; Rotfeld, A.D., "Does the OSCE Have a Future?" *op. cit.*, p. 37-38.

[720] The OSCE has fulfilled a range of border observance tasks, for example along the border between Georgia and Chechnya since 1999, in the Ingush Republic (Russian Federation) since 2001, and in Dagestan Republic (Russian Federation) since 2003 (Evers F., Kahl M., Zellner W., *The Culture of Dialogue*, *op. cit.*, p. 23). See also Меморандум о мерах по обеспечению безопасности и укреплению взаимного доверия между сторонами в

the auspices of the OSCE has been repeatedly discussed, *e.g.*, for the Transdniestria conflict, but no multinational forces have been established.[721]

It thus follows that the OSCE's role in the politico-military dimension of security involves primarily diplomatic means of dispute settlement, mediation, fact-finding, monitoring, conflict prevention, post-conflict peace-building, CSBMs, disarmament and control over arms.[722] As it is not focused on introducing or using military troops, the OSCE often acts as a political forum/coordinating institution. The further development of the OSCE is oriented toward the evolution of political, mediation, monitoring, expert and other capacities rather than toward having a military potential.[723]

CIS Activity

CIS politico-military cooperation includes border management, prevention and handling of natural disasters and environmental emergencies, management of joint systems, and struggles against new threats and challenges.[724] Similarly to the OSCE, the CIS focuses on CSBMs and

---

Грузино-Осетинском конфликте [Memorandum on Security and Confidence-Building Measures between the Parties of the Georgia-Ossetia Conflict], 16 May 1996, *Electronic Legal Database Konsul'tant Plus. Technologiia 3000*; *OSCE Handbook, op. cit.*, p. 56-57, 62-63, 72, 76-78; Neukirch C., "The OSCE Mission in Moldova," *OSCE Yearbook 2003*, (Hamburg; Nomos Verlagsgesellschaft, 2003), p. 149; Jakoby V., "The OSCE Mission in Georgia," *OSCE Yearbook 2003*, (Hamburg; Nomos Verlagsgesellschaft, 2003), p. 163-170; Stöber S., "The Failure of the OSCE Mission to Georgia – What Remains?" *OSCE Yearbook 2010*, (Hamburg: Nomos, 2011), p. 203, 205-207; Perspectives of the UN and Regional Organizations, *op. cit.*

[721] Neukirch C., "The OSCE Mission in Moldova," *op. cit.*, p. 158-160; Меморандум об основах нормализации отношений между Республикой Молдова и Приднестровьем [Memorandum on the Grounds for Normalization of Relations between Moldova and Transdnistria], 8 May 1997, *Russia-Ukraine (1990-2000) Documents and Materials,* vol. 2 (1996-2000), 2001, p. 97-98.

[722] Security Council Meeting 6257, *op. cit.*, p. 18 (speech of the Head of OSCE External Relations). See also Hummer W., Schweitzer M., "Article 52," *op. cit.*, p. 834; *OSCE Annual Report 2009, op. cit.*, p. 15, 17, 23-24, 50-51, 68-69, 96, 105; Charter for European Security 1999, *op. cit.*, para. 28; Cooperation between the United Nations and Regional Organizations/Arrangements, *op. cit.*

[723] Ackermann A., Salber H., "The OSCE "Corfu Process" – A Preliminary View of the Security Dialogue on Early Warning, Conflict Prevention and Resolution, Crisis Management, and Post-conflict Rehabilitation," *OSCE Yearbook 2010*, (Hamburg: Nomos, 2011), p. 197-202; Ackermann A., Crosby J., de Haan J., Falkehed E., "Developing an OSCE Mediation-Support Capacity: First Steps," *OSCE Yearbook 2010*, (Hamburg: Nomos, 2011), p. 369-376; Rotfeld, A.D., "Does the OSCE Have a Future?" *op. cit.*, p. 38.

[724] Cooperation of the CIS States in the Sphere of Security.

preventive actions (*e.g.*, development of general programs of action,[725] conclusion of international treaties,[726] establishment of information databases,[727] harmonization of legislation, training of personnel, research,

[725] See, *e.g.*, Программа сотрудничества государств-участников СНГ в противодействии незаконной миграции на 2009-2011 гг. [Program of Cooperation of the CIS Member States in the Suppression of Illegal Migration for 2009-2011], confirmed by the CIS CHS Decisions of 10 October 2008, *Electronic Legal Database Konsul'tant Plus. Technologiia 3000*; Concept of the Coordinated Border Policy, *op. cit.*; План мероприятий по реализации согласованной пограничной политики государств-участников СНГна 2011-2015 гг. [Plan of Actions on the Realization of the Concept of the Coordinated Border Policy of the CIS Member-States to 2011-2015], confirmed by the CIS CHS Decision of 10 December 2010, *Electronic Legal Database Konsul'tant Plus. Technologiia 3000*; Концепция военного сотрудничества государств-участников СНГ до 2015 г. [Concept of Military Cooperation of the CIS Member States until 2015], Confirmed by the CIS CHS Decisions of 10 December 2010, *Electronic Legal Database Konsul'tant Plus. Technologiia 3000*; Программа сотрудничества государств-участников СНГ в борьбе с незаконным оборотом наркотических веществ, психотропных вещетв и их прекурсоров, и противодействии наркомании на 2011-2013 гг. [Program of Cooperation of the CIS Member States in the Struggle against the Illegal Traffic in Drugs, Psychotropic Substances, and their Precursors, and Opposition to Drug Addiction for 2011-2013], confirmed by the CIS CHS Decision of 10 December 2010, *Electronic Legal Database Konsul'tant Plus. Technologiia 3000*; Межгосударственная программа мер по борьбе с преступностью на 2011-2013 гг. [Inter-State Program of Joint Action in the Struggle against Criminality for 2011-2013], confirmed by the CIS CHS Decisions of 10 December 2010, *Electronic Legal Database Konsul'tant Plus. Technologiia 3000*; Программа сотрудничества государств-участников СНГ в борьбе с терроризмом и иными насильственными проявлениями экстремизма на 2011-2013 [Program of Cooperation of the CIS Member States in the Struggle against Terrorism and Other Violent Forms of Extremism for 2011-2013], confirmed by the CIS CJS Decision of 10 December 2010, *Electronic Legal Database Konsul'tant Plus. Technologiia 3000.*

[726] See Concept of the Coordinated Border Policy, *op. cit.*, part I, II; Соглашение об обмене информацией в сфере борьбы преступностью [Agreement on the Information Exchange in the Struggle against Criminality], 22 May 2009, *Electronic Legal Database Konsul'tant Plus. Technologiia 3000*; Договор государств-участников СНГ о противодействии легализации преступных доходов и финансировании терроризма [Treaty of the CIS Member States on the Suppression of Money Laundering and Financing of Terrorism], 5 October 2007, *Electronic Legal Database Konsul'tant Plus. Technologiia 3000*; Соглашение государств-участников СНГ по обеспечению стабильного положения на их внешних границах [Agreement of the CIS Member States on the Guarantees of Stability on their External Borders], 9 October 1992, *Sodruzhestvo*, (1992, 7); Договор о сотрудничестве государств-участников СНГ в борьбе с терроризмом [Treaty on the Cooperation of the CIS Member States in the Struggle against Terrorism], 4 June 1999, *Sodruzhestvo*, (1999, 2).

[727] *E.g.*, the specialized databank of the Bureau on the Coordination of the Struggle against Organized Crime, the Joint Databank of Illegal Migrants and Other Persons whose Entry into the Territory of States Parties to the Agreement on Cooperation in the Struggle against Illegal Migration is Prohibited; see Организационно-правовой механизм сотрудничества в противодействии транснациональной преступности в рамках Содружества Независимых Государств [Institutionalized Legal Mechanism of Cooperation in the Struggle against Transboundary Crimes within the CIS].

maneuvers,[728] consultations, fact-finding, mutual inspections[729]), rather than on the use of military forces for peacekeeping or peace enforcement. At the same time, art. 11-12 of the CIS Statute provides for the possibility of using military and collective peace-maintenance forces to ensure peace and security in the region, *inter alia* in collective self-defense. The latter provision, however, is uncertain; it has never been mentioned in later CIS documents.

By contrast, repeated attempts have been made to establish the potential and modalities of *peacekeeping* activity.[730] This activity is to be decided and supervised by the CIS Council of the Heads of State (hereafter, CIS CHS), which decides on starting a particular peacekeeping or peace-support operation, determines its competence, authority, composition, purposes and terms, and appoints a head of the mission, commander-in-chief or head of the group of military observers.[731] With priority given to diplomatic means for the prevention or settlement of conflicts, groups of military observers and collective forces for the maintenance of peace are assigned to the separate conflicting parties, control observance of the cease-

---

[728] Информация о деятельности базовых организаций (учреждений) в сфере безопасности в СНГ [Information on the Activity of the Base Education Institutions in the Sphere of Security]; Concept of the Coordinated Border Policy, *op. cit.*, part I, II.

[729] Agreement of the CIS Member States on the Guarantees of Stability on their External Borders, *op. cit.*, art. 3, 7-8.

[730] Соглашение о группах военных наблюдателей и коллективных силах по поддержанию мира в СНГ [Agreement on Groups of Military Observers and Collective Peace-Maintenance Forces in the CIS], 20 March 1992, *Sodruzhestvo*, (1992, 4); Протокол о комплектовании, структуре, материально-техничестком и финансовом обеспечении групп наблюдателей и коллективных сил по поддержанию мира в СНГ [Protocol on the Recruitment Structure, Material and Financial Procurement of the CIS Military Observers and Collective Peace-Maintenance Forces], 15 May 1992, *Sodruzhestvo*, (1992(5)); Соглашение о коллективных миротворческих силах и совместных мерах по их материально-техническому обеспечению [Agreement on Collective Peacekeeping Forces and their Maintenance], 24 September 1993, *Sodruzhestvo*, (1993, 4).; Положение о коллективных силах по поддержанию мира в СНГ [Regulation on the CIS Collective Peace-Maintenance Forces], 19 January 1996, *Electronic Legal Database Konsul'tant Plus. Technologiia 3000*; Соглашение о социальных и правовых гарантиях персонала коллективных сил по поддержанию мира в СНГ [Agreement on Social and Legal Guarantees to the Personnel of the CIS Collective Peace-Maintenance Forces], 5 October 2007 (not in force), *Electronic Legal Database Konsul'tant Plus. Technologiia 3000*; Соглашение о порядке финансового, технического и тылового обеспечения деятельности и персонала коллективных сил по поддержанию мира [Agreement on the Order of Financial, Technical and Rear Procurement of the Activity and Personnel of the CIS Collective Peace-Maintenance Forces], 5 October 2007, *Electronic Legal Database Konsul'tant Plus. Technologiia 3000.* On this point, see also MacFarlane S.N., "The CIS and Regional Security," in *Multilateralism and Regional Security*, ed. M. Fortmann, S.N. MacFarlane, S. Roussel, (Toronto: The Canadian Peacekeeping Press, 1997), p. 229-230.

[731] Concept 1996, *op. cit.*, para. 5.

fire or the armistice agreements, ensure conditions for the peaceful settlement of international disputes, assist in the promotion and protection of human rights, and provide humanitarian assistance, including in cases of natural disasters and environmental emergencies.[732] Conflict prevention and conflict settlement activity can only be exercised with the consent of the parties to the conflict (Concept 1996, paras.1-2).

CIS documents also set forth the possibility of exercising *enforcement actions* in accordance with the authorization of the UN Security Council (Concept 1996, chapter 2)[733] and to apply *sanctions* (Concept, para. 1). The latter, however, can only be applied upon the agreement of the parties to the conflict, and thus cannot be viewed as sanctions of an international organization. The CIS documents do not refer to the possibility of initiating an enforcement action.

It should be noted, however, that the CIS peacekeeping and peace-enforcement mechanisms are very skeletal and uncertain. No permanent contingents have ever been formed, and personnel is to be provided by the interested states.[734] The Regulation on Collective Peacekeeping Forces in the CIS, 1996, provides for unified systems of training and recruiting methods but does not oblige states to have certain personnel available for participation in collective operations.

Between 1992 and 2011 the CIS was involved in a variety of situations in which peace and security in the region were threatened. After an official cease-fire in the *Georgia-Abkhazian conflict*[735] resulted from the negotiating efforts of the UN, OSCE and Russian Federation,[736] the CIS Collective military forces (hereafter, CMF) were deployed in the area[737] to

---

[732] Agreement on Groups of Military Observers, *op. cit.*, art. 1, 3.

[733] Korkelia K., "The CIS Peace-Keeping Operations," *op. cit.*, p. 24.

[734] Agreement on Groups of Military Observers, *op. cit.*, art. 4. An attempt to establish collective CIS peacekeeping forces (Agreement on Collective Peacekeeping Forces, *op. cit.*) failed, as Russia, the chief supplier of military personnel and facilities, refused to participate.

[735] See Statement on Measures for a Political Settlement of the Georgia-Abkhazian Conflict, 4 April 1994, *Diplomatic Herald*, (1994, 9-10), para. 3; Соглашение о прекращении огня и разъединении сил в зоне Грузино-Абхазского конфликта [Agreement on the Cease-Fire and Separation of Forces in the Zone of the Georgia-Abkhazian Conflict], 14 May 1994 (hereafter, Moscow Agreement), *Electronic Legal Database Konsul'tant Plus. Technologiia 3000.*

[736] See Statement on Measures for a Political Settlement of the Georgia-Abkhazian Conflict, *op. cit.*, para. 1.

[737] Their involvement in the Georgia-Abkhazian conflict started in 1994 on the basis of a CIS CHS decision; see Об использовании коллективных вооруженных сил для поддержания мира в зоне Грузино-Абхазского конфликта [On the Use of Collective Military Forces to Maintain Peace in the Zone of the Georgia-Abkhazian Conflict], CIS CHS Decision of 22 August 1994, *Electronic Legal Database Konsul'tant Plus. Technologiia 3000.*

replace a Russian military contingent.[738] The arrangement called for the CIS CMF to be stationed in the security separation zone to separate the military forces of the parties in the conflict, to observe the withdrawal of troops as well as cease-fire and separation obligations, to patrol Kodor Canyon, to guarantee the safe return of internally displaced persons to their habitual places of residence, to assist in the restoration of the regions involved in the conflict, to secure the observance of human rights and humanitarian standards, and to cooperate with the UNMOS and other UN personnel.[739] The CIS CMF were to be withdrawn at any moment upon the request of any party to the conflict.[740]

Despite the repeated attention of the CIS to the situation in *Transdniestria*,[741] the only efforts toward the peaceful settlement of the dispute have been taken by interested states rather than by organs of the CIS.[742] The situation in *Tajikistan* has been considered within the CIS since 1992;[743] upon an initiative by Kyrgyzstan, CIS member states supplied military contingents (composed of forces from Kazakhstan, Kyrgyzstan, the Russian Federation and Uzbekistan) for stabilizing the situation at the Tajikistan-Afghan border.[744] In the absence of its own military border forces

---

[738] Декларация о политическом урегулировании Грузино-Абхазского конфликта [Declaration on the Political Settlement of the Georgia-Abkhazia Conflict], 4 April 1994, *Electronic Legal Database Konsul'tant Plus. Technologiia 3000*, para. 5.

[739] Moscow Agreement, *op. cit.,* paras. 2.2, 2.4; CIS CHS Decision On the Use of Collective Military Forces to Maintain Peace in the Zone of the Georgia-Abkhazian Conflict, *op. cit.*, para. 5.

[740] The mandate of the CIS CMF was prolonged repeatedly (*e.g.*, by the CIS CHS Decisions of 7 October 1999-7 January 2000, para. 1; 1 January 2000, para. 2; 21 June 2000, para. 1; 26 July-2 October 2002; 18 February-2 April 2003; 25 July 2003) and was terminated by the CIS CHS Decision of 10 October 2008 upon the request of Georgia (para. 1); Declaration on the Political Settlement of the Georgia-Abkhazia Conflict, *op. cit.*

[741] *E.g.*, Об информации Исполнительного комитета СНГ о ситуации в урегулировании конфликта в Приднестровье [On the Information of the CIS Executive Committee on the Settlement of Conflict in Transdniestria], Decision of the CIS CMFA, 24 January 2000, *Electronic Legal Database Konsul'tant Plus. Technologiia 3000.*

[742] See, *inter alia*, Memorandum on the Grounds for Normalization of Relations between Moldova and Transdnistria, *op. cit.*, p. 97-98; Совместное Российско-украинское заявление [Joint Russian-Ukrainian Statement], 20 March 1998, *Russia-Ukraine 1990-2000. Documents and Materials*. vol. 2 (1996-2000), (Moscow: International Relations, 2001), p. 237-238.

[743] Заявление государств-участников СНГ [Statements of the CIS Member States], 9 October 1992 and 22 January 1993, *Electronic Legal Database Konsul'tant Plus. Technologiia 3000.*

[744] О мерах по стабилизации обстановки на участке государственной границы Республики Таджикистан с Афганистаном [On the Measures to Stabilize the Situation at the Border between Tajikistan and Afghanistan], confirmed by the CIS CHS Decision of 22 January 1993, *Sodruzhestvo*, (1993, 1); prolonged by the Decisions of 19 January 1996, 29 March 1997.

in Tajikistan, Russia provided its contingents for a transitional period. Peacekeeping efforts in *Nagorno-Karabakh* have been undertaken by the Russian Federation. Mixed peacekeeping forces for *South Ossetia* were introduced in July 1992.[745] The CIS' attention to the situation in *Chechnya* has been limited to sending observers to the Chechnya presidential elections[746] and making several references to the situation in the course of fighting terrorism and organized crime.

The mechanisms for *peaceful settlement of international disputes* in the CIS are rather poor. The only available mechanisms are obligatory mutual consultations in the case of any threat to international peace and security in order to coordinate activity on the matter (CIS Statute, art. 12), and negotiations aimed, *inter alia*, at deciding on the particular means of dispute settlement (art. 17). Parties to a dispute may also submit it to the CIS CHS (art. 17(3)), whose competence is formulated analogously to the competences of the UN Security Council as set forth in art. 36(1) of the UN Charter: "*to recommend appropriate procedures or methods of adjustment*" of disputes which could endanger international peace and security in the region (CIS Statute, art. 18). This mechanism, however, is very skeletal and has never been used. Specific accords sometimes provide for the possibility of mutual assistance in the settlement of existing conflicts upon the consent of the parties involved (CIS Statute, art. 16), or (exceptionally) establish particular forms of dispute settlement (Agreement of the CIS Member States on the Guarantees of Stability on their External Borders, 9 October 1992, art. 3, 7-8).

The CIS states are absolutely unwilling to submit their disputes for international adjudication.[747] The CIS Economic Court, despite its very limited competence,[748] has a certain intermediate impact on the peaceful

---

[745] Cornell S.E., "Russia's Gridlock in Chechnya: 'Normalization' or Deterioration?" *OSCE Yearbook 2004*, (Hamburg: Nomos, 2005), p. 251-253.

[746] О направлении наблюдателей от СНГ на выборы Президента Чеченской Республики, Российская Федерация [On the Sending of CIS Observers to the Elections of the President of the Chechen Republic, Russian Federation], CIS CHS Decision of 19 September 2003, *Electronic Legal Database Konsul'tant Plus. Technologiia 3000.*

[747] In particular, no CIS member state has recognized compulsory jurisdiction of the International Court of Justice on the basis of Art. 36 of the ICJ Statute; see Declarations Recognizing the Jurisdiction of the Court as Compulsory. Six states are parties to the OSCE Convention on Conciliation and Arbitration of 1992 (Armenia, Belarus, Moldova, Tajikistan, Ukraine, Uzbekistan); see List showing signatures and ratifications or accessions with respect to the Convention on Conciliation and Arbitration within the OSCE. The Convention's mechanisms have never been used. Six states are currently members of the of the Agreement on the CIS Economic Court; see История Суда [Court's History].

[748] From 1994 to 2010, only 11 applications for dispute settlement had been submitted to the CIS EC. In five cases, the Court found that it had no jurisdiction, either ratione personae

settlement of international disputes through its right to interpret "*provisions of international agreements, CIS acts and legal acts of the former USSR in the period of their mutual application*" at the request of state authorities, Supreme economic courts of CIS member states or CIS institutions.[749] Repeated attempts to broaden its jurisdiction or to establish a CIS Court with broader competence[750] have failed.

It thus follows that basic attention in the sphere of maintenance of international peace and security within the CIS is paid to the issues of border management, management of joint systems and the struggle against particular types of crimes. Attempts to establish a valid peacekeeping system within the CIS have failed because of skeletal legal regulation, discrepancies within the CIS lawmaking process,[751] the unwillingness of states to cooperate actively within the CIS and to implement their commitments in the sphere,[752] the overwhelming influence of Russia, and a loose and confusing institutional structure.[753] At the same time, the positive impact of the CIS CMF in Abkhazia and Tajikistan is acknowledged.[754]

(Orders No. 01–1/4–2000 of 20 December 2000, No. C–1/8–96 of 9 April 1996, No. 01–1/3–2000 of 7 July 2000; No. 01–1/5–03 of 19 November 2003) or ratione materiae (Order No. C–1/16–96 of 6 February 1996) (CIS Economic Court Archives, 2012).

[749] CIS Statute, *op. cit.*, art. 32; Соглашение о статусе Экономического Суда СНГ [Agreement on the Status of the CIS Economic Court], 6 July 1992, *Sodruzhestvo*, 6 (1992), para. 5. As of May 2012, the CIS EC had made 93 decisions and advisory opinions and seven orders interpreting earlier decisions and advisory opinions; see Обзор судебной практики [Overview of Court's Practice].

[750] See, *e.g.*, О создании и принципах Межгосударственного Суда СНГ [On the Establishment and Principles of the CIS Interstate Court], Decision of the CIS CHS, 22 January 1993, *Sodruzhestvo*, (1993, 1); Draft Statute of the CIS Court 1995, CIS EC Archives, 1995; Draft Protocol to the Agreement on the CIS EC of 2008; Draft Statute of the CIS Court 2008, CIS EC Archives, 2008.

[751] *E.g.*, the Decision on the Stay of Collective Peace-Maintenance Forces in Abkhazia, 19 September 2003, prolonging the CMF mandate (para. 1) came into force at different times for different states.

[752] *E.g.*, Belarus rejected sending its military forces to the Collective Peacekeeping Forces, whose military contingents have been primarily provided by the Russian Federation. See also Korkelia K., "The CIS Peace-Keeping Operations," *op. cit.*, p. 34.

[753] CIS states took until September 2004 to make their first attempt to develop a joint position for talks within the OSCE; see Evers F., Zellner W., "Regional Interests in Maintaining and Diversifying the OSCE Field Operations: Supporting a Trend," *OSCE Yearbook 2004*, (Hamburg: Nomos, 2005), p. 448-449. The first decision was only made on 10 December 2010 (Решение о взаимодействии государств-участников СНГ в рамках ОБСЕ [Decision of the CIS CHS on Interaction of the CIS Member States within OSCE], 10 December 2010).

[754] See, *e.g.*, UN Security Council Resolutions 1150 (1998), *op. cit.*, preamble; 1187 (1998), *op. cit.*, preamble; 1255 (1999), *op. cit.*, preamble; 1311 (2000), *op. cit.*, preamble; 1427 (2002), *op. cit.*, preamble; 1554 (2004), *op. cit.*, preamble; 1615 (2005), *op. cit.*, preamble; Supplement to an Agenda for Peace, *op. cit.*, para. 86(d); UN Press Release PI/1668 – United Nations, Regional Organizations Agree on Stronger Partnership in Facing Peace Security

CSTO Activity

The CSTO has a rather narrow competence. It is aimed at the establishment of an effective collective security system and the struggle against new threats and challenges (*e.g.*, CSTO Charter, art. 7-8), and is not involved in any other areas of activity.[755]

The CSTO derived from a collective defense pact (TCS, art. 4), and thus *collective self-defense* is enshrined as one of the organization's purposes in the CSTO Charter (art. 3). It is disappointing, however, that until recently the CSTO documents referred to aggression rather than to an armed attack as a ground for self-defense,[756] which provided a wide possibility for abuse. An additional misunderstanding arose from the wording of art. 2(3) of the Agreement on the CSTO Collective Rapid Reaction Forces of 14 June 2009 (hereafter, CRRF Agreement) providing for the "*prevention and repelling of an armed attack including aggression*"[757] as part of the CRRF's tasks. Currently, the CSTO institutions are taking steps to fill the gaps and eliminate technical and legal mistakes in documents. In particular, the

---

Challenges. Sixth High-Level Meeting of UN, Regional, Intergovernmental Bodies Set for Headquarters on 25-26 July 2005; Cooperation between the United Nations and Regional Organizations/Arrangements, *op. cit.*

[755] CSTO Secretary-General N. Bordyuzha includes the following in the CSTO's activities: military cooperation (harmonization of legislation of member states, mutual help in the development of armed forces, *etc.*); coordination of positions on politico-military issues; operational and military preparation and training; formation and development of coalition and regional joint groupings of forces; establishment of CSTO collective forces and combined military systems; military technical and military economic cooperation; combating contemporary challenges and threats; cooperation in emergency situations arising from natural and environmental disasters; information security (Bordyuzha N., "The Collective Security Treaty Organization," *op. cit.*, p. 342-346). For details on cooperation within the CSTO, see Rozanov A.A., Dovgan E.F., *Collective Security Treaty Organization (2002-2009)*. DCAF Regional Program Series No. 6 (Geneva/Minsk: Procon, 2010), p. 19-36.

[756] See in particular Соглашение об основных принципах военно-техническткого сотрудничества между сторонами Договора о коллективной безопасности [Agreement on the Main Principles of Military-Technical Cooperation among the Parties to the Treaty on Collective Security] of 20 June 2000 with Protocol of 19 September 2003, *Bulletin of International Treaties*, 12 (2005), p. 26-31, art. 10; План имплементации Концепции коллективной безопасности государств-участников ДКБ [Plan for Implementation of the Concept for Collective Security of the TCS Member States], confirmed by the CSC Decision of 26 May 1995, *Sodruzhestvo*, (1995, 2), para. 2.3; Положение о Совете коллективной безопасности [Regulations on the Council of Collective Security], confirmed by the CSC Decision of 28 April 2003, *Electronic Legal Database Konsul'tant Plus. Technologiia 3000*, paras. 5.3, 6; Положение о Совете министров обороны ОДКБ [Regulations on the Council of Defence Ministers], confirmed by the CSC Decision of 28 April 2003, *Electronic Legal Database Konsul'tant Plus. Technologiia 3000*, para. 5.1.2.

[757] Соглашение о коллективных силах оперативного реагирования ОДКБ [Agreement on the CSTO Collective Rapid Reaction Forces (CRRF Agreement)], 14 June 2009, *Electronic Legal Database Konsul'tant Plus. Technologiia 3000.*

Protocol on Amendment of the TSC adopted on 10 December 2010 specified the meaning and scope of the notion "aggression" in art. 4 of the TCS, which is currently understood as an "armed attack threatening security, stability, territorial integrity and sovereignty" (Protocol, para. 1b).[758] Other agreements signed on 10 December 2010 use the term "armed attack (aggression)."[759]

Contrary to the CIS and OSCE, the idea of *establishing collective military forces* was inherent in the CSTO from the moment the TCS had been concluded. The Concept of Collective Security of 1995 provided for the creation of coalition armed forces, which could be established by the CSTO Collective Security Council (hereafter, CSC) for peacekeeping operations envisaged in the decisions of the UN Security Council and OSCE (part. II).[760] In accordance with art. 2(1) of the Agreement on Status of Forces and Facilities of the Collective Security System of 11 October 2000, its parties could send military contingents to each other's territory upon the request of the state concerned.[761] The same agreement regulates the decision-making procedure and the status of military forces established to repel an armed attack against TCS states. At the CSC session in May 2001, it was decided to establish the CRRF in Central Asia.

Treaties concluded within the CSTO provide for several types of collective forces: peacekeeping forces established in accordance with the Agreement on the Peacekeeping Activity of the CSTO of 6 October 2007[762] and the CRRF (CRRF Agreement). These types of collective forces, together with regional joint forces (military contingents formed on the basis of bilateral and multilateral agreements concluded within the CSTO sub-regions); military, police, security, emergency and special purpose personnel of the CSTO member states; and groups of joint military systems (*e.g.*, joint air-defense system, intelligence, *etc.*) will form the CSTO system of

---

[758] Протокол к Договору о коллективной безопасности [Protocol to the TCS], 10 December 2010, *Electronic Legal Database Konsul'tant Plus. Technologiia 3000.*

[759] Agreement on the Order of Formation and Functioning of Forces, *op. cit.*, art. 2, 3, 5; Соглашение о статусе формирований, сил и средств системы коллективной безопасности [Agreement on Status of Forces and Facilities of the Collective Security System], art. 2, 11 October 2000, *Bulletin of International Treaties*, (2002, 5).

[760] Концепция коллективной безопасности государств-участников ДКБ [Concept of the Collective Security of the TCS Parties], confirmed by the CSC Decision of 10 December 1995, *Sodruzhestvo,* (1995, 1).

[761] Agreement on Status of Forces, *op. cit.*, p. 19-26.

[762] Соглашение о миротворческой деятельности ОДКБ [Agreement on the Peacekeeping Activity of the CSTO (CSTO Peacekeeping Agreement)], 6 October 2007, *Bulletin of International Treaties*, (2009, 6), p. 23-27.

collective security as soon as the corresponding agreements come into force.[763]

The CSTO peacekeeping forces may consist of military, police and civilian personnel. They can be utilized for conflict prevention, peace-making, peacekeeping and peace enforcement[764] but are not designed for peace-building or collective self-defense (CSTO Peacekeeping Agreement, art. 1). The CRRF are designed for protecting the territorial integrity and political independence of the CSTO member states, countering terrorism and ameliorating the consequences of natural disasters (CRRF Agreement, art. 2(3)).

All types of CSTO collective forces can be qualified as quasi-permanent formations. They remain under the national jurisdictions of the CSTO member states until their commanders report to the central command on crossing the border into the host state.[765] The decision on the use of collective forces or facilities is taken by the CSC[766] upon the request of the host country.[767] The CSTO peacekeeping forces can be used beyond the region's borders under authorization of the UN Security Council (CSTO Peacekeeping Agreement, art. 3-4) or for non-forcible peacekeeping operations of regional organizations (CSTO Peacekeeping Agreement, art. 7).[768]

In accordance with art. 51 and 54 of the UN Charter, the CSTO has repeatedly expressed its commitment to inform the UN Security Council on measures taken in self-defense and other steps related to the maintenance of international peace and security.[769] Until now, neither the CSTO peacekeeping forces nor the CRRF have ever been used in field operations,

---

[763] Agreement on the Order of Formation and Functioning of Forces, *op. cit.*, art. 1, 5-10.

[764] For the framework of UN classifications, see *United Nations Peacekeeping Operations*, *op. cit.*, p. 17-19.

[765] CSTO Peacekeeping Agreement, *op. cit.*, art. 2; CRRF Agreement, *op. cit.*, art. 7.

[766] CSTO Peacekeeping Agreement, *op. cit.*, art. 3; CRRF Agreement, *op. cit.*, art. 4; Agreement on Status of Forces, *op. cit.*, art. 2(4).

[767] CSTO Peacekeeping Agreement, *op. cit.*, art. 3(1); CRRF Agreement, *op. cit.*, art. 4; Agreement on the Order of Formation and Functioning of Forces, *op. cit.*, art. 12(1); Agreement on Status of Forces, *op. cit.*, art. 2(1), 3(1).

[768] Art. 6 of the TCS (with Protocol of 10 December 2010) provides for the possibility of using the forces and facilities of the CSTO system of collective security beyond the CSTO borders in accordance with the UN Charter. Unlike the CSTO peacekeeping forces, the CRRF can perform tasks only within the territory of the CSTO member states (CRRF Agreement, *op. cit.*, art. 2(3), Agreement on the Order of Formation and Functioning of Forces, *op. cit.*, art. 1, 6.

[769] TCS, *op. cit.* (with Protocol of 10 December 2010), art. 4(3); CSTO Peacekeeping Agreement, *op. cit.*, art. 4; CRRF Agreement, *op. cit.*, art. 4.

although requests for their application have been made (*e.g.*, by Kyrgyzstan in August 2010)[770] and their joint maneuvers take place annually.[771]

The CSTO's cooperation in the *struggle against international crime* is directed against international terrorism and extremism, illegal migration and illicit trafficking in arms and drugs. To combat these types of crimes, the CSTO has established special working groups, holds regular meetings of the heads of corresponding institutions of member states,[772] produces program documents[773] and maintains a common list of terrorist and extremist organizations.[774] The CRRF are involved in counterterrorism activities (CRRF Agreement, art. 2(3)) in the course of maneuvers. In practice, however, the CSTO does not go much further than the framework for cooperation that has been established. Most of the activities in this area are carried out through the systems and mechanisms of the CIS.

CSTO documents and mechanisms are poorly adapted for the *peaceful settlement of disputes* in accordance with art. 52 of the UN Charter. The CSTO Peacekeeping Agreement lists "*peaceful means and measures aimed at resolution of disputes*" among other peacekeeping activities (art.1), but does not provide for any mechanism. Different types of consultations (regular consultations toward framing a common security policy; joint

---

[770] See Подай оружие. Киргизия ждет от ОДКБ военной помощи [Give weapons. Kisgizia is Waiting for SCTO Military Help]; Ситуация в Кыргызстане. ОДКБ ждет решения Беларуси [Situation in Kyrgyzstan. SCTO is Waiting for Belarus' Decision].

[771] Collective self-defense maneuvers – Rubezh 2008 (military contingents of Armenia and the Russian Federation); counter-terrorist operations – Rubezh 2009, Rubezh 2010, Cobalt 2010; joint tasks – complex joint maneuvers in the CSTO sub-regions, Vzaimodejstvie 2009, Vzaimodejstvie 2010; Strategic and tactical maneuvers of CRRF – Center 2011, Central-Asian region 2012 (accessed 20 August 2012, http://www.odkb-csto.org/training).

[772] Положения о рабочих группах по борьбе с терроризмом и противодействии незаконной миграции при Комитете секретарей Советов безопасности ОДКБ [Provisions on Working Groups on Counter-Terrorism and Illegal Migration Issues at the Committee of the Secretaries of CSTO Security Councils], approved by the Decision of the CSTO CSSC of 22 June 2005, *Electronic Legal Database Konsul'tant Plus. Technologiia 3000.*

[773] План коллективных действий государств-членов ОДКБ по имплементации Контртеррористической стратегии ООН на период 2008-2012 гг. [Plan for Collective Actions of the CSTO Member States in the Implementation of the UN Counter-terrorism Strategy for the Period of 2008-2012], confirmed by the CSC Decision of 5 September 2008, *Electronic Legal Database Konsul'tant Plus. Technologiia 3000*; Agreement on the Main Principles of Military-Technical Cooperation, *op. cit.*

[774] О практических мерах по усилению роли ОДКБ в борьбе с терроризмом, религиозным экстремизмом, нелегальной миграцией и транснациональной преступностью [On the Practical Measures to Enhance the CSTO's Role in the Struggle against Terrorism, Religious Extremism, Illegal Migration and Transborder Crimes], CSTO CSSC Decision of 8 December 2003, *Electronic Legal Database Konsul'tant Plus. Technologiia 3000.*

consultations on issues related to emerging threats to national security, the territorial integrity of states, international peace and security; *etc.*)[775] are the only feasible means of dispute settlement within the organization. The same generally holds true for disputes related to the implementation or interpretation of the CSTO Charter or other international treaties signed within the CSTO framework.[776] Only one instrument provides for the possibility of establishing a mediation commission (Agreement on the Status of Forces, art. 16(2)), and two provide for transferring disputes to the CSC (Agreement on the Status of Forces, art. 16(3); CSTO Charter, art. 27).

The CSTO is thus a regional organization of collective security that is given a rather narrow competence, yet one that nevertheless includes the possibility of establishing and using military forces. The CMF established within the organization have not been used yet in field operations. Moreover, prospects for their impartial and effective use are also not clear, particularly in view of the unwillingness of Uzbekistan and the remoteness of Belarus to take part even in maneuvers. Serious gaps exist also in the areas of dispute settlement and the promotion and protection of human rights. (The latter is also true for the CIS; for example, the CIS Convention on Rights and Fundamental Freedoms of 26 May 1995 has come into force in only four states.[777]) Despite the numerous claims by UN organs on the primary role of human rights while countering international terrorism,[778] neither the CIS nor the CSTO documents provide for human rights guarantees in the sphere.[779]

---

775 TCS, *op. cit.* (with Protocol of 10 December 2010), art.2; Положение о порядке проведения консультаций между государствами-участниками ДКБ [Provision on the Procedure for Conducting Consultations], approved by the CSC Decision of 28 May 1997, *Electronic Legal Database Konsul'tant Plus. Technologiia 3000*; Положение о функционировании механизма координации внешне-политической деятельности государств-членов ОДКБ [Regulations on the Functioning of the Coordination Mechanism of the Foreign Policy Activity of the CSTO], of 19 November 2003, *Electronic Legal Database Konsul'tant Plus. Technologiia 3000*, part I(2), II(3).

776 CSTO Charter, *op. cit.*, art. 27; Agreement on the Main Principles of Military-Technical Cooperation, *op. cit.*, art. 11; Соглашение о правовом статусе ОДКБ [Agreement on the CSTO Status], 7 October 2002, Bulletin of International Treaties, 3 (2004), 10 *et seq.*, art. 31, *Electronic Legal Database Konsul'tant Plus. Technologiia 3000*; Соглашение о подготовке военных кадров для государств-членов ОДКБ [Agreement on Training of Military Personnel of the CSTO Member-States], 23 June 2005, art. 16, *Electronic Legal Database Konsul'tant Plus. Technologiia 3000*; CSTO Peacekeeping Agreement, *op. cit.* (note 160), art. 11; CRRF Agreement, *op. cit.* (note 155), art.14; Agreement on the Order of Formation and Functioning of Forces, *op. cit.* (note 86), art. 16.

777 Belarus, Kyrgyzstan, Russian Federation, Tajikistan (*Electronic Legal Database Konsul'tant Plus. Technologiia 3000*).

778 Uniting against Terrorism: Recommendations for a Global Counter-Terrorism Strategy. Report of the UN Secretary-General. Res A/60/825, para.118; Uniting against Terrorism:

5.3 Cooperation with the UN and Regional Organizations

The OSCE, CIS and CSTO are rather open to cooperating with the UN and other organizations in the maintenance of international peace and security. As noted above, all of them have observer status in the UN General Assembly, and they also participate in high-level meetings with the UN and other international and regional organizations as well as in thematic debates on cooperation between the UN and regional organizations,[780] *etc.*

OSCE

The OSCE has identified the following areas of activity as falling within the shared UN-OSCE agenda: anti-terrorism initiatives, conflict settlement and peace-building, early warning and conflict prevention, small arms and light weapons, border management, environmental and economic aspects of security, anti-trafficking, democratization and human rights, and freedom of the media.[781] Contacts take place through mechanisms of high-level dialogue, coordination and information-sharing at the staff level.

As the most representative organization in the region, the OSCE positions itself as a forum for cooperation with regional and sub-regional organizations and initiatives in its area.[782] Thus, the Charter for European Security describes the OSCE as a "*flexible co-coordinating framework to foster co-operation, through which various organizations can reinforce each other drawing on their particular strengths*" (para. 12). Legal grounds for cooperation between the OSCE and other regional organizations and institutions found their way into the Common Concept for the Development

---

Recommendations for a Global Counter-Terrorism Strategy. Report of the UN Secretary-General. Res A/60/825, part IV; 2005 World Summit Outcome, *op. cit.*, para. 85.

[779] See Plan for Collective Actions of the CSTO Member States in the Implementation of the UN Counter-terrorism Strategy for the Period of 2008-2012, *op. cit.*; Treaty on the Cooperation of the CIS Member States in the Struggle against Terrorism, *op. cit.*; Программа совместных действий ОДКБ, направленных на борьбу с терроризмом и транспортировкой наркотиков [CSTO Program of Joint Actions Aimed at Suppressing Terrorism and Drug Trafficking], adopted by the CSC on 23 June 2006, *Electronic Legal Database Konsul'tant Plus. Technologiia 3000*; Program of Cooperation of the CIS Member States in the Struggle against Terrorism and Other Violent Forms of Extremism for 2011-2013, *op. cit.*

[780] CIS since 2004 (Security Council Update Report, 23 March 2007, No. 3, *op. cit.*).

[781] External Co-operation: United Nations.

[782] Helsinki Summit Declaration 1992, *op. cit.*, para. 19; Charter for European Security 1999, *op. cit.*, para. 9; Corfu Informal Meeting, *op. cit.*, para. 5.

of Co-operation between Mutually Reinforcing Institutions of 1997[783] and were developed in the Platform for Co-operative Security, which sets forth principles and modalities of cooperation.[784]

Aware of the insufficiency of its competences and facilities for peacekeeping operations, the CSCE already in 1992 asserted its readiness "*to seek, on a case-by-case basis, the support of international institutions and organizations, such as the EC, NATO and WEU, as well as other institutions and mechanisms, including the peacekeeping mechanism of the CIS*" (Helsinki Summit Declaration of 1992, para. 20). In paras. 52-53 of Decision III of the Helsinki summit in 1992, the CSCE asserted its right to request the EC, NATO and WEU to make their resources available in order to support it in carrying out peacekeeping activities, and to ask the CIS and other institutions to support peacekeeping in the CSCE region. The wording of the Charter of European Security is more reasonable: the OSCE asserts its readiness rather than right to deploy the forces of other organizations in its operations, and clearly states that no sort of hierarchy, subordination or final division of labor between organizations is to be established (para. 12).[785]

The CIS and CSTO are viewed by the OSCE as being among its partners for cooperation,[786] which involves, *inter alia*, participation by OSCE representatives in summits and ministerial meetings convened by these organizations, bilateral and multilateral meetings of high-ranking officials, and inviting CIS and CSTO representatives to take part in OSCE Ministerial Council meetings, OSCE conferences and other relevant events.[787]

CIS

Although the CIS has repeatedly engaged in cooperation with the UN, OSCE and other organizations,[788] the only instrument regulating

[783] Common Concept for the Development of Co-operation between Mutually Reinforcing Institutions, 1997, Annex to MC(6).DEC/5.
[784] The Charter for European Security 1999, *op. cit.*, paras. 1, 12-13; part III.
[785] See also Evers F., Kahl M., Zellner W., *The Culture of Dialogue*, *op. cit.*, p. 18; Hummer W., Schweitzer M., "Article 52," *op. cit.*, p. 834.
[786] OSCE Cooperation with Other Organizations.
[787] *OSCE Annual Report 2009, op. cit.*, p. 91, 104, 108; OSCE Cooperation with Other Organizations, *op. cit.*; *OSCE Annual Report 2001 on Interaction Between Organizations and Institutions in the OSCE Area*, SEC.DOC/2/01, (Vienna: OSCE, 2001), p. 8.
[788] Concept 1996, *op. cit.*, para. 4; The CIS' adherence to cooperation with the UN and OSCE found its way into the CIS CHS Decision On the Use of Collective Military Forces to Maintain Peace in the Zone of the Georgia-Abkhazian Conflict, *op. cit.*, preamble, paras. 5(e), 6; Decisions of 8 February-22 March 2002, para. 5; 19 September 2003, para.6 (documents

possible mechanisms of cooperation is Concept 1996. It provides for consultations, support of peacekeeping operations of the UN and OSCE and cooperation with their missions, cooperation in the political settlement of disputes, information exchanges, informing the UN Security Council and appropriate OSCE organs on decisions in the sphere of maintenance of international peace and security, participation in the consideration of situations on CIS territory in the UN Security Council and OSCE organs, participation in the development of legal regulation in the sphere of peacekeeping, and joint operations under the authority of the UN Security Council (para. 5). The CIS commitment to the OCSE's objectives was set forth in the Helsinki Summit Declaration of 1992 (part I, para. 10).

In the Georgia-Abkhazian conflict, CIS (initially Russian) military troops actively cooperated with the UNMOG. In April 1994, the CIS turned to the UN Security Council and OSCE Secretary-General to consider the possibility of cooperation by the UN and OSCE with the CIS CMF.[789] The Cease-fire and Separation Agreement between Georgia and Abkhazia (1994) expressly divided tasks between the CIS CMF and the UN military observers (paras. 2.4, 2.7). At the same time, the CIS has not taken part in recent cooperation activities within the UN, transferring the chief responsibility in this area to the CSTO.

CSTO

The CSTO Charter sets forth its readiness to cooperate with international organizations involved in the maintenance of international peace and security (art. 4). As one form of cooperation, these organizations can be granted observer status in the CSTO,[790] although this option has never been used.

As for cooperation with the UN, the CSTO Secretary-General takes part in the meetings of the UN General Assembly and UN Security Council. Upon the visit of the UN Secretary-General to the CSTO headquarters

---

accessed at *Electronic Legal Database Konsul'tant Plus. Technologiia 3000*); Комплексный план по урегулированию ситуации на Таджико-Афганской границе [Complex Plan of Action on the Settlement of the Situation at Tajikistan-Afghan Border] adopted by the CIS CHS Decision of 26 May 1995, *Sodruzhestvo*, (1995, 2), para. 3.

[789] О сроке пребывания, составе и задачах коллективных миротворческих сил в Республике Таджикистан [On the Terms of Deployment, Composition and Tasks of the Collective Peacekeeping Forces in Tajikistan], Decision of the CIS CHS, 15 April 1994, *Sodruzhestvo*, (1994,1), para. 5.

[790] CSTO Charter, *op. cit.*, art. 21; Правила процедуры органов ОДКБ [Rules of Procedure of the CSTO Organs], adopted by the CSC Decision of 18 June 2004, *Electronic Legal Database Konsul'tant Plus. Technologiia 3000,* rule 15.

(March 2010), a Memorandum of Cooperation between the UN and CSTO Secretariats[791] was signed. Cooperation with the CSTO is included in the agenda of the UN General Assembly and has been repeatedly considered by the latter.[792] The CSTO supports the use of its peacekeeping personnel in UN operations[793] and cooperates with various UN institutions in addition to the main UN organs.

The CSTO lays an emphasis on cooperation with the OSCE.[794] Officials of these organizations take part in each other's activities through visits of their Secretaries-General or cooperation at the working level (*e.g.*, with the OSCE Conflict Prevention Center's Action against Terrorism unit).[795] CSTO countries coordinate their positions to express at the OSCE meetings.[796]

Special attention is also paid to cooperation with other regional and sub-regional organizations (the CIS, ShCO, EurAsEC). Meeting together on 12 October 2010, these organizations decided to cooperate in security, economic and social areas and to establish a special group responsible for interaction between them.[797]

Conclusions

International organizations involved in the maintenance of international peace and security in the CIS region (the OSCE, CIS and CSTO) differ in composition, competences, tasks and activities. All of them, however, can be qualified under Chapter VIII. Despite the reasonable

---

791 Joint Declaration on UN/CSTO Secretariat Cooperation, Moscow, 18 March 2010; Cooperation between the United Nations and Regional and Other Organizations, *op. cit.*, paras. 56, 125.

792 Cooperation between the United Nations and Regional and Other Organizations, *op. cit.*

793 ОДКБ выступает за использование своего миротворческого потенциала в операциях ООН [CSTO Stands for the Use of its Peacekeeping Forces in the UN Operations].

794 Expressed in the speech of the CSTO Secretary General at the joint meeting of the OSCE Permanent Council and Forum for Security Co-operation, Vienna, 15 April 2010; see CSTO Secretary General says Cooperation with OSCE Crucial for Security; Bordyuzha N., "The Collective Security Treaty Organization," *op. cit.*, p. 347-349.

795 Secretaries General of the OCSE and CSTO Discussed Co-operation of Organizations, press release, 26 March 2009.

796 Written contribution by the CSTO SG, Mr. N. Bordyuzha (SUM.DEL/23/10), 1 December 2010.

797 Joint Statement of High Officials of EurAsEC, CSTO, CIS and ShCO, 12 October 2010; see also Cooperation with Other International Organizations and Structures; Bordyuzha N., "The Collective Security Treaty Organization," *op. cit.*, p. 345.

criticism regarding their unwillingness to act;[798] inadequate material, military or technical facilities; the use of double standards; insufficient transparency in the course of operations; overwhelming Russian dominance over politics in the region (or state interests of principal members);[799] low effectiveness of states within the CIS that results in the low effectiveness of the organizations;[800] poor legal technique and expertise; as well as an "emptiness of commitments" (in particular within the CIS and CSTO), it is maintained here that the prerequisites for the establishment of an effective system of regional security do already exist.

It would be rather naive to expect that the situation will change instantly and drastically, but it has already gradually evolved during the last decade. The CIS states have become accustomed to new circumstances, and have developed necessary state institutions and legal systems. Despite the existing negligence to the legal technique and expertise, attempts have been made to review, clarify and structure the CIS and CSTO databases.

If we look at the system of regional organizations acting in the region, it appears that the OCSE has already developed and introduced a very detailed and comprehensive system of CSBMs as well as mechanisms for the diplomatic settlement of international disputes. Its expertise and commitments in human, economic and environmental matters could be very helpful in ensuring the rule of law in the CIS states. The CIS possesses a structured system of responses to the new threats and challenges in the post-Soviet territory. The CSTO has established a system of collective forces to be used for self-defense, peacekeeping and peace enforcement, in natural and environmental emergencies, and in the struggle against new threats and challenges. While announcements about the establishment of an effective system of regional security are undoubtedly premature, existing organizations (due to the complementarity of their tasks, competences and facilities) could together establish such a comprehensive system. This, however, requires less theatrics and care about national interests and more willingness to cooperate with each other and with the UN institutions.

---

[798] An example occurred during the unrest in Kyrgyzstan in 2010, when the CSTO did not participate in joint declarations that were made by the UN, OSCE and EU (Statements by the Special Envoys of UN, OSCE and EU on Kyrgyzstan – 16 June 2010; 14 September 2010; 22 November 2010).

[799] Evers F., Zellner W., "Regional Interests in Maintaining and Diversifying the OSCE Field Operations," *op. cit.*, p. 448-462 ; MacFarlane S.N., "The CIS and Regional Security," *op. cit.*, p. 233. Russian works about the CIS and CSTO largely focus on safeguarding Russian interests and accuse others of attempting to undermine these structures; see, *e.g.*, Vozzhenikov A.V., ed., *Regional Security*, *op. cit.*, p. 82-102.

[800] MacFarlane S.N., "The CIS and Regional Security," *op. cit.*, p. 227.

CONCLUSION

Visions of security and collective security have come a long way, including in the period since the UN Charter was adopted. The concepts have developed from the absence of international conflicts to the prevention and settlement of internal conflicts, the prevention of even the hypothetical possibility of any conflict, and the struggle against contemporary threats and challenges.

At the same time, a comprehensive vision of security as including economic, environmental, social and other components is inapplicable to the activity of the UN Security Council and regional organizations of collective security. On one hand, the competences, functions and tasks of the Security Council and regional organizations under Chapter VIII are much broader today that those envisaged in the UN Charter. On the other hand, a too-expansive approach would risk being used as a new excuse for advancing national interests rather than as an active mechanism for the maintenance of international peace.

As a result, the definitions of collective security and of the system of collective security cited by numerous publicists[801] are largely outdated today. Currently, the system of collective security is based on the prohibition of the use of force and other principles of international law, and on a universal state-oriented institutionalized mechanism of maintenance of international peace and security that provides for (1) the possibility of centralized collective enforcement in response to the use or threat of force or acts of aggression, and (2) the application of multilevel measures aimed at eliminating or minimizing potential reasons for conflicts and suppressing threats to international peace and security in accordance with the purposes and principles of the UN Charter as well as obligations under the Charter.

The system includes the following elements: principles of international law, mechanisms of peaceful settlement of international disputes, centralized mechanisms of enforcement, self-defense, regional arrangements and agencies, peacekeeping, disarmament and control over armaments, security and confidence-building measures, and mechanisms of cooperation in the struggle against contemporary threats and challenges.

---

[801] See, *e.g.*, Thompson K.W., "Collective Security Reexamined," *op. cit.*, p. 285; Jessup Ph.C., *International Security*, *op. cit.*, p. 110; Sakrasena K.P., *The United Nations and Collective Security*, *op. cit.*, p. 4-5; Kelsen H., "Collective Security and Collective Self-Defense," *op. cit.*, p. 783; *etc.*

Unquestionably, it is high time to see collective security as having a new face, with a redistribution of roles in the maintenance of international peace and security. Despite the formal adherence to mechanisms proposed by the UN's founders more than 65 years ago, the Security Council is clearly unable to handle conflicts around the world alone. Regional organizations, meanwhile, are determined to grab as much autonomy and authority as they can. So the question is not whether the face of collective security has changed or is currently changing – that is already obvious. The question is what face we see, both now and in the future. In the worst case, we may return to a system of alliances in which self-selected "better" states or regional organizations will arbitrarily decide what is moral or immoral, legitimate or fallacious, with little or no regard to legality or the rule of law, although this might not work as well today as it did before the UN was created. Weapons, technology and machinery have developed to the point that even the smallest state (not to mention non-state actors) may cause serious threats and problems to the biggest and strongest ones.

In view of the extreme interdependence of actors in today's world, the only way forward is cooperation and interaction based on the principles and peremptory rules of general international law, norms of the UN Charter, and respect and observance of the rule of law.

The UN Charter was drafted as – and has proved to be – a flexible document that is able to adapt to the challenges, factors and problems of newer periods. We thus need to reinterprete its provisions, but in conformity with its purposes, principles and spirit and with strict observance of peremptory rules.

Given the primary purpose of the UN Charter with respect to cooperation with other organizations in the maintenance of international peace and security – to subordinate the activity of regional organizations to that of the United Nations and at least to the minimal standards of Chapter VIII of the UN Charter – any collective activity in this sphere should be fulfilled by regional organizations, arrangements and entities within the framework of Chapter VIII. Regional organizations are to be viewed in the broadest way and include any collective entities acting in the security area regardless of their scope of competences, their *ad hoc* or permanent character, the existence of constituent documents, *etc.* This functional approach, however, does not predestinate special attention being paid to the activity of permanent institutions in the security area, the need to develop mechanisms of cooperation between them, or issues of responsibility for any breaches of international law that may take place in the course of this activity.

The issue of responsibility falls outside the scope of the present research. Neither the qualification of certain activity as being subject to the rules of Chapter VIII nor the exemption of particular organizations from the scope of security organizations as perceived by some authors may be decisive in this respect. Without prejudice to existing or future studies, the issue of responsibility for breaches of international law committed in the course of activity aimed at the maintenance of international peace and security may only be decided after careful consideration of all circumstances of a particular operation, including whether the actors involved possess legal personality, authorization, or general and operational control. In this era of mixed operations, one may only state the possibility of invoking the responsibility of clearly identifiable subjects of international law, which may be either states as members of a specific arrangement or entity, or regional organizations if they possess their own personnel and exercise general and operational control over specific operations.

The stable functioning of the system of collective security may only be achieved if we move away from the idealistic ideas about the possibility of total control by the UN Security Council and its sufficiency, but at the same time do not run to the other extreme – that of recognizing the rights of regional organizations to decide unilaterally on any activity to be taken for the maintenance of international peace and security. The potential for malificence on their part is illustrated by attempts already taken by some organizations (AU, ECOWAS) to decide on military invasions of their member states without authorization of the UN Security Council, basing these decisions on provisions of their constituent and other documents. Previously, no operations of this sort took place, probably because of internal awareness of their illegality.

The system of collective security can only be effective if it combines both subsidiarity and complementarity approaches. It should be accepted that the Security Council is unable to settle alone all conflicts around the world. Moreover, there is no need for it to do so. The Security Council is to preserve its authorization, control and assessment functions. It should remain the only organ able to decide on the use of enforcement measures of any sort (military or non-military) taken by states and/or regional organizations, apart from measures which may legally be taken by states in accordance with international law. The Security Council should retain overall control over operations conducted by states and regional organizations for the maintenance of international peace and security (this does not, however, mean full operational control), be able to decide on the legality of actions taken and play a role of coordinator in the sphere.

Regional organizations, through their autonomy in non-enforcement activity, become major in-field players and thus complement the powers of the Security Council. Horizontal applications of the principle of complementarity in relations between regional organizations will prevent them from having to develop identical mechanisms in every organization and may guarantee that in cases of emergency at least some participant that is willing and able to act will be found. These purposes, however, may only be achieved through the development of stable mechanisms of cooperation between the UN and regional organizations and between regional organizations acting in the same area, with the elaboration of algorithms of cooperation between organizations in case of emergency – preferably under the auspices of the United Nations. Any disregard for certain countries or regions, or a refusal to cooperate with them, may never serve a good service to the maintenance of peace and security either in a specific region or around the world.

None of the above steps needs formal amendent of the UN Charter. They all may be achieved in the course of functional reform of the Security Council and, more importantly, with the shift in awareness about the comprehensiveness of responsibility for maintenance of peace and security rather than security alone. Observance of, and respect for, the rule of law accepts no exceptions, especially when maintenance of international peace and security is concerned. Legitimacy will hardly be achieved if it is exercised at the expence of legality.

Formally, then, the system of collective security envisaged by the UN's founders still remains the same. It prohibits the use of force in international relations and allots to the Security Council primary responsibility in the sphere. At the same time, 67 years after the UN Charter was adopted, it may be viewed as rather different – with a much more comprehensive approach to security and a reliance on the active role of regional organizations. It seems logical and necessary to accept both of its faces to make all actors work on behalf of peace, security and stability.

ANNEX 1

CHAPTER VIII OF THE UN CHARTER: REGIONAL ARRANGEMENTS

Article 52

Nothing in the present Charter precludes the existence of regional arrangements or agencies for dealing with such matters relating to the maintenance of international peace and security as are appropriate for regional action provided that such arrangements or agencies and their activities are consistent with the Purposes and Principles of the United Nations.

The Members of the United Nations entering into such arrangements or constituting such agencies shall make every effort to achieve pacific settlement of local disputes through such regional arrangements or by such regional agencies before referring them to the Security Council.

The Security Council shall encourage the development of pacific settlement of local disputes through such regional arrangements or by such regional agencies either on the initiative of the states concerned or by reference from the Security Council.

This Article in no way impairs the application of Articles 34 and 35.

Article 53

The Security Council shall, where appropriate, utilize such regional arrangements or agencies for enforcement action under its authority. But no enforcement action shall be taken under regional arrangements or by regional agencies without the authorization of the Security Council, with the exception of measures against any enemy state, as defined in paragraph 2 of this Article, provided for pursuant to Article 107 or in regional arrangements directed against renewal of aggressive policy on the part of any such state, until such time as the Organization may, on request of the Governments concerned, be charged with the responsibility for preventing further aggression by such a state.

The term enemy state as used in paragraph 1 of this Article applies to any state which during the Second World War has been an enemy of any signatory of the present Charter.

Article 54

The Security Council shall at all times be kept fully informed of activities undertaken or in contemplation under regional arrangements or by regional agencies for the maintenance of international peace and security.

ANNEX 2

SYSTEM OF REGIONAL "SECURITY" ORGANIZATIONS IN EUROPE

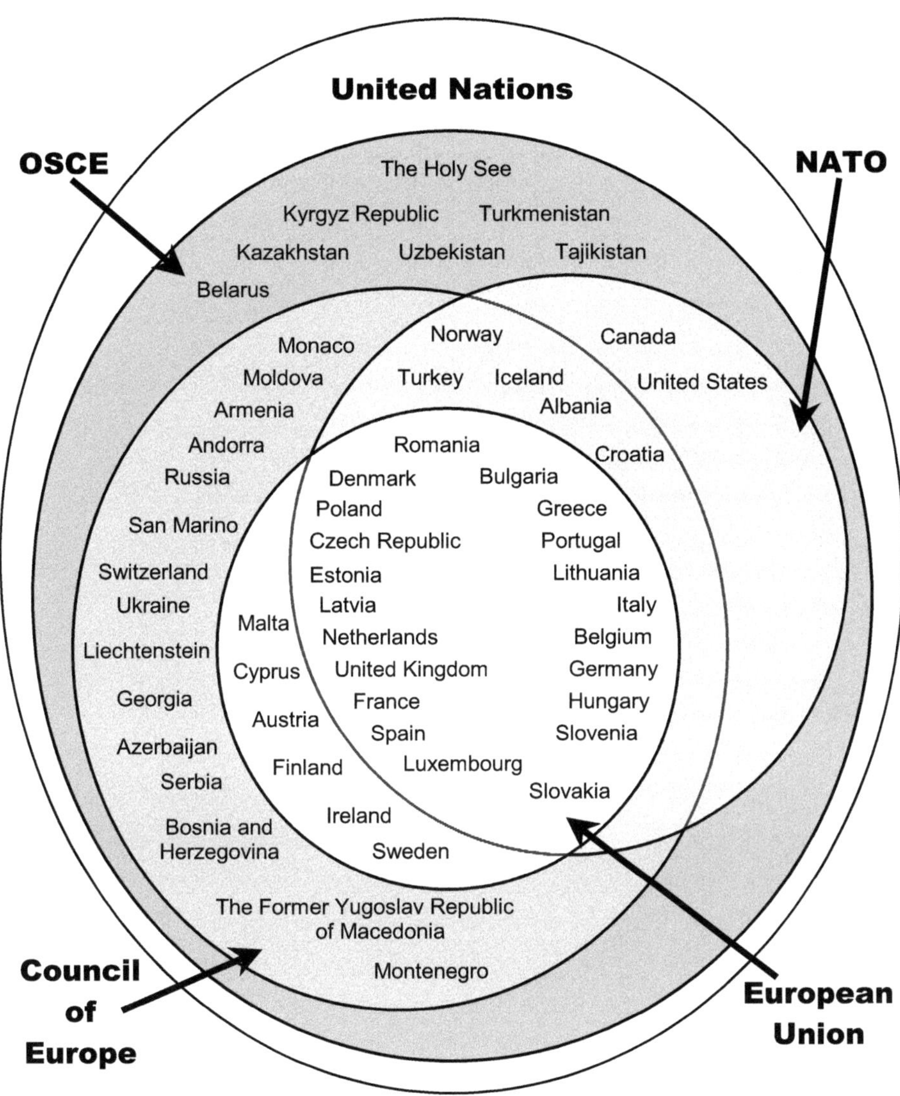

(Adapted from NATO)

ANNEX 3

SYSTEM OF REGIONAL ORGANIZATIONS IN EUROPE-CENTRAL ASIA

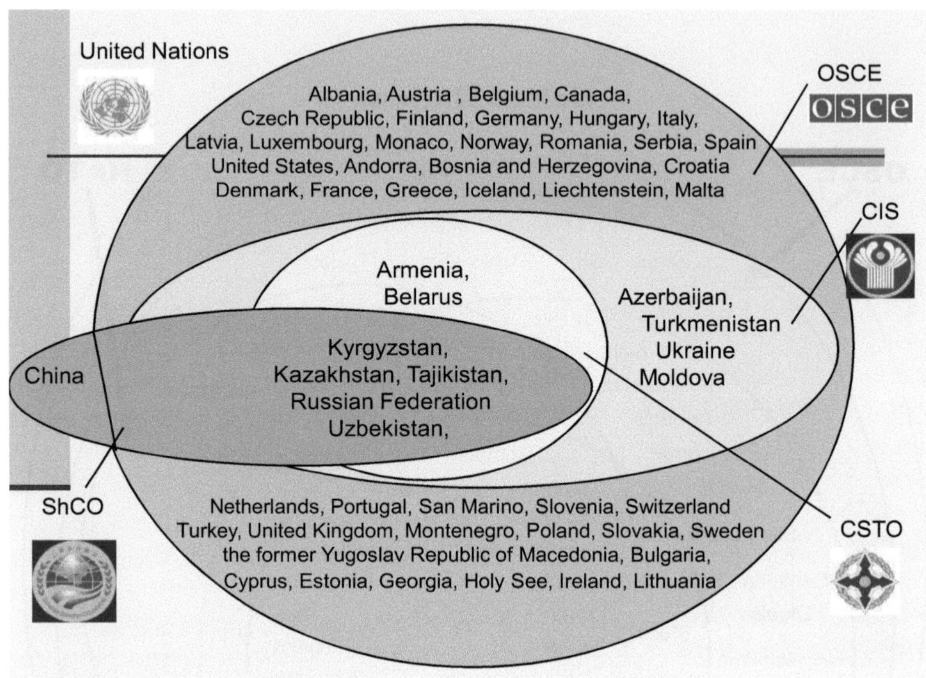

(Alena F. Douhan)

ANNEX 4

ORGANIZATIONS INVOLVED IN THE MAINTENANCE OF PEACE AND SECURITY IN EUROPE-CENTRAL ASIA

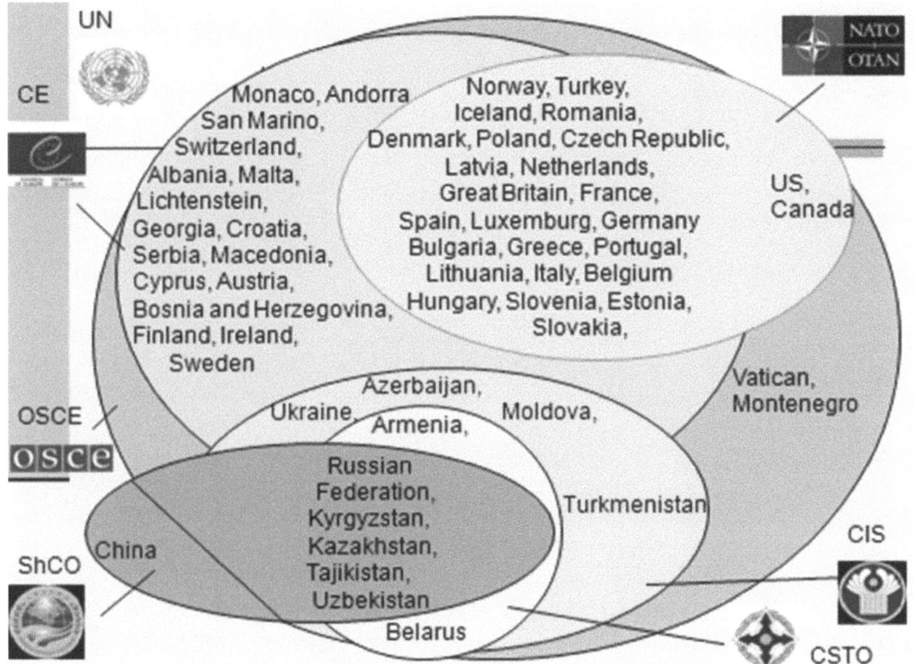

(Alena F. Douhan)

BIBLIOGRAPHY

Monographs

Abass A., *Regional Organizations and the Development of Collective Security: Beyond Chapter VIII of the UN Charter* (Oxford/Portland: Hart Publishing, 2004), 239 p.

Alexandrov S.A., *Self-defense Against the Use of Force in International Law* (The Hague: Kluwer Law International, 1996), 359 p.

Alvarez J.E., *International Organizations as Law-Makers* (New York: Oxford University Press, 2005), 660 p.

Amerasinghe C.F., *Principles of the Institutional Law of International Organizations*, 2nd ed. (Cambridge: Cambridge University Press, 2005), 535 p.

Belatchew A., *Prohibition of Force under the UN Charter: A Study of Art. 2(4)* (Uppsala: Iustus Förlag, 1991), 275 p.

Ball J.H., *Collective Security: The Why and How* (Boston: World Peace Foundation, 1943), 60 p.

Bentwich N., Martin A., *A Commentary on the Charter of the United Nations* (London: Routledge & Kegan Paul Ltd., 1950), 239 p.

Brzoska M., ed., *Design and Implementation of Arms Embargoes and Travel and Aviation Related Sanctions: Results of the Bonn-Berlin Process* (Bonn, BICC, 2001), 114 p.

Commission to Study the Organization of Peace: *Regional Arrangements for Security and the United Nations*. Eighth Report and Papers Presented to the Commission (New York, 1953), 144 p.

Conte A., *Handbook on Human Rights Compliance While Countering Terrorism* (Washington: Center on Global Counterterrorism Cooperation, 2008), 31 p.

Crawford J., *The International Law Commission's Articles on State Responsibility: Introduction, Text and Commentaries* (Cambridge: Cambridge University Press, 2007), 387 p.

Evers F., Kahl M., Zellner W., *The Culture of Dialogue: The OSCE Acquis 30 Years after Helsinki* (Hamburg: CORE, 2005), 72 p.

Farral J.M., *United Nations Sanctions and the Rule of Law* (Cambridge: Cambridge University Press, 2009), 542 p.

Faust D.A., *Effektive Sicherheit. Analyse des Systems kollektiver Sicherheit der Vereinten Nationen und Entwurf eines alternativen Sicherheitssystems* (Wiesbaden: Westdeutscher Verlag, 2002), 428 p.

Geyrhalter B., *Friedenssicherung durch Regionalorganizationen ohne Beschluß des Sicherheitsrates* (Cologne: LIT, 2001), 239 p.

Ghebali V-Y., Lambert A., *The OSCE Code of Conduct on Politico-Military Aspects of Security: Anatomy and Implementation* (Leiden: Matinus Nijhoff Publishers, 2005), 428 p.

Goodrich L.M., Hambro E., *Charter of the United Nations: Commentary and Documents,* 3rd ed. (Boston: World Peace Foundation, 1946), 413 p.

Haas E.B., *Collective Security and the Future International System* (Denver: University of Denver, 1967), 117 p.

Handbook on Criminal Justice and Responses to Terrorism, Criminal Justice Handbook Series (New York: United Nations, 2009), 127 p.

Henkin L., *How Nations Behave: Law and Foreign Policy*, 2nd ed., (New York: Columbia University Press, 1979), 400 p.

Hogan W.N., *International Conflict and Collective Security: The Principle of Concern in International Organization* (Lexington: University of Kentucky Press, 1955), 202 p.

Jennings R., Watts A., ed., *Oppenheim's International Law*, 9th ed., vol.1. Peace. Introduction and Part 1 (Harlow: Longman, 1992), 554 p.

Jessup Ph.C., *International Security: The American Role in Collective Action for Peace* (New York: Council on Foreign Relations Inc., 1935), 157 p.

Karns M.P., Mingst K.A., *International Organizations: The Politics and Processes of Global Governance* (Boulder/London: Lynne Rienner Publishers, 2010), 632 p.

Kelsen H., *Collective Security under International Law* (Washington: US Government Printing Office, 1954), 275 p.

Kelsen H., *The Law of the United Nations* (London: Stevens and Sons, 1964), 994 p.

Kewenig W.A., Heini A., *Die Anwendung wirtschaftlicher Zwangsmaßnahmen im Völkerrecht und im internationalen Privatrecht* (Heidelberg: Müller, Juristische Verlag, 1982), 104 p.

Körbs H., *Die Friedensdicherung duech die Vereinten Nationen und Regionalorganizationen nach Kapitel VIII der Satzung der Vereinten Nationen* (Bochum: UVB – Unversitätsverlag Dr. N. Brockmeyer, 1997), 595 p.

Kreutz J., *Hard Measures by a Soft Power? Sanctions Policy of the European Union.* Paper 45, Bonn International Center for Conversation (Bonn: Bonn International Center for Conversation, 2005), 50 p.

Lachowski Z., *Confidence and Security Building Measures in the New Europe*, SIPRI Research Report No. 18 (New York: OUP, 2004), 224 p.

Lind K., *The Revival of Chapter VIII of the UN Charter: Regional Organizations and Collective Security* (Stockholm: PrintCenter, 2004), 341 p.
Liska G., *Nations in Alliance: the Limits of Interdependence* (Baltimore: The John Hopkins Press, 1962), 301 p.
Lorenz J.P., *Peace, Power, and the United Nations: A Security System for the Twenty-first Century* (Oxford: Westview Press, 1999), 185 p.
Lowe V., ed., *The United Nations Security Council and War: The Evolution of Thought and Practice since 1945* (Oxford: Oxford University Press, 2008), 793 p.
Malanczuk P., *Humanitarian Intervention and the Legitimacy of the Use of Force* (The Hague: Het Spinhuis, 1993), 60 p.
Nincic M., Wallensteen P., ed., *Dilemmas of Economic Coercion: Sanctions in World Politics* (New York: Praeger Publishers, 1983), 250 p.
Nye J.S., *Understanding International Conflicts: An Introduction to Theory and History,* 3rd ed. (New York: Longman, 2000), 244 p.
Orakhelashvili A., *Peremptory Norms in International Law* (New York: Oxford University Press, 2008), 622 p.
Organski A.F.K., *World Politics* (New York: Alfred A. Knopf, 1958), 461 p.
Pernice R., *Die Sicherung des Weltfriedens durch Regionale Organisationen und die Vereinten Nationen (eine Untersuchung zur Kompetenzverteilung nach Kapitel VIII der UN-Charta*) (Hamburg: Hansischer Gildenverlag, Joachim Heitmann & Co., 1972), 178 p.
Rajan M.S., *United Nations and Domestic Jurisdiction*, 2nd ed. (London: Asia Publishing House, 1961), 540 p.
Rozanov A.A., Dovgan E.F., *Collective Security Treaty Organization (2002-2009).* DCAF Regional Program Series No. 6 (Geneva/Minsk: Procon, 2010), 92 p.
Rothstein R.L., *Alliances and Small Powers* (New York: Columbia University Press, 1968), 331 p.
Sakrasena K.P., *The United Nations and Collective Security: A Historical Analysis* (Delhi: D.K. Publishing House, 1977), 450 p.
Sarooshi D., *The United Nations and the Development of Collective Security (The Delegation by the UN Security Council of its Chapter VII Powers)* (Oxford: Clarendon Press, 1999), 311 p.
Schneider P., Müller-Wort T.-J.A., *The Court of Conciliation and Arbitration within OSCE*: Working Methods, Procedures and Composition. CORE Working paper 16 (Hamburg: CORE, 2007), 66 p.
Shaw M.N., *International Law*, 6th ed. (Cambridge: Cambridge University Press, 2008), 1542 p.

Simma B., ed., *The Charter of the United Nations: A Commentary* (New York: Oxford University Press Inc., 1995), 1258 p.

Sparrow G., *Sanctions* (London: Knightly Vernon Ltd., 1972), 58 p.

Targeted Financial Sanctions: A Manual for Design and Implementation. Contributions from the Interlaken Process (Institute for International Studies, 2001), 114 p.

Thakur R., *The United Nations, Peace and Security: From Collective Security to Responsibility to Protect* (Cambridge: Cambridge University Press, 2006), 388 p.

Verzijl J.H.W., *International Law in Historical Perspective* (Leiden: A.W. Sijhoff, 1968), vol. 1, 575 p.

Wallensteen, P. Stainbano C., ed., *International Sanctions: Between Words and Wars in the Global System* (London: Frank Cass, 2005), 251 p.

Walter C., *Vereinte Nationen und Regional Organisationen: Eine Untersuchung zu Kapitel VIII der Satzung der Vereinten Nationen* (Berlin: Springer Verlag, 1995), 407 p.

Weintraub S., ed., *Economic Coercion and U.S. Foreign Policy: Implications of Case Studies from the Johnson Administration* (Boulder: Westview Press, Inc., 1982), 234 p.

Weiss T.G., ed., *Beyond UN Subcontracting: Task-Sharing with Regional Security Arrangements and Service-Providing NGOs* (New York: St. Martin's Press, Inc., 1998), 266 p.

Weiss T.G., Forsythe D.R., Coate R.A., Pease K.-K., *The United Nations and Changing World Politics,* 5th ed. (Boulder: Westview Press, 2007), 416 p.

Wolfrum R., Kojima C., ed., *Solidarity: A Structural Principle of International Law* (Heidelberg: Springer, 2010), 238 p.

Zacher M.W., *International Conflicts and Collective Security, 1946-1977: The United Nations, Organization of American States, Organization of African Unity, and Arab League* (New York: Praeger Publishers, 1979), 297 p.

Zotiades G.B., Intervention by Treaty Right: Its Legality in Present Day International Law (Nicosia: Geka Press, 1965), 41 p.

Аречага Э.Х. де, *Современное международное право* [Arechaga H. de, *Modern International Law*] (Moscow: Progress, 1983), 480 p.

Бекяшева К.А., Отв. ред., *Международное публичное право*: *Учебник* [Bekjashev K.A., ed., *International Public Law: Textbook*] (Moscow: Prospect, 1999), 608 p.

Бровки Ю. П., Лепешкова Ю. А., Павловой Л. В., Отв. ред., *Международное публичное право. Особенная часть* [Brovka Y.P., Lepeshkov Y.A., Pavlova L.V., ed., *International Public Law. Special Part*] (Minsk: Amalfea, 2011), 688 p.

Возжеников А.В., Отв. ред., *Региональная безопасность: геополитический и геоэкономический подходы (теория и практика)* [Vozzhenikov A.V., ed., *Regional Security: Geopolitical and Geoeconomic Approaches*] (Moscow: Russian Academy of State Service, 2006), 262 p.

Додонов В.Н., Панов В.П., Румянцев О.Г.; Трофимова В.Н., Отв. ред., *Международное право. Словарь-справочник* [Dodonov V.N., Panov V.P., Rumjantsev O.G.; Trofimov V.N., ed., *International Law: Dictionary-Handbook*] (Moscow: INFRA-M, 1997), 368 p.

Игнатенко Г. В., Тиунов О. И., Отв. ред., *Международное право: учебник для ВУЗов* [Ignatenko G.V., Tiunov O.I., ed., *International Law: Textbook for Universities*] (Moscow: Norma, 2005), 720 p.

Каламкарян Р.А., *Кодификация международного права и современный миропорядок* [Kalamkarjan R.A., *Codification of International Law and Contemporary Legal Order*] (Moscow: Science, 2008), 274 p.

Каламкарян Р.А., Мигачев Ю.И., *Международное право: учебное пособие* [Kalamkarjan R.A., Migachev, Y.I., *International Law*] (Moscow: Yurlitinform, 2003), 424 p.

Клименко Б.М., Отв. ред., *Всеобъемлющая международная безопасность… Международно-правовые принципы и нормы: справочник.* [Klimenko B.M., ed., *Comprehensive International Security… International Legal Principles and Norms: Handbook*] (Moscow: International Relations, 1990), 328 p.

Ковалева, А.А., Черниченко, С.В., Отв. ред., *Международное право: Учебник для студентов ВУЗов* [Kovalev A.A., Chernichenko S.V., ed., *International Law*] (Moscow: Omega, 2008), 832 p.

Колосов Ю.М., Кривчикова Э.С., Отв. ред., *Международное право: Учебник* [Kolosov Y.M., Krivchikova, E.S., ed., *International Law*] (Moscow: International Relations, 2003), 720 p.

Лукашук И.И., *Право международной ответственности* [Lukashuk I.I., *Law of International Responsibility*] (Moscow: Walters Kluwer, 2004), 432 p.

Скакунов Э.И., *Самооборона в международном праве* [Skakunov E.I., *Self-Defense in International Law*] (Moscow: International Relations, 1973), 176 p.

Собакин В.К., *Коллективная безопасность – гарантия мирного сосуществования* [Sobakin V.K., *Collective Security – A Guarantee of Peaceful Coexistence*] (Moscow: International Relations, 1962), 518 p.

Тахир М., *Правовые проблемы коллективной безопасности* [Tahir M., *Legal Problems of Collective Security*] (St. Petersburg: St. Petersburg University Publishers, 2004), 208 p.

Тункин Т.И., *Право и сила в международной системе* [Tunkin T.I., *Law and Force in International Relations*] (Moscow: International Relations, 1983), 200 p.

Ушаков Н.А., *Невмешательство во внутренние дела государств* [Ushkov N.A., *Non-Intervention into Domestic Affairs*] (Moscow: International Relations, 1971), 168 p.

Черниченко С.В., *Теория международного права* [Chernichenko S.V., *Theory of International Law*], vol. 1 (Moscow: NIMP, 1999), 336 p.

Articles and Chapters

Abass A., "The New Collective Security Mechanism of ECOWAS: Innovations and Problems," *Journal of Conflict and Security Law*, 5(2) (2000), p. 211-229.

Ackermann A., Crosby J., de Haan J., Falkehed E., "Developing an OSCE Mediation-Support Capacity: First Steps," *OSCE Yearbook 2010*, (Hamburg: Nomos, 2011), p. 369-376.

Ackermann A., Salber H., "The OSCE "Corfu Process" – A Preliminary View of the Security Dialogue on Early Warning, Conflict Prevention and Resolution, Crisis Management, and Post-conflict Rehabilitation," *OSCE Yearbook 2010*, (Hamburg: Nomos, 2011), p. 197-202.

Akehurst M., "Enforcement Action of Regional Organizations with Special Reference to the Organization of American States," *British Yearbook of International Law,* 42 (1967), p. 175-228.

Alagappa M., "Regional Arrangements, the UN and International Security: A Framework for Analysis," in *Beyond Subcontracting: Task Sharing with Regional Security Arrangements and Service-Providing NGOs,* ed. Th. Weiss (Basingstoke: MacMillan, 1998), p. 3-29.

Andreopoulos G., "Collective Security and the Responsibility to Protect," in *United Nations Reform and the New Collective Security*, ed. P.G. Danchin, H. Fisher (Cambridge: Cambridge University Press, 2010), p. 155-172.

Arnold R., "Human Rights in Times of Terrorism," *Zeitschrift für Ausländisches Öffentliches Recht und Völkerrecht*, 66 (2006), p. 297-319.

Benvenisti E., "The US and the Use of Force: Double-edged Hegemony and Management of Global Emergencies," *European Journal of International Law*, 15 (2004), p. 677-700.

Bernhardt G., "Article 103," in *The Charter of the United Nations: A Commentary,* 2nd ed., vol. 1, ed. B. Simma (Munich: Verlag C.H. Beck, 2002), p. 1292-1302.

Beyerlin U., "Regional Arrangements," in *United Nations: Law, Politics and Practice*, ed. R. Wolfrum, vol. I (Munich: Verlag C.H. Beck, 1995), p. 1040-1058.

Bianchi A., "Assessing the Effectiveness of the UN Security Council's Anti-terrorism Measures: The Quest for Legitimacy and Cohesion," *European Journal of International Law*, 17(5) (2007), p. 881-919.

Biersteker T.J., "Targeted Sanctions and Individual Human Rights," *International Journal*, 65 (2009-2010), p. 99-118.

Blokker N., "Towards the Second Enlargement of the Security Council? A Comparative Perspective," in *The Security Council and the Use of Force: Theory and Reality – A Need for Challenge?*, ed. N. Blokker and N. Schrijver, (Leiden/Boston: Martinus Nijhoff Publishers, 2005), p. 253-260.

Bordyuzha N., "The Collective Security Treaty Organization: A Brief Overview," *OSCE Yearbook,* 16 (2010), p. 339-350.

Borelli S., Olleson S., "Obligations Relating to Human Rights and Humanitarian Law," in *The Law of International Responsibility*, ed. J. Crawford, A. Pellet, S. Olleson (Oxford: Oxford University Press, 2010), p. 1177-1195

Borgen C.J., "The Theory and Practice of Regional Organization in Civil Wars," *New York University Journal of International Law and Politics*, 26 (1994), 799-835.

Bother N., "Peace-keeping," in *The Charter of the United Nations: A Commentary,* ed. B. Simma, vol. 1 (Munich: Verlag C.H. Beck, 2002), p. 648-700.

Brunnée J., "International Law and Collective Concerns: Reflections on the Responsibility to Protect," in *Law of the Sea, Environmental Law and Settlement of Disputes,* ed. T.M. Ndiaye, R. Wolfrum, (Leiden/Boston: Martinus Nijhoff Publishers, 2007), p. 35-51.

Brunneé J., "The Security Council and Self-Defence: Which Way to Global Security?" in *The Security Council and the Use of Force: Theory and Reality – the Need for Change*, ed. N. Blokker, N. Schrijver, (Leiden: Martinus Nijhoff Publishers, 2005), p. 107-132.

Byers M., "Terrorism, the Use of Force and International Law after 11 September 2001," *International and Comparative Law Quarterly*, 51 (2002), part 2, p. 401-414.

Calamita N.J., "Sanctions, Countermeasures, and the Iranian Nuclear Issue," *Vanderbilt Journal of Transnational Law,* 42(5) (2009), p. 1393-1442.

Cameron I., "Protecting Legal Rights: On the (In)security of Targeted Sanctions," in *International Sanctions: Between Words and Wars in the Global System*, ed. P. Wallensteen, C. Staibano (London/New York: Frank Cass, 2005), p. 141-206.

Cannizaro E., "A Machiavellian Moment? The UN Security Council and the Rule of Law," *International Organizations Law Review*, 3 (2006), p. 189-224.

Cassese A., "Ex Iniuria ius oritus: Are we Moving Toward International Legitimation of Forcible Humanitarian Countermeasures in the World Community?" *European Journal of International Law*, 10(1) (1999), p. 23-30.

Cassese A., "The Character of the Violated Obligation," in *The Law of International Responsibility*, ed. J. Crawford, A. Pellet, S. Olleson, (Oxford: Oxford University Press, 2010), p. 415-420.

Chesterman S., "UNaccontable? The United Nations, Emergency Powers, and the Rule of Law," *Vanderbilt Journal of Transnational Law*, 42(5) (2009), p. 1509-1541.

Cornell S.E., "Russia's Gridlock in Chechnya: 'Normalization' or Deterioration?" *OSCE Yearbook 2004*, (Hamburg: Nomos, 2005), p. 251-260.

Cuéllar M.F., "Reflections on Sovereignty and Collective Security," *Stanford Journal of International Law*, 40(1) (2004), p. 211-257.

Damrosch L.F., "Sanctions against the Perpetrators of Terrorism," *Houston Journal of International Law* 22(1) (1999), p. 63-76.

Danchin P.G., "Things Fall Apart: The Concept of Collective Security in International Law," in *United Nations Reform and the New Collective Security*, ed. P.G. Danchin, H. Fischer (Cambridge: Cambridge University Press, 2010), p. 35-75.

Danchin P.G., Fischer H., "Introduction: The New Collective Security," in *United Nations Reform and the New Collective Security*, ed. P.G. Danchin, H. Fischer (Cambridge: Cambridge University Press, 2010), p. 1-31.

de Luca S.M., "The Gulf Crisis and Collective Security under the United Nations Charter," *Pace Yearbook of International Law*, 3(1) (1991), p. 267-307.

de Vries A.W., Hazelzet H., "The EU as a New Actor on the Sanctions Scene," in *International Sanctions: Between Words and Wars in the Global System*, ed. P. Wallensteen, C. Staibano (London/New York: Frank Cass, 2005), p. 95-107.

de Wet E., Wood M. "Collective Security," *Max Planck Encyclopedia of Public International Law.* Accessed 11 November 2011, www.mpepil.de

Dicke K., "Reform of the United Nations," in *United Nations: Law, Politics and Practice*, ed. R. Wolfrum, (Munich: Verlag C.H. Beck, 1995), p. 1012-1024.

Doehring K., "Collective Security," in *United Nations: Law, Politics and Practice*, ed. R. Wolfrum, vol. I (Munich: Verlag C.H. Beck, 1995), p. 110-115.

Doehring K., "Unlawful Resolutions of the Security Council and Their Legal Consequences," *Max Planck Yearbook of United Nations Law*, 1 (1997), p. 91-109.

Eagleton C., "The North Atlantic Treaty Organization," in *Commission to Study the Organization of Peace: Regional Arrangements for Security and the United Nations*. Eighth Report and Papers Presented to the Commission (New York, 1953), p. 91-99.

Eide A., "Peace-keeping and Enforcement by Regional Organizations: Its Place in the UN System," *Journal of Peace Research*, 3(2) (1966), p. 125-145.

Eitel T., "The UN Security Council and its Future Contribution in the Field of International Law," *Max Planck Yearbook of United Nations Law*, 2000, p. 53-71.

Elaraby N., "Some Reflections on the Role of the Security Council and the Prohibition of the Use of Force in International Relations: Article 2(4) Revisited in Light of Recent Developments," in *Verhandeln für den Frieden,* ed. J.A. Frowein (Berlin: Springer, 2003), p. 41-67.

Eriksson M., "EU Sanctions: Three Cases of Targeted Sanctions," in *International Sanctions: Between Words and Wars in the Global System,* ed. P. Wallensteen, C. Staibano, (London/New York: Frank Cass, 2005), p. 108-125.

Evers F., Zellner W., "Regional Interests in Maintaining and Diversifying the OSCE Field Operations: Supporting a Trend," *OSCE Yearbook 2004*, (Hamburg: Nomos, 2005), p. 447-465.

Farer T., "Political and Economic Coercion in Contemporary International Law," *American Journal of International Law*, 75 (1985), p. 405-413.

Farer T.J., "A Paradigm of Legitimate Intervention," in *Enforcing Restraint: Collective Intervention in Internal Conflicts*, ed. L.F. Damrosch, (New York: Council on Foreign Relations Press, 1993), p. 316-347.

Farer T.J., "The United States as Guarantor of Democracy in the Caribbean Basin: Is There a Legal Way?" *Human Rights Quarterly*, 10(1) (1988), p. 157-176.

Fawcett L., "The Evolving Architecture of Regionalization," in *The United Nations and Regional Security: Europe and Beyond,* ed. M. Pugh and W.P. Singh Sidhu (Boulder/London: Lynne Rienner Publishers, 2003), p. 11-30.

Forteau M., "Regional Co-operation," in *Max Planck Encyclopedia of Public International Law.* Accessed 11 November 2011, www.mpepil.com

Franck T.M. "Collective Security and UN Reform: Between the Necessary and the Possible," *Chicago Journal of International Law*, 6(2) (2005-2006), p. 597-611.

Frowein J.A., "Legal Consequences for International Law Enforcement in Case of Security Council Inaction," in *The Future of International Law Enforcement. New Scenarios – New Law?*, ed. J. Delbrück (Berlin: Duncker & Humblot, 1993), p. 111-124.

Frowein J.A., "Reactions by Not Directly Affected States to Breaches of Public International Law," in *Recueil des Cours/Collected Courses of the Hague Academy of International Law*, 248 (1994, IV) (Dordrecht: Martinus Nijhoff Publishers, 1995), p. 345-437.

Frowein J.A., "Zwangsmaßnahmen von Regionalorganizationen," in *Recht zwischen Umbruch und Bewahrung*, ed. U. Beyerlin, M. Bothe, R. Hofmann, E.-U. Petersman (Berlin: Springer Verlag, 1995), p. 57-69.

Frowein J.A., Krisch N., "Introduction to Chapter VII," in *The Charter of the United Nations: A Commentary*, 2nd ed., vol. 1, ed. B. Sinna (Munich: Verlag C.H. Beck, 2002), p. 703-716.

Frowein J.A., Krisch N., "Article 39," in *The Charter of the United Nations: A Commentary*, 2nd ed., vol. 1, ed. B. Simma, (Munich: Verlag C.H. Beck, 2002), p. 717-728.

Frowein J.A., Krisch N., "Article 41," in *The Charter of the United Nations: A Commentary*, 2nd ed., vol. 1, ed. B. Simma (Munich: Verlag C.H. Beck, 2002), p. 735-749.

Frowein J.A., Krisch N., "Article 42," in *The Charter of the United Nations: A Commentary*, 2nd ed., vol. 1, ed. B. Sinna (Munich: Verlag C.H. Beck, 2002), p. 749-759.

Galtung J., "On the Effects of International Economic Sanctions," in *Dilemmas of Economic Coercion: Sanctions in World Politics*, ed. M. Nincic, P. Wallensteen, (New York: Praeger Publishers, 1983), p. 17-60.

Gelber L., "The Commonwealth and the United Nations," in *Commission to Study the Organization of Peace: Regional Arrangements for Security and the United Nations*. Eighth Report and Papers Presented to the Commission (New York, 1953), p. 49-64.

Gowlland-Debbas V., “The Limits of Unilateral Enforcement of Community Objectives in the Framework of UN Peace Maintenance,” *European Journal of International Law*, 11(2) (2000), p. 361-383.

Graham K., “Regionalism and Responses to Armed Conflict, with Special Focus on Conflict Prevention and Peace-keeping,” in *Regionalisation and Global Governance: The Taming of Globalization?*, ed A.F. Cooper, Chr.W. Hughes, Ph. de Lombaerde (London/New York: Routledge Taylor and Francis Group, 2008), p. 159-186.

Grünfeld F., “The Effectiveness of United Nations Economic Sanctions,” in *United Nations Sanctions: Effectiveness and Effects, Especially in the Field of Human Rights: A Multidisciplinary Approach,* ed. W.J. van Genugten, (Antwerp: Intersentia, 1999), p. 113-134.

Hannay D., “Collective Security and the Use of Force,” *International Organizations Law Review*, 2(2) (2005), p. 367-372.

Heiskanen V., “The Rationality of the Use of Force and the Evolution of International Organizations,” in *The Legitimacy of International Organizations*, ed. J.-M. Coicaud and V. Heiskanen (Tokyo/NY/Paris: UN University Press, 2001), p. 155-185.

Henkin L., “The Invasion in Panama Under International Law: A Gross Violation,” *Columbia Journal of Transnational Law*, 29(2) (1991), p. 293-317.

Herik L. van den, “The Security Council’s Targeted Sanctions Regimes: In Need of Better Protection of the Individual,” *Leiden Journal of International Law*, 20 (2007), p. 797-807.

Herndl K. “Reflections on the Role, Functions and Procedures of the Security Council of the United Nations,” *Recueil des Cours/Collected Courses of the Hague Academy of International Law*, 206 (1987, VI), (Dordrecht: Martinus Nijhoff Publishers, 1991), p. 289-395.

Hoffmann S., “Is There an International Order?” in *Janus and Minerva: Essays in the Theory and Practice of International Politics* (Boulder: Westview Press, 1985), p. 85-121.

Hummer W., Schweitzer M., “Article 52,” in *The Charter of the United Nations: A Commentary*, 2nd ed., vol. 1, ed. B. Sinna (München: Verlag C.H. Beck, 2002), p. 807-853.

Jackamo T.J., “From the Cold War to the New Multilateral World Order: The Evolution of Covert Operations and the Customary International Law of Non-intervention. Note,” *Virginia Journal of International Law*, 32(4) (1992), p. 929-977

Jacobi S., “The OSCE Court: An Overview,” *Leiden Journal of International Law*, 10(2) (1997), p. 281-294.

Jakoby V., “The OSCE Mission in Georgia,” *OSCE Yearbook 2003*, (Hamburg; Nomos Verlagsgesellschaft, 2003), p. 163-170.

Jamnerjad M., Wood M., “The Principle of Non-Intervention,” *Leiden Journal of International Law*, 22(2) (2009), p. 345-381.

Johnson C.H., Niemeyer G., “Collective Security: The Validity of an Ideal,” *International Organizations*, 1 (1954), p. 19-35.

Karns M.P., “The Challenges of Maintaining Peace and Security in the 21st Century: The United Nations and Regional Organizations,” in *The United Nations: Past, Present and Future: Proceedings of the 2007 Francis Marion University UN Symposium*, ed. S Kaufman, A. Warters (New York: Nova Science Publishers Inc., 2009), p. 115-146.

Kelsen H., “Collective Security and Collective Self-Defense under the Charter of the United Nations,” *American Journal of International Law*, 42(4) (1948), p. 783-796.

Kelsen H., “Is the North Atlantic Treaty a Regional Arrangement?” *American Journal of International Law*, 45(1) (1951), p. 162-166.

Klabbers J., “The Politics of Institutional Reform,” in *United Nations Reform and the New Collective Security*, ed. P.G. Danchin, H. Fisher, (Cambridge: Cambridge University Press, 2010), p. 76-93.

Knight W.A., “Towards a Subsidiarity Model for Peacemaking and Preventive Diplomacy: Making Chapter VIII of the UN Operational,” *Third World Quarterly*, 17(1) (1996), p. 31-52.

Korkelia K., “The CIS Peace-Keeping Operations in the Context of International Legal Order.” Accessed 15 March 2011, http://www.nato.int/acad/fellow/97-99/korkelia.pdf

Koskenniemi M., “The Place of Law in Collective Security,” *Michigan Journal of International Law*, 17(2) (1995-1996), p. 455-490.

Kourula E., “Peace-keeping and Regional Arrangements,” in *United Nations Peace-keeping: Legal Essays,* ed. A. Cassese (Alphen aan den Rijn: Stijthoff & Noordhoff International Publishers, 1978), p. 95-123.

Kunig P., “Intervention, Prohibition of.” Accessed 2 November 2011, www.mpeil.com

Kupchan Ch.A., Kupchan C.A., “The Promise of Collective Security,” *International Security*, 20(1) (1995), p. 52-61.

Legault A., “Euro-Atlantic Multilateral Regimes,” in *Multilateralism and Regional Security,* ed. M. Fortmann, S.N. MacFarlane, S. Roussel (Toronto: The Canadian Peacekeeping Press, 1997), p. 149-165.

Luck E.C., “Regional Arrangements, the United Nations and the Japanese-American Security Treaty,” *Asia Survey*, 35(3) (1995), p. 237-252.

MacFarlane S.N., "The CIS and Regional Security," in *Multilateralism and Regional Security*, ed. M. Fortmann, S.N. MacFarlane, S. Roussel, (Toronto: The Canadian Peacekeeping Press, 1997), p. 224-237.

Mälksoo L., "Great Powers Then and Now: Security Council Reform and Responses to Threats to Peace and Security," in *United Nations Reform and the New Collective Security,* ed. P.G. Danchin, H. Fisher, (Cambridge: Cambridge University Press, 2010), p. 94-113.

Meeker L.C., "Defensive Quarantine and the Law," *American Journal of International Law*, 57(3) (1963), p. 515-524.

Morris J., "UN Security Council Reform: A Counsel for the 21st Century," *Security Dialogue*, 31(3) (2000), p. 265-277.

Morrison F.L., "The Role of Regional Organizations in the Enforcement of International Law," in *Allocation of Law Enforcement Authority in the International System* (Proceedings of an International Symposium of the Kiel Institute of International Law, 23-25 March 1994), ed. J. Delbrück (Berlin: Dunker and Humblot, 1994), p. 39-56.

Müllerson R., "Jus ad Bellum: Plus ça change (le Monde) plus c'est la même chose (le droit)?," *Journal of Conflict and Security Law*, 7(2) (2002), p. 149-189.

Müllerson R., Scheffer, D.J., "Legal Regulation of the Use of Force," in *Beyond Confrontation: International Law for the Post-Cold War Era*, ed. L.F. Damrosh, G.M. Danilenko, R. Müllerson (Boulder: Westview Press, 1995), p. 93-139.

Murdock J.O., "Collective Security Distinguished from Intervention," *American Journal of International Law,* 56(2) (1962), p. 500-503.

Neuhold H., "Collective Security after 'Operation Allied Force,'" *Max Planck Yearbook of United Nations Law*, 4 (2000), p. 73-106.

Neukirch C., "The OSCE Mission in Moldova," *OSCE Yearbook 2003*, (Hamburg; Nomos Verlagsgesellschaft, 2003), p. 149-161.

Nincic M., Wallensteen P., "Economic Coercion and Foreign Policy," in *Dilemmas of Economic Coercion: Sanctions in World Politics*, ed. Nincic and P. Wallensteen (New York: Praeger Publishers, 1983), p. 1-15.

Nolte G., "Intervention by Invitation." Accessed 2 November 2011, www.mpeil.com

O'Connell M.A., "The United Nations Security Council and the Authorization of Force: Renewing the Council through Law Reform," in *The Security Council and the Use of Force: Theory and Reality – A Need for Challenge?*, ed. N. Blokker and N. Schrijver, (Leiden/Boston: Martinus Nijhoff Publishers, 2005), p. 47-63.

Omorogbe E., "The African Union and the United Nations: Conflict or Cooperation?" Accessed 30 July 2011, http://uttv.ee/naita?id=5481

Orakhelashvili A., "The Impact of Peremptory Norms on the Interpretation and Application of United Nations Security Council Resolutions," *European Journal of International Law*, 16(1) (2005), p. 59-88.

Pronk J., "United Nations: Changes, Challenges, Chances," in *The Role of the United Nations in Peace and Security, Global Development and World Governance: An Assessment of the Evidence,* ed. M. Hordijk, M. van Eerd, K. Hofman (Lewinston: The Edwin Mellen Press, 2007), p. 236-253.

Randelzhofer A., "Use of Force," in *Encyclopedia of Public International Law,* vol. 4, ed. R. Bernhard (Amsterdam: North-Holland Publishing Co., 1982), p. 265-275.

Reeve R., "The OSCE Mission to Georgia – Activities in 2004," *OSCE Yearbook, 2004*, 10 (2005), p. 155-161.

Reinisch A., "Developing Human Rights and Humanitarian Law of the Security Council for the Imposition of Economic Sanctions," *American Journal of International Law*, 95 (2001), p. 851-872.

Reisman M.W., "Termination of the USSR's Treaty Right of Intervention in Iran," *American Journal of International Law*, 74(1) (1980), p. 144-154.

Reisman M.W., "The Constitutional Crisis in the United Nations," *American Journal of International Law,* 87(1) (1993), p. 83-100.

Ress G., Bröhmer J., "Article 53," in *The Charter of the United Nations: A Commentary*, ed. B. Simma, 2nd ed., vol. 1 (Munich: Verlag C.H. Beck, 2002), p. 854-879.

Röling B.V.A., "Definition of Aggression," in *The Current Legal Regulation of the Use of Force*, ed. A. Cassese (Dordrecht: Martinus Nijhoff Publishers, 1986), p. 413-421.

Röling B.V.A., "International Law and the Maintenance of Peace," *Netherlands Yearbook of International Law*, IV (1973), p. 1-103.

Ronzitti N., "The Report of the High-Level Panel on Threats, Challenges and Change, the Use of Force and the Reform of the United Nations," *Italian Yearbook of International Law*, XIV (2004), (Leiden/Boston: Martinus Nijhoff Publishers, 2005), p. 3-22.

Rotfeld, A.D., "Does the OSCE Have a Future?" *OSCE Yearbook 2003*, 9 (2003), p. 31-42.

Schreuer C., "Regionalization," in *United Nations: Law, Politics and Practice,* ed. R. Wolfrum, vol. I (Munich: Verlag C.H. Beck, 1995), p. 1059-1067.

Siekmann R., "Commentary: OSCE versus UN Peacekeeping," *Helsinki Monitor,* 3(4) (1992), p. 18-20.

Simma B., "Does the UN Charter Provide an Adequate Legal Basis for Individual or Collective Responses to Violations of Obligations Erga Omnes?" in *The Future of International Law Enforcement: New Scenarios – New Law?*, ed. J. Delbruck (Berlin: Dunker and Humblot, 1993), p. 125-146.

Simma B., "From Bilateralism to Community Interest in International Law," *Recueil des Cours/Collected Courses of the Hague Academy of International Law*, 250 (1994), (The Hague: Martinus Nijhoff Publishers, 1994), p. 217-384.

Simon S., Benjamin D., "America and the New Terrorism," *Survival (The IISS Quarterly)*, 42(1) (2000), p. 59-75.

Staibano C., "Trends in UN Sanctions: From ad hoc Practice to Institutional Capacity Building," in *International Sanctions: Between Words and Wars in the Global System*, ed. P. Wallensteen, C. Staibano, (London/New York: Frank Cass, 2005), p. 31-54.

Stöber S., "The Failure of the OSCE Mission to Georgia – What Remains?" *OSCE Yearbook 2010*, (Hamburg: Nomos, 2011), p. 203-220.

Stromberg R.N., "The Idea of Collective Security," in *From Collective Security to Preventive Diplomacy: Readings in International Organization and the Maintenance of Peace*, ed J. Larus (New York: John Wiley & Sons, Inc., 1965), p. 273-284.

Tams Ch.J., "All's Well that Ends Well: Comments on the ILC's Articles on State Responsibility," *Zeitschrift für ausländisches öffentliches Recht und Völkerrecht*, 62 (2002), p. 759-808.

Thakur R., van Langenhove L., "Enhancing Global Governance through Regional Integration," in *Regionalisation and Global Governance: The Taming of Globalization?*, ed. A.F. Cooper, C. W. Hughes, Ph. de Lombaerde (London/New York: Routledge Taylor and Francis Group, 2008), p. 17-42.

Thompson K.W., "Collective Security Reexamined," in *From Collective Security to Preventive Diplomacy: Readings in International Organization and the Maintenance of Peace*, ed. J. Larus (New York: John Wiley & Sons, Inc., 1965), p. 285-303.

United Nations Peacekeeping Operations: Principles and Guidelines (New York: UN Department of Peacekeeping Operations, 2010), 98 p.

Vaur-Chaumette A.-L., "The International Community as a Whole," in *The Law of International Responsibility*, ed. J. Crawford, A. Pellet, S. Olleson, (Oxford: Oxford University Press, 2010), p. 1023-1028.

Villani U., "The Security Council's Authorization of Enforcement Action by Regional Organizations," *Max Planck Yearbook of United Nations Law*, 6 (2002), p. 535-557.

Waldock C.H.M., "The Regulation of the Use of Force by Individual States in International Law," *Recueil des cours/Collected Courses of the Hague Academy of International Law*, 1952 (II), p. 455-517.

Walter C., "Security Council Control over Regional Action," *Max Planck Yearbook of United Nations Law,* 1 (1997), p. 129-193.

Ward C.A., "The Counter-Terrorism Committee: Its Relevance for Implementing Targeted Sanctions," in *International Sanctions: Between Words and Wars in the Global System*, ed. P. Wallensteen, C. Staibano, (London/New York: Frank Cass, 2005), p. 167-180.

Wellens K., "Theoretical Aspects of the Implementation Processes: General Observations," in *Public Interest Rules of International Law: Towards Effective Implementation*, ed. T. Komori, K. Wellens, (Farnham: Ashgate Publishing Ltd, 2009), p. 15-52.

Wilson G., "Regional Arrangements as Agents of the UN Security Council: Some African and European Organizations Contrasted," *Liverpool Law Review,* 29(2) (2008), p. 183-204.

Winfield P.H., "The Grounds of Intervention in International Law," *British Yearbook of International Law*, 5 (1924), p. 149-162.

Wippman D., "Treaty-Based Intervention: Who Can Say No?" *The University of Chicago Law Review*, 62(4) (1995), p. 607-687.

Wolfrum R., "Der Beitrag regionaler Abmachungen zur Friedenssicherung: Möglichkeiten und Grenzen," *Zeitschrift für Ausländisches Öffentliches Recht und Völkerrecht*, 1 (1993), p. 576-602.

Xinmin MA, "Statement on Responsibility of States for Internationally Wrongful Acts," *Chinese Journal of International Law*, 7(2) (2008), p. 563-566.

Zwanenburg M., "Regional Organizations and the Maintenance of International Peace and Security: Three Recent Regional African Peace Operations," *Journal of Conflict & Security Law,* 11(3) (2006), p. 483-508.

Андреев М.В., "Современные проблемы обеспечения Евразийской безопасности в контексте выработки нового межгосударственного соглашения" [Andreev M.V., "Contemporary Problems of Ensuring European Security in the Context of the Elaboration of a New Interstate Agreement"], *International Security and Control over Armaments. Herald of the Diplomatic Academy of the MFA of Russia*, (2010), p. 84-89.

Бордюжа Н. "Организация Договора о коллективной безопасности" [Bordyuzha N., "The Collective Security Treaty Organization"], *International Life*, 2 (2005), p. 72-82.

Валеев Р.М., “Роль контроля в системе международного сотрудничества государств в XXI веке” [Valeev R.M., “The Role of Control in the System of International Cooperation in the XXI Century”], *Russian Yearbook of International Law*, 2001, p. 35-64.

Гольцов С.Д., Малеев Ю.Н., “Применение вооруженной силы государствами как мера превентивной самозащиты ad hoc от внешней угрозы” [Goltsov S.D., Maleev Y.N., “Use of Military Force by States as a Means of *ad hoc* Preventive Self-Help against the External Threat”], *Moscow Journal of International Law*, 4 (2004), p. 45-58.

Кирн Р., “Глава VIII Устава ООН: необходимость более широкой интерпретации” [Kirn R., “Chapter VIII of the UN Charter: The Need for Broader Interpretation”], *International Public and Private Law*, 1 (2003), p. 12-13.

Лазарев М.И., “Международные правоотношения и международные силоотношения в конце XX – в канун XXI века” [Lazarev M.I., “International Relations in Law and Force at the End of the XXth – Eve of XXIst Centuries], *Russian Yearbook of International Law*, 1998-1999 (Saint Petersburg: Russia-Neva, 1999), p. 334-337.

Малеев Ю.Н., “Реабилитация адекватного и пропорционального применения силы” [Maleev Y.N., “Rehabilitation of the Adequate and Proportional Use of Force”], *Moscow Journal of International Law*, 3 (2004), p. 31-47

Нешатаева Т.Н., “Понятие санкций международных организаций” [Neshataeva T.N., “The Notion of Sanctions of International Organizations”], *Jurisprudence*, 6 (1984), p. 94-98.

Николаенко В., “10 лет Договору о коллективной безопасности” [Nikolaenko V., “10 Years of the Treaty of Collective Security”], *International Life*, 3 (2003), p. 60-66.

Пирадов А.С., Старушенко Г.Б., “Принцип невмешательства в современном международном праве” [Piradov A.S., Starushenko G.B., “The Principle of Non-Intervention in Modern International Law”], *Soviet Yearbook of International Law*, 1958 (Moscow: USSR Academy of Sciences, 1959), p. 230-253.

Рекута А.Л., “Организация Договора о коллективной безопасности: проблемы и пути развития по предотвращению угроз безопасности в Центрально-Азиатском регионе” [Rekuta A.L., “The Collective Security Treaty Organization: Challenges and Perspectives of Development to Prevent the Threats to Security in the Central Asian Region”], *Military Thought* 11, (2006), p. 2-9.

Шибаева Е.А., “Международные организации в системе международно-правового регулирования” [Shibaeva E.A., “International Organizations in the System of International Legal Regulation”], *Soviet Yearbook of International Law*, 1978 (Moscow: Nauka, 1980), p. 214-224.

Academic papers

Joensson J.H., *Understanding Collective Security in the 21st Century: A Critical Study of UN Peacekeeping in the Former Yugoslavia*, doctoral thesis in political and social sciences, European University Institute (Florence, 2010), 279 p.

Korkelia K., “The CIS Peace-Keeping Operations in the Context of International Legal Order.” Accessed 20 November 2011, http://www.nato.int/acad/fellow/97-99/korkelia.pdf

Нешатаева Т.Н., *Международно-правовые санкции специализированных учреждений ООН* [Neshataeva T.N., *International Legal Sanctions of the UN Specialized Agencies*], extended abstract of PhD dissertation (Moscow: Moscow State University, 1985), 24 p.

Чиков П.В., *Военные санкции в международном праве* [Chikov P.V., *Military Sanctions in International Law*], extended abstract of PhD dissertation (Kazan: Kazan State University, 2003), 26 p.

Decisions of International Courts and Tribunals

Barcelona Traction, Light and Power Company, Ltd., *I.C.J. Reports 1970* (The Hague: I.C.J., 1970), p. 3-113.

Bosphorus Hava Yollari Turizm ve Ticaret AS v. Ireland, European Court of Human Rights, Decision of 13 September 2001 and Judgment of 30 June 2005. Accessed 12 March 2012, https://www.suepo.org/rights/public/archive/bosphorus.pdf

Case Concerning Armed Activities on the Territory of the Congo (Democratic Republic of the Congo v. Rwanda), Judgment of 3 February 2006, Separate Opinion of Judge Dugard, *I.C.J. Reports 2006* (The Hague: I.C.J., 2006), p. 86-94.

Case Concerning the Gabčíkovo-Nagymaros Project (Hungary v. Slovakia), Decision of 25 September 1997, *I.C.J. Reports 1997* (The Hague: I.C.J., 1997), p. 7-84.

Case Concerning the Application of the Genocide Convention (Bosnia and Herzegovina v. Yugoslavia), Order of 13 September 1993 on the Request for the Indication of Further Provisional Measures, Separate Opinion of Judge Lauterpacht, *I.C.J. Reports 1993*, (The Hague: I.C.J., 1993), p. 407-448.

Case Concerning Questions of Interpretation and Application of the 1971 Montreal Convention Arising from the Aerial Incident at Lockerbie, Judgment of 27 February 1998, Preliminary Objections, *I.C.J. Reports 1998*, (The Hague: I.C.J., 1998), p. 115-137.

Case Concerning Questions of Interpretation and Application of the 1971 Montreal Convention Arising from the Aerial Incident at Lockerbie, Separate Opinion of Judge Lachs, *I.C.J. Reports 1992*, (The Hague: I.C.J., 1992), p. 138-139.

Certain Expenses of the United Nations (Article 17, Paragraph 2, of the Charter), Advisory Opinion, *I.C.J. Reports 1962* (The Hague: I.C.J, 1962), p. 151-309.

East Timor (Portugal v. Australia), Judgment, *I.C.J. Reports 1995*, (The Hague: I.C.J., 1995), p. 90-106.

International Status of South-West Africa, Advisory Opinion, *I.C.J. Reports 1950* (The Hague: I.C.J., 1950), p. 128-145.

Interpretation of Peace Treaties, Advisory Opinion, *I.C.J. Reports 1950* (The Hague, I.C.J., 1950), p. 65-78.

Joined cases C-402/05 P and C-415/05 P, Kadi and Al Barakaat International Foundation v. Council of the European Union and Commission of the European Union. Accessed 30 March 2011, http://eur-lex.europa.eu/LexUriServ/LexUriServ.do?uri=CELEX:62005J0402:EN:HTML

Jose Maria Sison v. Council of the EU, Case T-47/03, Judgment of 11 July 2007. Accessed 30 March 2012, http://curia.europa.eu/jurisp/cqi-bin/form.pl?lango=en&Submit=Rechercher&alldocs=alldocs&docjo=docjo=docop&docor=docor&docj=docj&docrequire=&numaff=T-47/03%20&dafers=&dafer=&nomusuel=&domaine=&mots=&resmax=100

Joined Cases C-57/09, C-101/09, Judgment of the Court (Grand Chamber) of 9 November 2010. Accessed 30 March 2012, http://eur-lex.europa.eu/LexUriServ/LexUriServ.do?uri=CELEX:62009CJ0057:EN:HTML#Footnote*

Kadi v. Council and Commission, ECJ Case T 315/01 of 21 September 2005. Accessed 30 March 2011, http://eur-lex.europa.eu/LexUriServ/LexUriServ.do?uri=CELEX:62001A0315:EN:HTML

Legal Consequences of the Construction of a Wall in the Occupied Palestinian Territory, Advisory Opinion, *I.C.J. Reports 2004,* (The Hague: I.C.J., 2004), p. 136-203.

Military and Paramilitary Activities in and against Nicaragua (Nicaragua *v.* United States of America), Jurisdiction and Admissibility, Judgment, *I.C.J. Reports 1984,* p. 392-443.

Military and Paramilitary Activities in and against Nicaragua (Nicaragua v. United States of America), Merits, Judgment, *I.C.J. Reports* (The Hague: I.C.J., 1986), p. 14-150.

Mojahedines du people d'Iran, Case T-228/02, Judgment of 12 December 2006. Accessed 30 March 2012, http://eur-lex.europa.eu/LexUriServ/LexUriServ.do?uri=CELEX:62002A0228:EN:HTML

Naulilaa Portuguese Colonies Case, 1928, *UNRIAA*, vol. II, p. 1011 *et seq*.

Responsibility of Germany for acts committed subsequent to 31 July 1914 and before Portugal entered into the war, *RIAA*, 1930, vol. II, p. 1035 *et seq*.

Yusuf and al Barakaat International Foundation v. Council and Commission, CFI Case T306/01, 21 September 2005. Accessed 30 March 2011, http://eur-lex.europa.eu/LexUriServ/LexUriServ.do?uri=CELEX:62001A0306:EN:HTML

Zollman v. Great Britain, Application no. 62902/00 of 27 November 2003. Accessed 15 October 2011, http://cmiskp.echr.coe.int/tkp197/view.asp?action=html&documentId=671866&portal=hbkm&source=externalbydocnumber&table=F69A27FD8FB86142BF01C1166DEA398649

Documents

A More Secure World: Our Shared Responsibility. Report of the Secretary-General's High Panel on Threats, Challenges and Change (New York: United Nations, 2004), 129 p.

Annex B. International Security Cooperation Bodies, in *SIPRI Yearbook 2010: Armaments, Disarmament and International Security* (Oxford: Oxford University Press, 2010), p. 509-525.

Convention for the Protection of Human Rights and Fundamental Freedoms, 4 November 1950, *European Convention on Human Rights, COETS*, 5, p. 5-32.

Consolidated version of the Treaty on European Union (with Lisbon treaty), *Official Journal of the European Union*, 51 (2008), p. 13-46.

Documents of the UN Conference on International Organization, San Francisco, 1945, vol. I. General (London/New York, United Nations Information Organizations, 1945), 718 p.
Documents of the UN Conference on International Organization, San Francisco, 1945, vol. III. General (London/New York, United Nations Information Organizations, 1945), 710 p.
Documents of the UN Conference on International Organization, San Francisco, 1945, vol. XII. Commission III. Security Council (London/ New York: United Nations Information Organizations, 1945), 866 p.
Draft Articles on Responsibility of States for Internationally Wrongful Acts, 2001, *Yearbook of the International Law Commission*, 2001, vol. II, Part Two (New York/Geneva: United Nations, 2006), p. 43-59.
Draft Articles on Responsibility of States for Internationally Wrongful Acts, with commentaries, 2001, *Yearbook of the International Law Commission*, 2001, vol. II (New York/Geneva: United Nations, 2006), Part Two, p. 31-143.
Fourth Report on State Responsibility, by Mr. Gaetano Arangio-Ruiz, Special Rapporteur, Document A/CN.4/444 and Add. 1-3., in *Yearbook of the International Law Commission* (1992-II), Part I (New York/Geneva: United Nations, 1995), p. 1-50.
General Comment No. 29: Article 4: Derogations during a State of Emergency (CCPR/C/21/Rev.1/Add.11), in *General Comments and Recommendations*, vol. I, 4th ed. (Lund, 2003), p. 107-115.
OSCE Annual Report 2001 on Interaction Between Organizations and Institutions in the OSCE Area, SEC.DOC/2/01, (Vienna: OSCE, 2001), 93 p.
OSCE Annual Report 2009 (Vienna: OSCE, 2010), 120 p.
OSCE Handbook 2007 (Vienna: OSCE, 2007), 128 p.
OSCE Mechanisms and Procedures – Summary/Compedium (SEC.GAL/121/08), 20 June 2008, (Vienna: OSCE, 2011), 172 p.
Statement on Measures for a Political Settlement of the Georgia-Abkhazian Conflict, 4 April 1994, *Diplomatic Herald*, (1994, 9-10).
The Repertoire of Practice of the Security Council (Supplement 1989-1992) (United Nations: Department of Political Affairs, 1993), 1050 p.
Treaty on the Functioning of the European Union, *Official Journal of the European Union*, 51 (2008), p. 47-200.
UN International Law Commission Draft Articles on Prevention of Transboundary Harm from Hazardous Activities (2001), GAOR, 56th Session, Supplement 10, p. 370 *et seq.*

UN International Law Commission Draft Principles on the Allocation of Loss in the Case of Transboundary Harm Arising out of Hazardous Activities (with Commentaries) (2006), GAOR, 61st Session, Supplement 10, p. 106 *et seq*.

Vienna Convention on the Law of Treaties, 23 May 1969, *1155 UNTS*, 331 *et seq*.

Договор о коллективной безопасности [Treaty of Collective Security] of 15 May 1992 (with Protocol of 20 December 2010), *Electronic Legal Database Konsul'tant Plus: Technologiia 3000*

Заявление глав государств СНГ [Statement on the CIS CHS], 15 April 1994, *Sodruzhestvo*, (1994, 1).

Комплексный план по урегулированию ситуации на Таджико-Афганской границе [Complex Plan of Action on the Settlement of the Situation at Tajikistan-Afghan Border] adopted by the CIS CHS Decision of 26 May 1995, *Sodruzhestvo*, (1995, 2).

Концепция коллективной безопасности государств-участников ДКБ [Concept of the Collective Security of the TCS Parties], confirmed by the CSC Decision of 10 December 1995, *Sodruzhestvo,* (1995, 1).

Концепция предотвращения и урегулирования конфликтов на территории государств-участников СНГ [Concept of the Prevention and Settlement of Conflicts on the Territory of CIS Member States], confirmed by the CIS CHS Decision of 19 January 1996, *Sodruzhestvo* (1996, 1).

Меморандум об основах нормализации отношений между Республикой Молдова и Приднестровьем [Memorandum on the Grounds for Normalization of Relations between Moldova and Transdnistria], 8 May 1997, *Russia-Ukraine (1990-2000) Documents and Materials,* vol. 2 (1996-2000), 2001, p. 97-98.

Меморандум о поддержании мира и безопасности в СНГ [Memorandum on the Maintenance of Peace and Stability in the CIS], 10 February 1995, *Sodruzhestvo,* (1995, 1).

О мерах по стабилизации обстановки на участке государственной границы Республики Таджикистан с Афганистаном [On the Measures to Stabilize the Situation at the Border between Tajikistan and Afghanistan], confirmed by the CIS CHS Decision of 22 January 1993, *Sodruzhestvo*, (1993, 1).

О парламентском контроле за военной организацией государства [On Parliamentary Control over the Military Organization of the State], model law adopted 24 November 2001, *Information Bulletin "CIS Interparliamentary Assembly,"* 28 (2002).

О сроке пребывания, составе и задачах коллективных миротворческих сил в Республике Таджикистан [On the Terms of Deployment, Composition and Tasks of the Collective Peacekeeping Forces in Tajikistan], Decision of the CIS CHS, 15 April 1994, *Sodruzhestvo*, (1994,1).

Об участии государств-участников СНГ в миротворческих операциях [On Participation of the CIS Member States in Peacekeeping Operations], model law adopted 17 April 2004, *Information Bulletin "CIS Interparliamentary Assembly,"* 34 (2004).

План имплементации Концепции коллективной безопасности государств-участников ДКБ [Plan for Implementation of the Concept for Collective Security of the TCS Member States], confirmed by the CSC Decision of 26 May 1995, *Sodruzhestvo*, (1995, 2).

Проект Договора о европейской безопасности [Draft European Security Treaty], *International Security and Control over Armaments. Herald of Diplomatic Academy of the MFA of Russia*, (2010), p. 90-99.

Протокол о комплектовании, структуре, материально-техничестком и финансовом обеспечении групп наблюдателей и коллективных сил по поддержанию мира в СНГ [Protocol on the Recruitment Structure, Material and Financial Procurement of the CIS Military Observers and Collective Peace-Maintenance Forces], 15 May 1992, *Sodruzhestvo*, (1992(5)).

Совместное Российско-украинское заявление [Joint Russian-Ukrainian Statement], 20 March 1998, *Russia-Ukraine 1990-2000. Documents and Materials*. vol. 2 (1996-2000), (Moscow: International Relations, 2001), p. 237-238.

Соглашение о группах военных наблюдателей и коллективных силах по поддержанию мира в СНГ [Agreement on Groups of Military Observers and Collective Peace-Maintenance Forces in the CIS], 20 March 1992, *Sodruzhestvo*, (1992, 4).

Соглашение о коллективных миротворческих силах и совместных мерах по их материально-техническому обеспечению [Agreement on Collective Peacekeeping Forces and their Maintenance], 24 September 1993, *Sodruzhestvo*, (1993, 4).

Соглашение о миротворческой деятельности ОДКБ [Agreement on the Peacekeeping Activity of the CSTO], 6 October 2007, *Bulletin of International Treaties*, (2009, 6), p. 23-27.

Соглашение о создании Содружества Независимых Государств [Agreement on the Establishment of the Commonwealth of Independent States], 8 December 1991, *Sodruzhestvo,* (1992, 1).

Соглашение о статусе формирований, сил и средств системы коллективной безопасности [Agreement on Status of Forces and Facilities of the Collective Security System], 11 October 2000, *Bulletin of International Treaties*, (2002, 5), p.19-26.

Соглашение о статусе Экономического Суда СНГ [Agreement on the Status of the CIS Economic Court], 6 July 1992, *Sodruzhestvo*, 6 (1992).

Соглашение об основных принципах военно-техническтого сотрудничества между сторонами Договора о коллективной безопасности [Agreement on the Main Principles of Military-Technical Cooperation among the Parties to the Treaty on Collective Security] of 20 June 2000 with Protocol of 19 September 2003, *Bulletin of International Treaties*, 12 (2005), p. 26-31.

Соглашение об учреждении системы управления силами и средствами системы коллективной безопасности ОДКБ [Agreement on the Establishment of the System of Management of Forces and Means of the CSTO Collective Security System], 6 October 2007, *National Register of Legal Acts of Belarus* N 53, 3/2212.

Устав Организации Договора о коллективной безопасности [CSTO Charter], 17 October 2002, *Bulletin of International Treaties*, 3 (2004), p. 3-9.

Устав Содружества Независимых государств [CIS Statute], 22 January 1993, *Sodruzhestvo* (1993, 1).

Electronic documents

2005 World Summit Outcome, A/RES/60/1, 24 October 2005. Accessed 22 March 2011, http://globalr2p.org/media/pdf/WSOD_2005.pdf

Address to International Rescue Committee on the humanitarian impact of economic sanctions, UN Secretary-General, press release, SG/SM/7625, 15 November 2000. Accessed 15 February 2012, http://www.un.org/News/Press/docs/2000/20001115.sgsm7625.doc.html

African Union Convention for the Protection and Assistance of Internally Displaced Persons in Africa, 23 October 2009. Accessed 15 February 2012, http://www.au.int/en/sites/default/files/AFRICAN_UNION_CONVENTION_FOR_THE_PROTECTION_AND_ASSISTANCE_OF_INTERNALLY_DISPLACED_PERSONS_IN_AFRICA_%28KAMPALA_CONVENTION%29.pdf

Agreement on the Military Aspects of the Peace Settlement, Annex 1A. Accessed 12 March 2012, http://www.ohr.int/dpa/default.asp?content_id=368
An Agenda for Peace, "Preventive Diplomacy, Peacemaking and Peace-keeping," A/47/277- S/24111. Report of the UN Secretary-General, 17 June 1992. Accessed 15 March, 2012, http://www.un.org/Docs/SG/agpeace.html
Annex 2 to the Summary of Conclusions of the First CSCE Council of Ministers, Berlin, 1991. Accessed 31 May 2011, http://www.osce.org/mc/40234
Article 53. Supplement 1959-1966. Accessed 14 May 2012, http://untreaty.un.org/cod/repertory/art53/english/rep_supp3_vol2-art53_e.pdf
Astana Commemorative Declaration, "Towards a Security Community," 2010. Accessed 31 May 2011, http://www.osce.org/mc/73962
Basic Principles of the Use of Restrictive Measures (Sanctions), 10198/1/04 Rev. 1, 7 June 2004. Accessed 11 November 2011, http://register.consilium.europa.eu/pdf/en/04/st10/st10198-re01.en04.pdf
Bonn-Berlin Process: 1999-2001, Germany. Accessed 20 August 2011, www.smartsanctions.de
Charter for European Security 1999. Accessed 19 May 2011, http://www.unece.org/fileadmin/DAM/trans/osce/osceunece/istachart99e.pdf
Charter of the Organization of American States, 1948. Accessed 12 May 2011, http://www.oas.org/dil/treaties_A-41_Charter_of_the_Organization_of_American_States.htm
Charter of Paris for a New Europe, 1990. Accessed 20 March 2012, http://www.osce.org/mc/39516
Charter of the United Nations. Introductory Note. Accessed 20 March 2012, http://www.un.org/en/documents/charter/intro.shtml
Charter for European Security, 1999. Accessed 11 April 2011, http://www.osce.org/mc/17502
CIS Member States. Accessed 19 May 2011, http://www.cis.minsk.by/index.php?id=2
Commission on Human Rights Resolution 2003/17, "Human rights and Unilateral Coercive Measures," 22 April 2003. Accessed 20 March 2012, http://www.unhchr.ch/huridocda/huridoca.nsf/%28Symbol%29/E.CN.4.RES.2003.17.En?Opendocument

Common Concept for the Development of Co-operation between Mutually Reinforcing Institutions, 1997, Annex to MC(6).DEC/5. Accessed 20 March 2012, http://www.osce.org/mc/40427

Consolidated List, Resolution 1267. Accessed 30 April 2012, http://www.un.org/sc/committees/1267/consolist.shtmhttp://www.un.org/sc/committees/1267/pdf/AQList.pdf

Consolidated List, Resolution 1518, Individuals. Accessed 30 April 2012, http://www.un.org/sc/committees/1518/list_27jul2005.htm

Consolidated List, Resolution 1518, Entities. Accessed 30 April 2012, http://www.un.org/sc/committees/1518/pdf/List_of_Entities.pdf

Consolidated List, Resolution 1521. Accessed 30 April 2012, http://www.un.org/sc/committees/1521/pdf/1521_travel_ban_list.pdf

Consolidated List, Resolution 1521, 1532. Accessed 30 April 2012, http://www.un.org/sc/committees/1521/pdf/1521_assets_freeze_list.pdf

Consolidated List, Resolution 1533. Accessed 30 April 2012, http://www.un.org/sc/committees/1533/pdf/1533_list.pdf

Consolidated List, Resolution 1572. Accessed 30 April 2012, http://www.un.org/sc/committees/1572/pdf/listtable.pdf

Consolidated List, Resolution 1591. Accessed 30 April 2012, http://www.un.org/sc/committees/1591/pdf/Sudan_list.pdf

Consolidated List, Resolution 1718. Accessed 30 April 2012, http://www.un.org/sc/committees/1718/pdf/List%2016%20July%202009.pdf

Consolidated List, Resolution 1737. Accessed 30 April 2012, http://www.un.org/sc/committees/1737/pdf/1737ConsolidatedList.pdf

Consolidated List, Resolution 1844. Accessed 30 April 2012, http://www.un.org/sc/committees/751/pdf/1844_cons_list_12Apr10.pdf

Consolidated List, Resolution 1970. Accessed 30 April 2012, http://www.un.org/sc/committees/1970/pdf/List%20of%20Individuals%20and%20Entities.pdf

Constitutive Act of the African Union, 11 July 2000. Accessed October 19, 2011, http://www.uneca.org/daweca/conventions_and_resolutions/constitution.pdf

Cotonou Agreement, 25 July 1993. Accessed 19 October 2011, http://www.unhcr.org/refworld/docid/3ae6b5796.html

Convention (III) relative to the Treatment of Prisoners of War, Geneva, 12 August 1949. Accessed 30 April 2012, http://www.icrc.org/ihl.nsf/FULL/375?OpenDocument

Convention (IV) relative to the Protection of Civilian Persons in Time of War, Geneva, 12 August 1949. Accessed 30 April 2012, http://www.icrc.org/ihl.nsf/full/380

Convention on Conciliation and Arbitration within the CSCE, 1992. Accessed 29 April 2011, http://www.osce.org/mc/40342

Convention on the Prohibition of the Use, Stockpiling, Production and Transfer of Anti-personnel Mines and on their Destruction, 1997, with Protocol II. Accessed 30 April 2012, http://treaties.un.org/doc/Treaties/1997/09/19970918%2007-53%20AM/Ch_XXVI_05p.pdf

Cooperation of the CIS States in the Sphere of Security. Accessed 30 April 2012, http://www.cis.minsk.by/index.php?id=32

Cooperation between the UN and Regional and Other Organizations, Report of the UN Secretary-General, 20 September 2010 (A/65/382 – S/2010/490). Accessed 12 October 2011, http://daccess-dds-ny.un.org/doc/UNDOC/GEN/N10/542/44/PDF/N1054244.pdf

Cooperation between the United Nations and Regional Organizations/Arrangements in a Peacekeeping Environment: Suggested Principles and Mechanisms, March 1999. Accessed 30 April 2012, http://www.securitycouncilreport.org/atf/cf/%7B65BFCF9B-6D27-4E9C-8CD3-CF6E4FF96FF9%7D/UNRO%20Cooperation%20between%20the%20UN%20and%20Regional%20Organizations.pdf

Cooperation with Other International Organizations and Structures. Accessed 12 April 2012, http://www.dkb.gov.ru/start/index.htm

Corfu Informal Meeting of OSCE Foreign Ministers on the Future of European Security, Chair's Concluding Statements to the Press, 2009. Accessed 19 October 2011, http://www.osce.org/cio/37803

Cooperation between the United Nations and Regional and Other Organizations, Report of the UN Secretary-General, A/65/382-S/2010/490, 20 September 2010. Accessed 29 April 2011, http://daccess-ds.un.org/access.nsf/Get?OpenAgent&DS=A/65/382-S/2010/490&Lang=R

Council Common Position of 29 December 2001 on the Application of Specific Measures to Combat Terrorism 2001.931.CFSP. Accessed 4 September 2011, http://eur-lex.europa.eu/LexUriServ/LexUriServ.do?uri=OJ:L:2001:344:0093:0096:EN:PDF

Council Decision 2010/639/CFSP, 25 October 2010, concerning Restrictive Measures against Certain Officials of Belarus. Accessed 18 February 2012, http://eur-lex.europa.eu/LexUriServ/LexUriServ.do?uri=OJ:L:2010:280:0018:0028:EN:PDF

Council Decision 2010/127/CFSP, 1 March 2010. Accessed February 18, 2012, http://eur-lex.europa.eu/LexUriServ/LexUriServ.do?uri=OJ:L:2010:051:0019:0021:EN:PDF

Council Decision 2011/172/CFSP, 21 March 2011. Accessed February 18, 2012, http://eur-lex.europa.eu/LexUriServ/LexUriServ.do?uri=OJ:L:2011:076:0063:0067:EN:PDF

Council Decision 2011/173/CFSP, 21 March 2011. Accessed February 18, 2012, http://eur-lex.europa.eu/LexUriServ/LexUriServ.do?uri=OJ:L:2011:076:0068:0071:EN:PDF

Council Decision 2012/36/CFSP, 23 January 2012. Accessed February 18, 2012, http://eur-lex.europa.eu/LexUriServ/LexUriServ.do?uri=OJ:L:2012:019:0031:0032:EN:PDF

Council Regulation (EC) No 2271/96, 22 November 1996. Accessed 12 February 2012, http://eur-lex.europa.eu/LexUriServ/LexUriServ.do?uri=CELEX:31996R2271:EN:HTML

CSCE and the New Europe – Our Security is Indivisible. Ministerial Declaration of 1 December 1993. Accessed 15 October 2011, http://www.osce.org/mc/40401

CSTO Members. Accessed 11 April 2011, http://www.dkb.gov.ru/start/index.htm

CSTO Secretary General says Cooperation with OSCE Crucial for Security. Accessed 11 April 2011, http://www.osce.org/pc/69165

Declaration on the Enhancement of Cooperation between the UN and Regional Arrangements or Agencies (A/RES/49/57), 17 February 1995. Accessed 15 October 2011, http://www.un.org/documents/ga/res/49/a49r057.htm

Declarations Recognizing the Jurisdiction of the Court as Compulsory. Accessed 15 October 2011, http://www.icj-cij.org/jurisdiction/index.php?p1=5&p2=1&p3=3

Document of the Stockholm Conference on Confidence- and Security-Building Measures and Disarmament in Europe, Convened in Accordance with the Relevant Provisions of the Concluding Document of the Madrid Meeting of the Conference on Security and Co-operation in Europe of 19 September 1986. Accessed 11 October 2011, http://www.state.gov/t/isn/4725.htm

Draft Articles on Responsibility of International Organizations, 2011. Accessed 11 October 2011, http://untreaty.un.org/ilc/texts/instruments/english/draft%20articles/9_11_2011.pdf

Draft Articles on the Responsibility of International Organizations, 2011, with Commentaries. Accessed 12 October 2011, http://untreaty.un.org/ilc/texts/instruments/english/commentaries/9_11_2011.pdf

General Comment No. 31, The Nature of the General Legal Obligation Imposed by States Parties by the Covenant, 24 March 2004. Accessed 11 October 2011, http://daccess-dds-ny.un.org/doc/UNDOC/GEN/G04/419/56/PDF/G0441956.pdf.

External Co-operation: United Nations. Accessed 15 October 2011, http://www.osce.org/ec/43240

Fostering the Role of the OSCE as a Forum for a Political Dialogue, Decision No. 3 of the 9th Bucharest Ministerial Council, 4 December 2001. Accessed October 15, 2011, http://www.osce.org/mc/40515

Guidelines on Implementation and Evaluation of Restrictive Measures (Sanctions) in the Framework of the EU Common Foreign and Security Policy, 2 December 2005. Accessed 15 October 2011, http://registerconsilium.europa.eu/pdf/en/05/st15/st15114.en05.pdf

Helsinki Final Act, 1 August 1975. Accessed 11 March 2011, http://www.osce.org/mc/39501?download=true

Helsinki Summit Declaration 1992. Accessed 11 March 2011, http://www.osce.org/mc/39530

Human Rights and Unilateral Coercive Measures, draft resolution. Accessed May 21, 2012, http://daccess-dds-ny.un.org/doc/RESOLUTION/LTD/G12/120/71/PDF/G1212071.pdf

In Larger Freedom: Towards Development, Security and Human Rights for All: Report of the Secretary-General (A/59/2005). Accessed 21 April 2012, http://daccess-dds-ny.un.org/doc/UNDOC/GEN/N05/270/78/PDF/N0527078.pdf

Interlaken Process: Smart Sanctions – Targeted Sanctions. Accessed 20 May 2011, www.smartsanctions.ch

International Covenant on Civil and Political Rights, 16 December 1966. Accessed 21 April 2012, http://www2.ohchr.org/english/law/ccpr.htm

Joint Declaration on UN/CSTO Secretariat Cooperation, Moscow, 18 March 2010. Accessed 21 April 2012, http://www.mid.ru/brp_4.nsf/0/A11ED61A82FAD2FCC32576F0004904F4

Joint Action 96/668/CFSP of 22 November 1996. Accessed 21 April 2012, http://eur-lex.europa.eu/LexUriServ/LexUriServ.do?uri=CELEX:31996E0668:EN:HTML

Joint Statement of High Officials of EurAsEC, CSTO, CIS and ShCO, 12 October 2010. Accessed 21 April 2012, http://www.dkb.gov.ru/start/index.htm

Lisbon Declaration on a Common and Comprehensive Security Model for Europe for the Twenty-first Century, 1996. Accessed 21 April 2011, http://www.osce.org/mc/39539?download=true

List showing signatures and ratifications or accessions with respect to the Convention on Conciliation and Arbitration within the OSCE. Accessed 21 April 2011, http://www.osce.org/cca/40119

Meeting with countries contributing troops and police to the United Nations Integrated Mission in Timor-Leste – Official Communiqué, 9 February 2012. Accessed 22 April 2012, http://daccess-dds-ny.un.org/doc/UNDOC/GEN/N12/228/87/PDF/N1222887.pdf

Meeting with countries contributing troops and police to the United Nations Disengagement Observer Force – Official Communiqué, 12 December 2011. Accessed April 22, 2012, http://daccess-dds-ny.un.org/doc/UNDOC/GEN/N11/635/10/PDF/N1163510.pdf

Meeting with countries contributing troops and police to the UN Stabilization Mission in Haiti – Official Communiqué, 14 November 2011. Accessed 22 April 2012, http://daccess-dds-ny.un.org/doc/UNDOC/GEN/N11/498/29/PDF/N1149829.pdf

Meeting with countries contributing troops and police to the African Union-United Nations Hybrid Operation in Darfur – Official Communique, 18 July 2011. Accessed April 22, 2012, http://daccess-dds-ny.un.org/doc/UNDOC/GEN/N11/420/02/PDF/N1142002.pdf

North Atlantic Treaty, 4 April 1949. Accessed 12 May 2011, http://www.nato.int/cps/en/natolive/official_texts_17120.htm

Note by the President of the Security Council (S/25859), 28 May 1993. Accessed 12 May 2011, http://www.securitycouncilreport.org/atf/cf/%7B65BFCF9B-6D27-4E9C-8CD3-CF6E4FF96FF9%7D/RO%20S25859.pdf

Obligations erga omnes in international law: Resolution of the Institut de Droit International, 2005 Krakow. Accessed 12 May 2011, http://www.idi-iil.org/idiE/resolutionsE/2005_kra_01_en.pdf

OSCE Cooperation with Other Organizations. Accessed 12 May 2012, http://www.osce.org/ec/43244

OSCE Document on Small Arms and Light Weapons, 24 November 2000. Accessed 12 May 2011, http://www.osce.org/fsc/20783

OSCE Document on Stockpiles of Conventional Ammunition, 19 November 2003. Accessed 12 May 2011, http://www.osce.org/fsc/15792

OSCE Mechanisms and Procedures, Vienna, 8 June 2004. Accessed 12 May 2011, http://www.osce.org/cpc/39615

OSCE Members. Accessed 12 May 2011, http://www.osce.org/who/83

OSCE Stabilizing Measures for Localized Crisis Situations, 25 November 1993. Accessed 12 May 2011, http://www.osce.org/fsc/41316

Principles for Dispute Settlement and Provisions for a CSCE Procedure for Peaceful Settlement of Disputes, Valletta, 1991. Accessed 12 May 2011, http://www.osce.org/secretariat/30115

Principles Governing Conventional Arms Transfers, 25 November 1993. Accessed 12 May 2011, http://www.osce.org/fsc/42313

Principles of Nurnberg Tribunal, 1950. Accessed 12 May 2011, http://deoxy.org/wc/wc-nurem.htm

Proposals of the 6th High-Level Meeting. The Electronic Newsletter of the UN University CRIS. Accessed 22 March 2011, http://www.cris.unu.edu/fileadmin/newsletter/newsletter_aug_05.pdf

Protocol Additional to the Geneva Conventions of 12 August 1949, and relating to the Protection of Victims of International Armed Conflicts, 8 June 1977. Accessed 15 October 2011, http://www.icrc.org/ihl.nsf/FULL/470?OpenDocument

Protocol Additional to the Geneva Conventions of 12 August 1949, and relating to the Protection of Victims of Non-International Armed Conflicts, 8 June 1977. Accessed 15 October 2011, http://www.icrc.org/ihl.nsf/FULL/475?OpenDocument

Protocol on Amendment to the Constitutive Act of the African Union, 11 July 2003. Accessed 15 October 2011, http://www.africa-union.org/official_documents/Treaties_%20Conventions_%20Protocols/Protocol%20on%20Amendments%20to%20the%20Constitutive%20Act.pdf

Protocol Relating to the Mechanism of Conflict Prevention, Management, Resolution, Peacekeeping and Security, 10 December 1999. Accessed 15 October 2011, http://www.iss.co.za/af/regorg/unity_to_union/pdfs/ecowas/ConflictMecha.pdf

Protocol Relating to the Establishment of the Peace and Security Council of the African Union, 9 July 2002. Accessed 15 October 2011, http://www.africa-union.org/root/au/organs/psc/Protocol_peace%20and%20security.pdf

Perspectives of the UN and Regional Organizations on Preventive and Quiet Diplomacy, Dialogue, Facilitation and Mediation: Common Challenges and Good Practices, February 2011. Accessed 15 October 2011, http://www.osce.org/cpc/76015

Relationship between the United Nations and Regional Organizations, in Particular the African Union, in the Maintenance of International Peace and Security. Report of the UN Secretary-General, 7 April 2008 (S/2008/18). Accessed 30 May 2011, http://www.securitycouncilreport.org/atf/cf/%7B65BFCF9B-6D27-4E9C-8CD3-CF6E4FF96FF9%7D/UNRO%20S%202008%20186.pdf

Report of the Special Rapporteur on the Promotion and Protection of Human Rights and Fundamental Freedoms while Countering Terrorism, Martin Scheinin (A/HRC/4/26), 29 January 2007. Accessed 12 October 2011, http://daccess-dds-ny.un.org/doc/UNDOC/GEN/G07/105/07/PDF/G0710507.pdf

Report of the UN Secretary-General, 7 April 2008 (S/2008/18). Accessed 12 October 2011, http://daccess-dds-ny.un.org/doc/UNDOC/GEN/N08/206/66/PDF/N0820666.pdf

Resolution 1597 (2008) PACE United Nations Security Council and European Union Blacklists. Accessed 20 October 2011, http://www.assembly.coe.int/Main.asp?link=/Documents/AdoptedText/ta08/ERES1597.htm.

Resolution adopted by the Human Rights Council 12/22, "Human Rights and Unilateral Coercive Measures," 2 October 2009. Accessed 20 October 2011, http://daccess-dds-ny.un.org/doc/RESOLUTION/GEN/G09/167/31/PDF/G0916731.pdf

Responsibility of International Organizations, 2011: Draft Text with Commentaries Thereto. Accessed 30 January 2012, http://untreaty.un.org/ilc/sessions/61/2009_RIO_articles_and_commentaries%28e%29.pdf

Restrictive measures (sanctions) in force. European Commission List as of 17 April 2012. Accessed 10 May 2012, http://eeas.europa.eu/cfsp/sanctions/docs/measures_en.pdf

Secretaries General of the OCSE and CSTO Discussed Co-operation of Organizations, press release, 26 March 2009. Accessed 10 May 2011, http://www.dkb.gov.ru/start/index.htm

Security Council Meeting 6256, 13 January 2011 (S/PV.6256). Accessed 21 April 2012, http://daccess-dds-ny.un.org/doc/UNDOC/PRO/N10/207/93/PDF/N1020793.pdf

Security Council Meeting 6257 (S/PV.6257) – Cooperation between the United Nations and regional and sub-regional organizations in maintaining international peace and security, 13 January 2010. Accessed 21 April 2012, http://www.securitycouncilreport.org/atf/cf/%7B65BFCF9B-6D27-4E9C-8CD3-CF6E4FF96FF9%7D/RO%20SPV%206257.pdf

Security Council Meeting 6306, 4 May 2011 (S/PV.6303). Accessed 21 April 2012, http://daccess-dds-ny.un.org/doc/UNDOC/PRO/N10/344/11/PDF/N1034411.pdf

Security Council Meeting 6702, 12 January 2012 (S/PV.6702). Accessed 21 April 2012, http://daccess-dds-ny.un.org/doc/UNDOC/PRO/N12/205/79/PDF/N1220579.pdf

Security Council Report, "The UN and Regional Organizations: Historical Chronology." Accessed 21 April 2012, http://www.securitycouncilreport.org/site/c/glKWLeMTIsG/b.3504159

Security Council Update Report, "The United Nations and Regional Organizations," 23 March 2007, No. 3. Accessed 9 October 2011, http://www.securitycouncilreport.org/atf/cf/%7B65BFCF9B-6D27-4E9C-8CD3-CF6E4FF96FF9%7D/Update%20Report%2023%20Mar%202007_ROs.pdf

Security Council Update Report, "The United Nations and Regional Organizations," 18 September 2006, No. 3. Accessed 9 October 2011, http://www.securitycouncilreport.org/atf/cf/%7B65BFCF9B-6D27-4E9C-8CD3-CF6E4FF96FF9%7D/Update%20Report%2018%20Sep%202006_UN%20&%20ROs.pdf

Security Council Update Report No. 2, "UN Cooperation with Regional and Sub-regional Organizations and Conflict Prevention," 14 April 2008. Accessed 9 October 2011, http://www.securitycouncilreport.org/site/c.glKWLeMTIsG/b.4021779/k.EBAA/Update_Report_No_2br_UN_Cooperation_with_Regional_and_SubRegional_Organisations_and_Conflict_Preventionbr14_April_2008.htm#UND

ShCO Members. Accessed 11 April 2011, http://www.sectsco.org/RU/show.asp?id=453

Statement by the President of the Security Council, S/PRST/1994/22, 3 May 1994. Accessed 19 March 2012, http://daccess-dds-ny.un.org/doc/UNDOC/GEN/N94/202/90/PDF/N9420290.pdf

Statement by the President of the Security Council, S/PRST/2007/42, 6 November 2007. Accessed 19 March 2012, http://daccess-dds-ny.un.org/doc/UNDOC/GEN/N07/585/12/PDF/N0758512.pdf

Statement by the President of the Security Council, S/PRST/2010/1, 13 January 2010. Accessed 19 October 2011, http://www.italyun.esteri.it/NR/rdonlyres/7B89C1FC-5DEC-4187-AA04-B60727F10BF8/0/onueorgreg.pdf

Statement by the President of the Security Council, S/PRST/2010/4, 24 February 2010. Accessed 19 March 2012, http://daccess-dds-ny.un.org/doc/UNDOC/GEN/N10/250/67/PDF/N1025067.pdf

Statements by the Special Envoys of UN, OSCE and EU on Kyrgyzstan – 16 June 2010; 14 September 2010; 22 November 2010. Accessed 13 May 2011, http://www.consilium.europa.eu

Stockholm Process (2001-2002), Sweden. Accessed 20 August 2011, www.smartsanctions.se

Strategic Concept for the Defence and Security of the Members of the North Atlantic Treaty Organization, 2010. Accessed 19 October 2011, http://www.nato.int/cps/en/natolive/official_texts_68580.htm

Supplement to an Agenda For Peace, A/50/60 - S/1995/1, 3 March 1995. Accessed 18 October 2011, http://www.un.org/Docs/SG/agsupp.html#INSTRUMENT

Texts of the Panama Canal Treaties with United States Senate Modifications. Accessed 19 November 2011, http://lcweb2.loc.gov/frd/cs/panama/pa_appnb.html

The Covenant of the League of Nations, 28 June 1919. Accessed 22 March 2011, http://avalon.law.yale.edu

The Experience of the United Nations in Administering Arms Embargoes and Travel Sanctions, in Smart Sanctions, the Next Step: Arms Embargoes and Travel Sanctions, Second Expert Seminar, Berlin, 3-5 December 2000. Accessed 11 November 2011, http://www.un.org/Docs/sc/committees/sanctions/background.doc

The list of individuals and entities established pursuant to Security Council Resolution 1988 (2011). Accessed 30 April 2012, http://www.un.org/sc/committees/1988/pdf/1988List.pdf

OSCE Concept of Comprehensive and Cooperative Security: An Overview of Major Milestones (SEC.GAL/100/09), 17 June 2009. Accessed 30 April 2011, http://www.osce.org/cpc/37592

The Protection of Human Rights and the Principle of Non-Intervention in Internal Affairs of States. Institut de Droit International, Session in Santiago de Compostela, 1989. Accessed 30 April 2012, http://www.idi-iil.org/idiE/resolutionsE/1989_comp_03_en.PDF

The United Nations Global Counter-Terrorism Strategy, A/60/288, 20 September 2006. Accessed 12 March 2011, http://www.coe.int/t/dlapil/codexter/Source/UN%20Global%20CT%20Strategy%20e.pdf

Treaty of Guarantee, Nicosia, 16 August 1960. Accessed 19 November 2011, http://www.mfa.gov.cy/mfa/mfa2006.nsf/All/484B73E4F0736CFDC22571BF00394F11/$file/Treaty%20of%20Guarantee.pdf

Treaty of Westphalia, 24 October 1648. Accessed 22 March 2011, http://avalon.law.yale.edu/17th_century/westphal.asp

UN General Assembly Resolution A/RES/47/10. Cooperation between the United Nations and the Conference on Security and Cooperation in Europe, 28 October 1992. Accessed 2 April 2012, http://daccess-dds-ny.un.org/doc/RESOLUTION/GEN/NR0/023/78/IMG/NR002378.pdf

UN General Assembly Resolution A/RES/48/5. Observer status for the Conference on Security and Cooperation in Europe in the General Assembly, 13 October 1993. Accessed 2 April 2012, http://daccess-dds-ny.un.org/doc/RESOLUTION/GEN/NR0/710/89/IMG/NR071089.pdf

UN General Assembly Resolution A/RES/48/19. Cooperation between the United Nations and the Conference on Security and Cooperation in Europe, 16 November 1993. Accessed 2 April 2012, http://daccess-dds-ny.un.org/doc/RESOLUTION/GEN/NR0/711/03/IMG/NR071103.pdf

UN General Assembly Resolution A/RES/48/237. Observer status for the Commonwealth of Independent States in the General Assembly, 24 March 1994. Accessed 2 April 2012, http://daccess-dds-ny.un.org/doc/RESOLUTION/GEN/NR0/704/54/IMG/NR070454.pdf

UN General Assembly Resolution A/RES/49/13. Cooperation between the United Nations and the Conference on Security and Cooperation in Europe, 15 November 1994. Accessed 2 April 2012, http://daccess-dds-ny.un.org/doc/UNDOC/GEN/N94/600/75/PDF/N9460075.pdf

UN General Assembly Resolution A/RES/50/87. Cooperation between the United Nations and the Organization for Security and Co-operation in Europe, 18 December 1995. Accessed 2 April 2012, http://daccess-dds-ny.un.org/doc/UNDOC/GEN/N96/762/73/PDF/N9676273.pdf

UN General Assembly Resolution A/RES/51/57. Cooperation between the United Nations and the Organization for Security and Cooperation in Europe, 12 December 1996. Accessed 2 April 2012, http://daccess-dds-ny.un.org/doc/UNDOC/GEN/N97/762/25/PDF/N9776225.pdf

UN General Assembly Resolution A/RES/52/22. Cooperation between the UN and the Organization for Security and Cooperation in Europe, 25 November 1997. Accessed 2 April 2012, http://daccess-dds-ny.un.org/doc/UNDOC/GEN/N98/760/57/PDF/N9876057.pdf

UN General Assembly Resolution A/RES/53/85. Cooperation between the UN and the Organization for Security and Cooperation in Europe, 7 December 1998. Accessed 2 April 2012, http://daccess-dds-ny.un.org/doc/UNDOC/GEN/N99/763/75/PDF/N9976375.pdf

UN General Assembly Resolution A/RES/54/117. Cooperation between UN and OSCE, 15 December 1999. Accessed 2 April 2012, http://daccess-dds-ny.un.org/doc/UNDOC/GEN/N00/281/76/PDF/N0028176.pdf

UN General Assembly Resolution A/RES/55/3. Cooperation between UN and Council of Europe, 20 October 2000. Accessed 2 April 2012, http://daccess-dds-ny.un.org/doc/UNDOC/GEN/N00/559/57/PDF/N0055957.pdf

UN General Assembly Resolution A/RES/55/179. Cooperation between UN and OSCE, 19 December 2000. Accessed 2 April 2012, http://daccess-dds-ny.un.org/doc/UNDOC/GEN/N00/570/13/PDF/N0057013.pdf

UN General Assembly Resolution A/RES/56/43. Cooperation between the UN and the Council of Europe, 7 December 2001. Accessed 2 April 2012, http://daccess-dds-ny.un.org/doc/UNDOC/GEN/N01/483/40/PDF/N0148340.pdf

UN General Assembly Resolution A/RES/56/216. Cooperation between the UN and the Organization for Security and Cooperation in Europe, 21 December 2001. Accessed 2 April 2012, http://daccess-dds-ny.un.org/doc/UNDOC/GEN/N01/493/88/PDF/N0149388.pdf

UN General Assembly Resolution A/RES/57/156. Cooperation between the United Nations and the Council of Europe, 16 December 2002. Accessed 2 April 2012, http://daccess-dds-ny.un.org/doc/UNDOC/GEN/N02/548/46/PDF/N0254846.pdf

UN General Assembly Resolution A/RES/57/298. Cooperation between the United Nations and the Organization for Security and Cooperation in Europe, 20 December 2002. Accessed 2 April 2012, http://daccess-dds-ny.un.org/doc/UNDOC/GEN/N02/561/17/PDF/N0256117.pdf

UN General Assembly Resolution A/RES/58/55. Promotion at the regional level in the Organization for Security and Cooperation in Europe of the United Nations programme of action on the illicit trade in small arms and light weapons in all its aspects, 8 December 2003. Accessed 2 April 2012, http://daccess-dds-ny.un.org/doc/UNDOC/GEN/N03/456/21/PDF/N0345621.pdf

UN General Assembly Resolution A/RES/59/50. Observer status for the Collective Security Treaty Organization in the Reports, Letters of the Secretary-General Assembly, 2 December 2004. Accessed 2 April 2012, http://daccess-dds-ny.un.org/doc/UNDOC/GEN/N04/479/26/PDF/N0447926.pdf

UN General Assembly Resolution A/RES/59/139. Cooperation between the United Nations and the Council of Europe, 17 February 2005. Accessed 2 April 2012, http://daccess-dds-ny.un.org/doc/UNDOC/GEN/N04/484/60/PDF/N0448460.pdf

UN General Assembly Resolution A/RES/61/13. Cooperation between the United Nations and the Council of Europe, 8 December 2006. Accessed 2 April 2012, http://daccess-dds-ny.un.org/doc/UNDOC/GEN/N06/495/21/PDF/N0649521.pdf

UN General Assembly Resolution A/RES/64/183. Cooperation between the United Nations and the Shanghai Cooperation Organization, 18 December 2009. Accessed 2 April 2012, http://daccess-dds-ny.un.org/doc/UNDOC/GEN/N09/472/81/PDF/N0947281.pdf

UN General Assembly Resolution A/RES/64/256. Cooperation between the United Nations and the Collective Security Treaty Organization, 2 March 2010. Accessed 2 April 2012, http://daccess-dds-ny.un.org/doc/UNDOC/GEN/N09/477/19/PDF/N0947719.pdf ;

UN General Assembly Resolution A/RES/65/122. Cooperation between the United Nations and the Collective Security Treaty Organization, 13 December 2010. Accessed 2 April 2012, http://daccess-dds-ny.un.org/doc/UNDOC/GEN/N10/519/86/PDF/N1051986.pdf

UN General Assembly Resolution A/RES/65/124. Cooperation between the United Nations and the Shanghai Cooperation Organization, 13 December 2010. Accessed 2 April 2012, http://daccess-dds-ny.un.org/doc/UNDOC/GEN/N10/519/98/PDF/N1051998.pdf

UN General Assembly Resolution A/RES/65/130. Cooperation between the United Nations and the Council of Europe, 24 February 2011. Accessed 2 April 2012, http://daccess-dds-ny.un.org/doc/UNDOC/GEN/N10/520/34/PDF/N1052034.pdf

UN General Assembly Resolution A/RES/66/36. Regional Disarmament, 12 January 2012. Accessed 2 April 2012, http://daccess-dds-ny.un.org/doc/UNDOC/GEN/N11/460/98/PDF/N1146098.pdf

UN General Assembly Resolution A/RES/66/37. Conventional arms control at the regional and sub-regional levels, 12 January 2012. Accessed 2 April 2012, http://daccess-dds-ny.un.org/doc/UNDOC/GEN/N11/461/04/PDF/N1146104.pdf

UN General Assembly Resolution A/RES/66/38. Confidence-building measures in the regional and sub-regional context, 12 January 2012. Accessed 2 April 2012, http://daccess-dds-ny.un.org/doc/UNDOC/GEN/N11/461/10/PDF/N1146110.pdf

UN General Assembly Resolution A/RES/66/102. The rule of law at the national and international levels, 13 January 2012. Accessed 20 August 2012, http://daccess-dds-ny.un.org/doc/UNDOC/GEN/N11/464/94/PDF/N1146494.pdf?OpenElement

UN Press Release PI/1668 – United Nations, Regional Organizations Agree on Stronger Partnership in Facing Peace Security Challenges. Sixth High-Level Meeting of UN, Regional, Intergovernmental Bodies Set for Headquarters on 25-26 July 2005. Accessed 20 December 2011, http://www.un.org/News/Press/docs/2005/pi1668.doc.htm

UN Security Council Report, 5663rd Meeting, 17 April 2007. Accessed 12 October 2011, http://www.securitycouncilreport.org/atf/cf/%7B65BFCF9B-6D27-4E9C-8CD3-CF6E4FF96FF9%7D/CC%20SPV%205663.pdf

UN Security Council Report, 6587th Meeting, 20 July 2011. Accessed 12 October 2011, http://daccess-dds-ny.un.org/doc/UNDOC/PRO/N11/422/59/PDF/N1142259.pdf

UN Security Council Report, 3822nd Meeting, 8 October 1997, S/PV.3822. Accessed 12 October 2011, http://www.undemocracy.com/securitycouncil/meeting_3822

UN Security Council Report, 4128th Meeting, 17 April 2000, S/PV.4128. Accessed 10 April 2012, http://www.un.org/Docs/sc/committees/sanctions/spv4128.pdf

UN Security Council Resolution 161 (1961), 21 February 1961. Accessed 15 March 2012, http://www.un.org/english/documen/scresol/1961/res161.pdf

UN Security Council Resolution 221 (1966), 9 April 1966. Accessed 15 March 2012, http://daccess-dds-ny.un.org/doc/RESOLUTION/GEN/NR0/227/44/IMG/NR022744.pdf

UN Security Council Resolution 353 (1974), 20 July 1974. Accessed 2 April 2012, http://daccess-dds-ny.un.org/doc/RESOLUTION/GEN/NR0/289/72/IMG/NR028972.pdf

UN Security Council Resolution 360 (1974), 16 August 1974. Accessed 2 April 2012, http://daccess-dds-ny.un.org/doc/RESOLUTION/GEN/NR0/289/79/IMG/NR028979.pdf

UN Security Council Resolution 660 (1990), 25 September 1990. Accessed 2 April 2012, http://daccess-dds-ny.un.org/doc/RESOLUTION/GEN/NR0/289/79/IMG/NR028979.pdf

UN Security Council Resolution 661 (1990), 6 August 1990. Accessed 2 April 2012, http://daccess-dds-ny.un.org/doc/RESOLUTION/GEN/NR0/575/11/IMG/NR057511.pdf

UN Security Council Resolution 665 (1990), 25 August 1990. Accessed 2 April 2012, http://daccess-dds-ny.un.org/doc/RESOLUTION/GEN/NR0/575/15/IMG/NR057515.pdf

UN Security Council Resolution 678 (1990), 29 November 1990. Accessed 2 April 2012, http://daccess-dds-ny.un.org/doc/RESOLUTION/GEN/NR0/575/28/IMG/NR057528.pdf

UN Security Council Resolution 713 (1991), 25 September 1991. Accessed 2 April 2012, http://daccess-dds-ny.un.org/doc/RESOLUTION/GEN/NR0/596/49/IMG/NR059649.pdf

UN Security Council Resolution 724 (1991), 15 December 1991. Accessed 2 April 2012, http://daccess-dds-ny.un.org/doc/RESOLUTION/GEN/NR0/596/60/IMG/NR059660.pdf

UN Security Council Resolution 757 (1992), 30 May 1992. Accessed 2 April 2012, http://daccess-dds-ny.un.org/doc/RESOLUTION/GEN/NR0/011/16/IMG/NR001116.pdf

UN Security Council Resolution 775 (1992), 28 August 1992. Accessed 2 April 2012, http://daccess-dds-ny.un.org/doc/UNDOC/GEN/N92/410/10/IMG/N9241010.pdf

UN Security Council Resolution 786 (1992), 10 November 1992. Accessed 2 April 2012, http://daccess-dds-ny.un.org/doc/UNDOC/GEN/N92/689/74/IMG/N9268974.pdf

UN Security Council Resolution 787 (1992), 16 November 1992. Accessed 2 April 2012, http://daccess-dds-ny.un.org/doc/UNDOC/GEN/N92/723/03/IMG/N9272303.pdf

UN Security Council Resolution 788 (1992), 19 November 1992. Accessed 2 April 2012, http://daccess-dds-ny.un.org/doc/UNDOC/GEN/N93/010/46/IMG/N9301046.pdf

UN Security Council Resolution 792 (1992), 30 November 1992. Accessed 2 April 2012, http://daccess-dds-ny.un.org/doc/UNDOC/GEN/N92/760/95/IMG/N9276095.pdf

UN Security Council Resolution 794 (1992), 3 December 1992. Accessed 2 April 2012, http://daccess-dds-ny.un.org/doc/UNDOC/GEN/N92/772/11/PDF/N9277211.pdf

UN Security Council Resolution 798 (1992), 18 December 1992. Accessed 2 April 2012, http://daccess-dds-ny.un.org/doc/UNDOC/GEN/N92/828/82/IMG/N9282882.pdf

UN Security Council Resolution 812 (1993), 12 March 1993. Accessed 15 March 2012, http://daccess-dds-ny.un.org/doc/UNDOC/GEN/N93/146/16/IMG/N9314616.pdf

UN Security Council Resolution 816 (1993), 31 March 1993. Accessed 2 April 2012, http://daccess-dds-ny.un.org/doc/UNDOC/GEN/N93/187/17/IMG/N9318717.pdf

UN Security Council Resolution 822 (1993), 30 April 1993. Accessed 2 April 2012, http://daccess-dds-ny.un.org/doc/UNDOC/GEN/N93/247/71/IMG/N9324771.pdf

UN Security Council Resolution 841 (1993), 16 June 1993. Accessed 2 April 2012, http://daccess-dds-ny.un.org/doc/UNDOC/GEN/N93/354/58/IMG/N9335458.pdf

UN Security Council Resolution 853 (1993), 29 July 1993. Accessed 2 April 2012, http://daccess-dds-ny.un.org/doc/UNDOC/GEN/N93/428/34/IMG/N9342834.pdf

UN Security Council Resolution 864 (1993), 15 September 1993. Accessed 2 April 2012, http://daccess-dds-ny.un.org/doc/UNDOC/GEN/N93/502/71/PDF/N9350271.pdf

UN Security Council Resolution 875 (1993), 16 October 1993. Accessed 2 April 2012, http://daccess-dds-ny.un.org/doc/UNDOC/GEN/N93/560/55/PDF/N9356055.pdf

UN Security Council Resolution 913 (1994), 22 April 1994. Accessed 2 April 2012, http://daccess-dds-ny.un.org/doc/UNDOC/GEN/N94/190/97/PDF/N9419097.pdf

UN Security Council Resolution 929 (1994), 22 June 1994. Accessed 2 April 2012, http://daccess-dds-ny.un.org/doc/UNDOC/GEN/N94/260/27/PDF/N9426027.pdf

UN Security Council Resolution 934 (1994), 30 June 1994. Accessed 2 April 2012, http://daccess-dds-ny.un.org/doc/UNDOC/GEN/N94/271/83/PDF/N9427183.pdf

UN Security Council Resolution 937 (1994), 21 July 1994. Accessed 2 April 2012, http://daccess-dds-ny.un.org/doc/UNDOC/GEN/N94/298/25/PDF/N9429825.pdf

UN Security Council Resolution 940 (1994), 31 July 1994. Accessed 2 April 2012, http://daccess-dds-ny.un.org/doc/UNDOC/GEN/N94/298/25/PDF/N9429825.pdf

UN Security Council Resolution 942 (1994), 23 September 1994. Accessed 2 April 2012, http://daccess-dds-ny.un.org/doc/UNDOC/GEN/N94/372/72/PDF/N9437272.pdf

UN Security Council Resolution 943 (1994), 23 September 1994. Accessed 2 April 2012, http://daccess-dds-ny.un.org/doc/UNDOC/GEN/N94/372/78/PDF/N9437278.pdf

UN Security Council Resolution 959 (1994), 19 November 1994. Accessed 2 April 2012, http://daccess-dds-ny.un.org/doc/UNDOC/GEN/N94/458/34/PDF/N9445834.pdf

UN Security Council Resolution 993 (1995), 12 May 1995. Accessed 2 April 2012, http://daccess-dds-ny.un.org/doc/UNDOC/GEN/N95/144/49/PDF/N9514449.pdf

UN Security Council Resolution 999 (1995), 16 June 1995. Accessed 2 April 2012, http://daccess-dds-ny.un.org/doc/UNDOC/GEN/N95/180/23/PDF/N9518023.pdf

UN Security Council Resolution 1022 (1995), 22 November 1995. Accessed 2 April 2012, http://daccess-dds-ny.un.org/doc/UNDOC/GEN/N95/368/65/PDF/N9536865.pdf

UN Security Council Resolution 1030 (1995), 14 December 1995. Accessed 2 April 2012, http://daccess-dds-ny.un.org/doc/UNDOC/GEN/N95/368/65/PDF/N9536865.pdf

UN Security Council Resolution 1031 (1995), 15 December 1995. Accessed 2 April 2012, http://daccess-dds-ny.un.org/doc/UNDOC/GEN/N95/405/26/PDF/N9540526.pdf

UN Security Council Resolution 1036 (1996), 12 January 1996. Accessed 2 April 2012, http://daccess-dds-ny.un.org/doc/UNDOC/GEN/N96/006/33/PDF/N9600633.pdf

UN Security Council Resolution 1061 (1996), 14 June 1996. Accessed 2 April 2012, http://daccess-dds-ny.un.org/doc/UNDOC/GEN/N96/148/73/PDF/N9614873.pdf

UN Security Council Resolution 1065 (1996), 12 July 1996. Accessed 2 April 2012, http://daccess-dds-ny.un.org/doc/UNDOC/GEN/N96/173/21/PDF/N9617321.pdf

UN Security Council Resolution 1089 (1996), 13 December 1996. Accessed 2 April 2012, http://daccess-dds-ny.un.org/doc/UNDOC/GEN/N96/363/16/PDF/N9636316.pdf

UN Security Council Resolution 1127 (1997), 28 August 1997. Accessed 2 April 2012, http://daccess-dds-ny.un.org/doc/UNDOC/GEN/N96/363/16/PDF/N9636316.pdf

UN Security Council Resolution 1132 (1997), 8 October 1997. Accessed 20 November 2010, http://daccess-dds-ny.un.org/doc/UNDOC/GEN/N97/267/13/PDF/N9726713.pdf

UN Security Council Resolution 1150 (1998), 30 January 1998. Accessed 2 April 2012, http://daccess-dds-ny.un.org/doc/UNDOC/GEN/N98/019/80/PDF/N9801980.pdf

UN Security Council Resolution 1167 (1998), 14 May 1998. Accessed 2 April 2012, http://daccess-dds-ny.un.org/doc/UNDOC/GEN/N98/134/03/PDF/N9813403.pdf

UN Security Council Resolution 1174 (1998), 15 June 1998. Accessed 2 April 2012, http://daccess-dds-ny.un.org/doc/UNDOC/GEN/N98/167/58/PDF/N9816758.pdf

UN Security Council Resolution 1187 (1998), 30 July 1998. Accessed 2 April 2012, http://daccess-dds-ny.un.org/doc/UNDOC/GEN/N98/223/13/PDF/N9822313.pdf

UN Security Council Resolution 1203 (1998), 24 October 1998. Accessed 2 April 2012, http://daccess-dds-ny.un.org/doc/UNDOC/GEN/N98/321/21/PDF/N9832121.pdf

UN Security Council Resolution 1206 (1998), 12 November 1998. Accessed 2 April 2012, http://daccess-dds-ny.un.org/doc/UNDOC/GEN/N98/348/88/PDF/N9834888.pdf

UN Security Council Resolution 1225 (1999), 28 January 1999. Accessed 2 April 2012, http://daccess-dds-ny.un.org/doc/UNDOC/GEN/N99/020/97/PDF/N9902097.pdf

UN Security Council Resolution 1240 (1999), 15 May 1999. Accessed 2 April 2012, http://daccess-dds-ny.un.org/doc/UNDOC/GEN/N99/143/81/PDF/N9914381.pdf

UN Security Council Resolution 1247 (1999), 18 August 1999. Accessed 2 April 2012, http://daccess-dds-ny.un.org/doc/UNDOC/GEN/N99/143/81/PDF/N9914381.pdf

UN Security Council Resolution 1255 (1999), 30 July 1999. Accessed 2 April 2012, http://daccess-dds-ny.un.org/doc/UNDOC/GEN/N99/223/74/PDF/N9922374.pdf

UN Security Council Resolution 1267 (1999), 15 October 1999. Accessed 2 April 2012, http://daccess-dds-ny.un.org/doc/UNDOC/GEN/N99/300/44/PDF/N9930044.pdf

UN Security Council Resolution 1274 (1999), 12 November 1999. Accessed 2 April 2012, http://daccess-dds-ny.un.org/doc/UNDOC/GEN/N99/143/81/PDF/N9914381.pdf

UN Security Council Resolution 1287 (2000), 31 January 2000. Accessed 2 April 2012, http://daccess-dds-ny.un.org/doc/UNDOC/GEN/N00/270/43/PDF/N0027043.pdf

UN Security Council Resolution 1298 (2000), 17 May 2000. Accessed 2 April 2012, http://daccess-dds-ny.un.org/doc/UNDOC/GEN/N00/437/11/PDF/N0043711.pdf

UN Security Council Resolution 1305 (2000), 21 June 2000. Accessed 2 April 2012, http://daccess-dds-ny.un.org/doc/UNDOC/GEN/N00/491/85/PDF/N0049185.pdf

UN Security Council Resolution 1311 (2000), 28 July 2000. Accessed 2 April 2012, http://daccess-dds-ny.un.org/doc/UNDOC/GEN/N00/558/19/PDF/N0055819.pdf

UN Security Council Resolution 1339 (2001), 31 January 2001. Accessed 2 April 2012, http://daccess-dds-ny.un.org/doc/UNDOC/GEN/N01/234/10/PDF/N0123410.pdf

UN Security Council Resolution 1357 (2001), 21 June 2001. Accessed 2 April 2012, http://daccess-dds-ny.un.org/doc/UNDOC/GEN/N01/420/28/PDF/N0142028.pdf

UN Security Council Resolution 1364 (2001), 31 July 2001. Accessed 2 April 2012, http://daccess-dds-ny.un.org/doc/UNDOC/GEN/N01/474/79/PDF/N0147479.pdf

UN Security Council Resolution 1371 (2001), 26 September 2001. Accessed 2 April 2012, http://daccess-dds-ny.un.org/doc/UNDOC/GEN/N01/552/01/PDF/N0155201.pdf

UN Security Council Resolution 1373 (2001), 12 October 2001. Accessed 24 July 2012, http://daccess-dds-ny.un.org/doc/UNDOC/GEN/N01/557/43/PDF/N0155743.pdf?OpenElement

UN Security Council Resolution 1393 (2002), 31 January 2002. Accessed 2 April 2012, http://daccess-dds-ny.un.org/doc/UNDOC/GEN/N02/238/65/PDF/N0223865.pdf

UN Security Council Resolution 1423 (2002), 12 July 2002. Accessed 2 April 2012, http://daccess-dds-ny.un.org/doc/UNDOC/GEN/N02/477/85/PDF/N0247785.pdf

UN Security Council Resolution 1427 (2002), 29 July 2002. Accessed 2 April 2012, http://daccess-dds-ny.un.org/doc/UNDOC/GEN/N02/500/43/PDF/N0250043.pdf

UN Security Council Resolution 1462 (2003), 30 January 2003. Accessed 2 April 2012, http://daccess-dds-ny.un.org/doc/UNDOC/GEN/N03/231/34/PDF/N0323134.pdf

UN Security Council Resolution 1483 (2003), 22 May 2003. Accessed 2 April 2012, http://daccess-dds-ny.un.org/doc/UNDOC/GEN/N03/368/53/PDF/N0336853.pdf

UN Security Council Resolution 1511 (2003), 16 October 2003. Accessed 24 July 2012, http://daccess-dds-ny.un.org/doc/UNDOC/GEN/N01/557/43/PDF/N0155743.pdf?OpenElement

UN Security Council Resolution 1524 (2004), 30 January 2004. Accessed 2 April 2012, http://daccess-dds-ny.un.org/doc/UNDOC/GEN/N02/238/65/PDF/N0223865.pdf

UN Security Council Resolution 1551 (2004), 9 July 2004. Accessed 2 April 2012, http://daccess-dds-ny.un.org/doc/UNDOC/GEN/N04/419/37/PDF/N0441937.pdf

UN Security Council Resolution 1554 (2004), 29 July 2004. Accessed 2 April 2012, http://daccess-dds-ny.un.org/doc/UNDOC/GEN/N04/444/70/PDF/N0444470.pdf ,

UN Security Council Resolution 1572 (2004), 15 November 2004. Accessed 2 April 2012, http://daccess-dds-ny.un.org/doc/UNDOC/GEN/N04/607/37/PDF/N0460737.pdf

UN Security Council Resolution 1575 (2004), 22 November 2004. Accessed 2 April 2012, http://daccess-dds-ny.un.org/doc/UNDOC/GEN/N04/619/22/PDF/N0461922.pdf

UN Security Council Resolution 1582 (2005), 28 January 2005. Accessed 2 April 2012, http://daccess-dds-ny.un.org/doc/UNDOC/GEN/N05/223/15/PDF/N0522315.pdf

UN Security Council Resolution 1615 (2005), 29 July 2005. Accessed 2 April 2012, http://daccess-dds-ny.un.org/doc/UNDOC/GEN/N05/446/18/PDF/N0544618.pdf

UN Security Council Resolution 1631 (2005), 17 October 2005. Accessed 2 April 2012, http://daccess-dds-ny.un.org/doc/UNDOC/GEN/N05/556/42/PDF/N0555642.pdf

UN Security Council Resolution 1639 (2005), 21 November 2005. Accessed 2 April 2012, http://daccess-dds-ny.un.org/doc/UNDOC/GEN/N05/613/29/PDF/N0561329.pdf

UN Security Council Resolution 1666 (2006), 31 March 2006. Accessed 2 April 2012, http://daccess-dds-ny.un.org/doc/UNDOC/GEN/N06/293/33/PDF/N0629333.pdf

UN Security Council Resolution 1722 (2006), 21 November 2006. Accessed 2 April 2012, http://daccess-dds-ny.un.org/doc/UNDOC/GEN/N06/624/29/PDF/N0662429.pdf

UN Security Council Resolution 1785 (2007), 21 November 2007. Accessed 2 April 2012, http://daccess-dds-ny.un.org/doc/UNDOC/GEN/N07/608/63/PDF/N0760863.pdf

UN Security Council Resolution 1808 (2008), 15 April 2008. Accessed 2 April 2012, http://daccess-dds-ny.un.org/doc/UNDOC/GEN/N08/306/29/PDF/N0830629.pdf

UN Security Council Resolution 1809 (2008), 16 April 2008. Accessed 2 April 2012, http://www.info.gov.za/speeches/2008/08041712451003.htm

UN Security Council Resolution 1822 (2008), 30 June 2008. Accessed 2 April 2012, http://daccess-dds-ny.un.org/doc/UNDOC/GEN/N08/404/90/PDF/N0840490.pdf

UN Security Council Resolution 1838 (2008), 7 October 2008. Accessed 2 April 2012, http://daccess-dds-ny.un.org/doc/UNDOC/GEN/N08/538/84/PDF/N0853884.pdf

UN Security Council Resolution 1845 (2008), 20 November 2008. Accessed 2 April 2012, http://daccess-dds-ny.un.org/doc/UNDOC/GEN/N08/612/49/PDF/N0861249.pdf

UN Security Council Resolution 1856 (2008), 22 December 2008. Accessed 2 April 2012, http://daccess-dds-ny.un.org/doc/UNDOC/GEN/N08/666/94/PDF/N0866694.pdf

UN Security Council Resolution 1857 (2008), 22 December 2008. Accessed 2 April 2012, http://daccess-dds-ny.un.org/doc/UNDOC/GEN/N08/666/43/PDF/N0866643.pdf ,

UN Security Council Resolution 1863 (2009), 16 January 2009. Accessed 2 April 2012, http://daccess-dds-ny.un.org/doc/UNDOC/GEN/N09/211/65/PDF/N0921165.pdf

UN Security Council Resolution 1895 (2009), 18 November 2009. Accessed 2 April 2012, http://daccess-dds-ny.un.org/doc/UNDOC/GEN/N09/612/34/PDF/N0961234.pdf

UN Security Council Resolution 1948 (2010) от 18 November 2010. Accessed 2 April 2012, http://daccess-dds-ny.un.org/doc/UNDOC/GEN/N10/643/53/PDF/N1064353.pdf

UN Security Council Resolution 1973 (2011), 17 March 2011. Accessed 2 April 2012, http://daccess-dds-ny.un.org/doc/UNDOC/GEN/N11/268/39/PDF/N1126839.pdf

UN Security Council Resolution 2033 (2012), 12 January 2012. Accessed 2 April 2012, http://daccess-dds-ny.un.org/doc/UNDOC/GEN/N12/206/23/PDF/N1220623.pdf

United Nations Members. Accessed 11 April 2011, http://www.un.org/en/members

United Nations Millennium Declaration, A/55/2, 8 September 2000. Accessed 19 November 2011, http://www.un.org/millennium/declaration/ares552e.htm

United Nations Security Council and European Union Blacklists, PACE doc. 11454, 16 November 2007: Explanatory Memorandum. Accessed 11 November 2011, http://assembly.coe.int/main.asp?Link=/documents/workingdocs/doc07/edoc11454.htm

Uniting against Terrorism: Recommendations for a Global Counter-Terrorism Strategy. Report of the UN Secretary-General. Res A/60/825. Accessed 15 November 2011, http://daccess-dds-ny.un.org/doc/UNDOC/GEN/N06/330/88/PDF/N0633088.pdf

Update of the EU Best Practices for the Effective Implementation of Restrictive Measures, EU Council 8666/1/08 rev. 1, 24 April 2008. Accessed 15 November 2011, http://registerconsilium.europa.eu/pdf/en/08/st08/st08666-re01.en08.pdf

Vienna Document of Negotiations on Confidence- and Security Building Measures, 16 November 1999. Accessed 15 November 2011, http://www.osce.org/fsc/41276

What is OSCE? Factsheet. Accessed 15 November 2011, http://www.osce.org/secretariat/35775

Written contribution by the CSTO SG, Mr. N. Bordyuzha (SUM.DEL/23/10), 1 December 2010. Accessed 15 November 2011, http://www.dkb.gov.ru/start/index.htm

Декларация государств-членов ОДКБ о совершенствовании и усилении эффективности деятельности ОДКБ [Declaration of the CSTO Members on the Improvement and Enhancement of Effectiveness of CSTO Activity], 23 June 2006, *Electronic Legal Database Konsul'tant Plus. Technologiia 3000.*

Декларация о политическом урегулировании Грузино-Абхазского конфликта [Declaration on the Political Settlement of the Georgia-Abkhazia Conflict], 4 April 1994, *Electronic Legal Database Konsul'tant Plus. Technologiia 3000.*

Договор государств-участников СНГ о противодействии легализации преступных доходов и финансировании терроризма [Treaty of the CIS Member States on the Suppression of Money Laundering and Financing of Terrorism], 5 October 2007, *Electronic Legal Database Konsul'tant Plus. Technologiia 3000.*

Договор о сотрудничестве государств-участников СНГ в борьбе с терроризмом [Treaty on the Cooperation of the CIS Member States in the Struggle against Terrorism], 4 June 1999, *Sodruzhestvo*, (1999, 2).

Заявление государств-участников СНГ [Statements of the CIS Member States], 9 October 1992 and 22 January 1993, *Electronic Legal Database Konsul'tant Plus. Technologiia 3000.*

Информация о деятельности базовых организаций (учреждений) в сфере безопасности в СНГ [Information on the Activity of the Base Education Institutions in the Sphere of Security]. Accessed 15 May 2012, http://www.cis.minsk.by/page.php?id=14338

История Суда [Court's History]. Accessed 15 May 2012, http://www.sudsng.org/about/history

Концепция военного сотрудничества государств-участников СНГ до 2015 г. [Concept of Military Cooperation of the CIS Member States until 2015], Confirmed by the CIS CHS Decisions of 10 December 2010, *Electronic Legal Database Konsul'tant Plus. Technologiia 3000.*

Концепция дальнейшего развития Содружества независимых государств. План реализации Концепции [Concept of the Future Development of the Commonwealth of Independent States, Plan of Actions], Decision of the CIS CHS of 5 October 2007, *Electronic Legal Database Konsul'tant Plus. Technologiia 3000.*

Концепция согласованной пограничной политики государств-участников СНГ [Concept of the Coordinated Border Policy of the CIS Member States], confirmed by the CIS CHS decision of 26 August 2005, *Electronic Legal Database Konsul'tant Plus. Technologiia 3000.*

Концепция формирования и функционирования миротворческого механизма ОДКБ [Concept of Formation and Functioning of the CSTO Peacekeeping Mechanism], 18 June 2004, *Electronic Legal Database Konsul'tant Plus. Technologiia 3000.*

Межгосударственная программа мер по борьбе с преступностью на 2011-2013 гг. [Inter-State Program of Joint Action in the Struggle against Criminality for 2011-2013], confirmed by the CIS CHS Decisions of 10 December 2010, *Electronic Legal Database Konsul'tant Plus. Technologiia 3000.*

Меморандум о мерах по обеспечению безопасности и укреплению взаимного доверия между сторонами в Грузино-Оссетинском конфликте [Memorandum on Security and Confidence-Building Measures between the Parties of the Georgia-Ossetia Conflict], 16 May 1996, *Electronic Legal Database Konsul'tant Plus. Technologiia 3000.*

О направлении наблюдателей от СНГ на выборы Президента Чеченской Республики, Российская Федерация [On the Sending of CIS Observers to the Elections of the President of the Chechen Republic, Russian Federation], CIS CHS Decision of 19 September 2003, *Electronic Legal Database Konsul'tant Plus. Technologiia 3000.*

О модели региональной системы коллективной безопасности [On the Model of the Regional System of Collective Security], Decision of the Collective Security Council, 24 May 2000, *Electronic Legal Database Konsul'tant Plus. Technologiia 3000.*

О создании и принципах Межгосударственного Суда СНГ [On the Establishment and Principles of the CIS Interstate Court], Decision of the CIS CHS, 22 January 1993, *Sodruzhestvo*, (1993, 1).

О практических мерах по усилению роли ОДКБ в борьбе с терроризмом, религиозным экстремизмом, нелегальной миграцией и транснациональной преступностью [On the Practical Measures to Enhance the CSTO's Role in the Struggle against Terrorism, Religious Extremism, Illegal Migration and Transborder Crimes], CSTO CSSC Decision of 8 December 2003, *Electronic Legal Database Konsul'tant Plus. Technologiia 3000.*

Об информации Исполнительного комитета СНГ о ситуации в урегулировании конфликта в Приднестровье [On the Information of the CIS Executive Committee on the Settlement of Conflict in Transdniestria], Decision of the CIS CMFA, 24 January 2000, *Electronic Legal Database Konsul'tant Plus. Technologiia 3000.*

Об использовании коллективных вооруженных сил для поддержания мира в зоне Грузино-Абхазского конфликта [On the Use of Collective Military Forces to Maintain Peace in the Zone of the Georgia-Abkhazian Conflict], CIS CHS Decision of 22 August 1994, *Electronic Legal Database Konsul'tant Plus. Technologiia 3000.*

Обзор судебной практики [Overview of Court's Practice]. Accessed 18 May 2012, http://www.sudsng.org/database/sudobzor/

ОДКБ выступает за использование своего миротворческого потенциала в операциях ООН [CSTO Stands for the Use of its Peacekeeping Forces in the UN Operations]. Accessed 20 August 2012, http://www.odkb-csto.org/international_org/detail.php?ELEMENT_ID=112

Организационно-правовой механизм сотрудничества в противодействии транснациональной преступности в рамках Содружества Независимых Государств [Institutionalized Legal Mechanism of Cooperation in the Struggle against Transboundary Crimes within the CIS]. Accessed 15 May 2012, http://www.cis.minsk.by/page.php?id=13962

План коллективных действий государств-членов ОДКБ по имплементации Контртеррористической стратегии ООН на период 2008-2012 гг. [Plan for Collective Actions of the CSTO Member States in the Implementation of the UN Counter-terrorism Strategy for the Period of 2008-2012], confirmed by the CSC Decision of 5 September 2008, *Electronic Legal Database Konsul'tant Plus. Technologiia 3000.*

План мероприятий по реализации согласованной пограничной политики государств-участников СНГна 2011-2015 гг. [Plan of Actions on the Realization of the Concept of the Coordinated Border Policy of the CIS Member-States to 2011-2015], confirmed by the CIS CHS Decision of 10 December 2010, *Electronic Legal Database Konsul'tant Plus. Technologiia 3000.*

Подай оружие. Киргизия ждет от ОДКБ военной помощи [Give weapons. Kisgizia is Waiting for SCTO Military Help]. Accessed 12 February 2012, http://www.centrasia.ru/newsA.php?st=1281667800.

Положение о коллективных силах по поддержанию мира в СНГ [Regulation on the CIS Collective Peace-Maintenance Forces], 19 January 1996, *Electronic Legal Database Konsul'tant Plus. Technologiia 3000.*

Положение о порядке проведения консультаций между государствами-участниками ДКБ [Provision on the Procedure for Conducting Consultations], approved by the CSC Decision of 28 May 1997, *Electronic Legal Database Konsul'tant Plus. Technologiia 3000.*

Положения о рабочих группах по борьбе с терроризмом и противодействии незаконной миграции при Комитете секретарей Советов безопасности ОДКБ [Provisions on Working Groups on Counter-Terrorism and Illegal Migration Issues at the Committee of the Secretaries of CSTO Security Councils], approved by the Decision of the CSTO CSSC of 22 June 2005, *Electronic Legal Database Konsul'tant Plus. Technologiia 3000.*

Положение о Совете коллективной безопасности [Regulations on the Council of Collective Security], confirmed by the CSC Decision of 28 April 2003, *Electronic Legal Database Konsul'tant Plus. Technologiia 3000.*

Положение о Совете министров обороны ОДКБ [Regulations on the Council of Defence Ministers], confirmed by the CSC Decision of 28 April 2003, *Electronic Legal Database Konsul'tant Plus. Technologiia 3000.*

Положение о функционировании механизма координации внешне-политической деятельности государств-членов ОДКБ [Regulations on the Functioning of the Coordination Mechanism of the Foreign Policy Activity of the CSTO], of 19 November 2003, *Electronic Legal Database Konsul'tant Plus. Technologiia 3000.*

Правила процедуры органов ОДКБ [Rules of Procedure of the CSTO Organs], adopted by the CSC Decision of 18 June 2004, *Electronic Legal Database Konsul'tant Plus. Technologiia 3000.*

Программа совместных действий ОДКБ, направленных на борьбу с терроризмом и транспортировкой наркотиков [CSTO Program of Joint Actions Aimed at Suppressing Terrorism and Drug Trafficking], adopted by the CSC on 23 June 2006, *Electronic Legal Database Konsul'tant Plus. Technologiia 3000.*

Программа сотрудничества государств-участников СНГ в борьбе с незаконным оборотом наркотических веществ, психотропных вещетв и их прекурсоров, и противодействии наркомании на 2011-2013 гг. [Program of Cooperation of the CIS Member States in the Struggle against the Illegal Traffic in Drugs, Psychotropic Substances, and their Precursors, and Opposition to Drug Addiction for 2011-2013], confirmed by the CIS CHS Decision of 10 December 2010, *Electronic Legal Database Konsul'tant Plus. Technologiia 3000.*

Программа сотрудничества государств-участников СНГ в борьбе с терроризмом и иными насильственными проявлениями экстремизма на 2011-2013 [Program of Cooperation of the CIS Member States in the Struggle against Terrorism and Other Violent Forms of Extremism for 2011-2013], confirmed by the CIS CJS Decision of 10 December 2010, *Electronic Legal Database Konsul'tant Plus. Technologiia 3000.*

Программа сотрудничества государств-участников СНГ в противодействии незаконной миграции на 2009-2011 гг. [Program of Cooperation of the CIS Member States in the Suppression of Illegal Migration for 2009-2011], confirmed by the CIS CHS Decisions of 10 October 2008, *Electronic Legal Database Konsul'tant Plus. Technologiia 3000.*

Протокол к Договору о коллективной безопасности [Protocol to the Treaty of Collective Security], 10 December 2010, *Electronic Legal Database Konsul'tant Plus. Technologiia 3000.*

Решение о взаимодействии государств-участников СНГ в рамках ОБСЕ [Decision of the CIS CHS on Interaction of the CIS Member States within OSCE], 10 December 2010. Accessed 11 May 2011, http://cis.minsk.by/reestr/com.qulix.reestr.Reestr/Reestr.html#reestr/view/text?doc=2966

Ситуация в Кыргызстане. ОДКБ ждет решения Беларуси [Situation in Kyrgyzstan. SCTO is Waiting for Belarus' Decision]. Accessed 12 February 2012, http://news.tut.by/politics/173663.html

Соглашение государств-участников СНГ по обеспечению стабильного положения на их внешних границах [Agreement of the CIS Member States on the Guarantees of Stability on their External Borders], 9 October 1992, *Sodruzhestvo*, (1992, 7).

Соглашение о коллективных силах оперативного реагирования ОДКБ [Agreement on the CSTO Collective Rapid Reaction Forces], 14 June 2009, *Electronic Legal Database Konsul'tant Plus. Technologiia 3000.*

Соглашение о подготовке военных кадров для государств-членов ОДКБ [Agreement on Training of Military Personnel of the CSTO Member-States], 23 June 2005, *Electronic Legal Database Konsul'tant Plus. Technologiia 3000.*

Соглашение о порядке финансового, технического и тылового обеспечения деятельности и персонала коллективных сил по поддержанию мира [Agreement on the Order of Financial, Technical and Rear Procurement of the Activity and Personnel of the CIS Collective Peace-Maintenance Forces], 5 October 2007, *Electronic Legal Database Konsul'tant Plus. Technologiia 3000.*

Соглашение о порядке формирования и функционирования сил и средств системы коллективной безопасности ОДКБ [Agreement on the Order of Formation and Functioning of Forces and Means of the CSTO System of Collective Security], 10 December 2010, *Electronic Legal Database Konsul'tant Plus. Technologiia 3000.*

Соглашение о правовом статусе ОДКБ [Agreement on the CSTO Status], 7 October 2002, Bulletin of International Treaties, 3 (2004), 10 *et seq.*, *Electronic Legal Database Konsul'tant Plus. Technologiia 3000.*

Соглашение о прекращении огня и разъединении сил в зоне Грузино-Абхазского конфликта [Agreement on the Cease-Fire and Separation of Forces in the Zone of the Georgia-Abkhazian Conflict], 14 May 1994, *Electronic Legal Database Konsul'tant Plus. Technologiia 3000.*

Соглашение о социальных и правовых гарантиях персонала коллективных сил по поддержанию мира в СНГ [Agreement on Social and Legal Guarantees to the Personnel of the CIS Collective Peace-Maintenance Forces], 5 October 2007 (not in force), *Electronic Legal Database Konsul'tant Plus. Technologiia 3000.*

Соглашение о статусе формирований сил и средств системы коллективной безопасности ОДКБ [Agreement on the Status of the Forces and Facilities of the CSTO System of Collective Security], 10 December 2010, *Electronic Legal Database Konsul'tant Plus. Technologiia 3000.*

Соглашение об обмене информацией в сфере борьбы преступностью [Agreement on the Information Exchange in the Struggle against Criminality], 22 May 2009, *Electronic Legal Database Konsul'tant Plus. Technologiia 3000.*

L'HARMATTAN, ITALIA
Via Degli Artisti 15; 10124 Torino

L'HARMATTAN HONGRIE
Könyvesbolt ; Kossuth L. u. 14-16
1053 Budapest

ESPACE L'HARMATTAN KINSHASA
Faculté des Sciences sociales,
politiques et administratives
BP243, KIN XI
Université de Kinshasa

L'HARMATTAN CONGO
67, av. E. P. Lumumba
Bât. – Congo Pharmacie (Bib. Nat.)
BP2874 Brazzaville
harmattan.congo@yahoo.fr

L'HARMATTAN GUINÉE
Almamya Rue KA 028, en face du restaurant Le Cèdre
OKB agency BP 3470 Conakry
(00224) 60 20 85 08
harmattanguinee@yahoo.fr

L'HARMATTAN CAMEROUN
BP 11486
Face à la SNI, immeuble Don Bosco
Yaoundé
(00237) 99 76 61 66
harmattancam@yahoo.fr

L'HARMATTAN CÔTE D'IVOIRE
Résidence Karl / cité des arts
Abidjan-Cocody 03 BP 1588 Abidjan 03
(00225) 05 77 87 31
etien_nda@yahoo.fr

L'HARMATTAN MAURITANIE
Espace El Kettab du livre francophone
N° 472 avenue du Palais des Congrès
BP 316 Nouakchott
(00222) 63 25 980

L'HARMATTAN SÉNÉGAL
« Villa Rose », rue de Diourbel X G, Point E
BP 45034 Dakar FANN
(00221) 33 825 98 58 / 77 242 25 08
senharmattan@gmail.com

L'HARMATTAN TOGO
1771, Bd du 13 janvier
BP 414 Lomé
Tél : 00 228 2201792
gerry@taama.net

527607 - Avril 2013
Achevé d'imprimer par